The Ideologies of Theory
Volume 2

Theory and History of Literature
Edited by Wlad Godzich and Jochen Schulte-Sasse

For other books in this series, see p. x.

The Ideologies of Theory
Essays 1971-1986
Volume 2: The Syntax of History

Fredric Jameson

Theory and History of Literature, Volume 49

University of Minnesota Press, Minneapolis

Published by the University of Minnesota Press
2037 University Avenue Southeast, Minneapolis, MN 55414.
Published simultaneously in Canada
by Fitzhenry & Whiteside Limited, Markam.
Printed in the United States of America.

Library of Congress Cataloging-in-Publication Data

Jameson, Fredric.
   The ideologies of theory : essays, 1971-1986 / Fredric Jameson.
     p.   cm. -- (Theory and history of literature ; v. 49)
   Includes bibliographies and indexes.
   Contents: -- v. 2. Syntax of history.
   ISBN 0-8166-1575-6 (v. 2)   ISBN 0-8166-1576-4 (pbk. : v. 2)
   ISBN 0-8166-1577-2 (set)   ISBN 0-8166-1578-0 (pbk. : set)
   1. Criticism. 2. Marxist criticism. 3. Hermaneutics. I. Title.
II. Series.
PN81.J285 1988
801'.95--dc19   88-4813

The following chapters are reprinted with permission of the publishers: Chapter 1, "The
Vanishing Mediator; or, Max Weber as Storyteller," from *New German Critique*, 1 (Winter
1973), pp. 52-89, copyright © 1973 by *New German Critique;* Chapter 2, "Architecture and
the Critique of Ideology," from *Architecture, Criticism, Ideology*, edited by J. Ockham, pp.
51-87, copyright © 1985 by Princeton Architectural Press and *Revisions;* an earlier version of
Chapter 2 was first given at the Institute for Architecture and Urban Studies (March 1982) at
the symposium "Architecture and Ideology," sponsored by *Revisions;* Chapter 3, "Pleasure:
A Political Issue," from *Formations of Pleasure*, Formation Series, vol. 1, pp. 1-14, published
by Routledge and Kegan Paul, London, copyright © 1983 by Formations Editorial Collec-
tive, reprinted with permission of Associated Book Publishers (U.K.); Chapter 4, "Of
Islands and Trenches: Neutralization and the Production of Utopian Discourse," from
diacritics, 7, no. 2 (June 1977), pp. 2-21, copyright © 1977 by the Johns Hopkins University
Press, Baltimore, Md.; four diagrams in Chapter 4, on pp. 86, 96, from Louis Marin,
Utopics: Spatial Play, trans. Robert A. Vollrath, pp. 43, 46, 47, 127, copyright © 1984 by
Humanities Press International, Inc., Atlantic Highlands, N.J., and the Macmillan Press,
Ltd., London and Basingstoke, Hampshire; Chapter 5, "The Politics of Theory: Ideological
Positions in the Postmodernism Debate," from *New German Critique*, 33 (Fall 1984), pp.
53-65, copyright © 1973 by *New German Critique;* Chapter 6, "Beyond the Cave: Demysti-
fying the Ideology of Modernism," from *Bulletin of the Midwest Modern Language Association*,
8, no. 1 (1975), pp. 1-20, copyright © 1975 by *The Journal of the Midwest Modern Language
Association*, originally delivered as a lecture at the 1974 meeting of the Midwest Modern
Language Association; Chapter 7, "Reflections on the Brecht-Lukács Debate," from
Aesthetics and Politics, pp. 196-213, copyright © 1977 by New Left Books, London; Chapter
8, "Marxism and Historicism," from *New Literary History*, no. 1 (Autumn 1979), pp. 41-72,
copyright © 1979 by *New Literary History*, The University of Virginia, Charlottesville,
reprinted with permission of the Johns Hopkins University Press; Chapter 9, "Periodizing
the 60s," from *The 60s without Apology*, pp. 178-209, copyright © 1984 by *Social Text*, New
York, published by the University of Minnesota Press, Minneapolis.

The University of Minnesota
is an equal-opportunity
educator and employer.

An die Nachgeborenen:
Cassie, Stacy, Cade, Charlotte

....so wird durch ebendenselben dialektischen Prozess jedes
Kategorienproblem wieder in ein geschichtliches Problem
verwandelt. Allerdings: in ein Problem der Universal
geschichte, die damit...gleichzeitig als methodisches Problem
und als Problem der Erkenntnis der Gegenwart erscheint.

....by the same dialectical process every problem of categories
becomes transformed into a historical problem. But (it should
be noted): into a problem of universal history which now
appears...simultaneously as a problem of method and a
problem of our knowledge of the present.

Georg Lukács, *History and Class Consciousness*

Contents

Contents of Volume 1: Situation of Theory

Introductory Note

This second volume of my collected theoretical essays marks a general—but not strictly chronological—shift from problems of textual interpretation to the rather different issues raised by cultural and historical analysis: the question of possible new forms of *spatial* analysis, the politics of historiography (including the writing of the history of our own period), and some first approaches to "postmodernism." The requirement for a certain kind of narrative analysis here obviously returns with a vengeance; but it is also worth suggesting the transmigration of the earlier concept of "meta-commentary," which was a reflexive operation proposed for staging the struggle within an individual literary and cultural text of various interpretations that are themselves so many "methods" or philosophies or ideological worldviews. When the polemic leaves the ground of an individual text (as it currently seems to have a tendency to do, not always with the happiest results), it seems to me increasingly desirable to stage such conflicts in terms of a rather different framework, which I will call *transcoding*.

This is, in my opinion, the most fruitful way in which theoretical polemics can be conducted in a situation characterized by the proliferation of theoretical codes of all kinds (a situation sometimes loosely characterized as "poststructuralism"). These codes (sometimes also more loosely called "methods") are henceforth a fact of life of our intellectual space, which determines a new kind of intellectual formation for our students that may be closer to the learning and practice of foreign languages than to any traditional philosophical formation oriented around "truth" or system. It will, in other words, today be less a question of finding a single system of truth to convert to, than it will of speaking the various theoretical codes experimentally, with a kind of Whorf-Sapir view toward determining what can and what cannot be said in each of those theoretical "private languages." What is blurred, left out, what does not compute or is "inexpressible," in this or that theoretical language may then be a more damaging indictment of the "theory" in question than traditional ontological or metaphysical critiques. This view has the additional merit of opening the door to the languages of the other disciplines, most notably the social sciences (the absence of Max Weber from our conventional humanistic formation strikes me as particularly deplorable, as the first essay in this volume may suggest). It also implies that whatever its own (very considerable) truth claims, Marxism must also take its chances on this polemic level and—even though it is neither a contemporary *theory*, in the historically specific sense of this word, nor a traditional *philosophy* (but rather, like Freud, that particular thing sometimes called a unity-of-theory-and-practice)—measure its range, by way of the transcoding operation, against its various methodological rivals or alternatives. What has sometimes in my own work been thought to be either eclectic or, still worse, synthesizing and "Hegelian," will generally be found to involve transcoding of this type, rather than random, but all-inclusionary system building.

Theory and History of Literature

The Ideologies of Theory
Volume 2

Chapter 1
The Vanishing Mediator; or, Max Weber as Storyteller

The sociological treaties of Max Weber form a corpus of narratives peculiarly suited for analytical techniques developed in the study of myths and other types of imaginative literature. Such an approach requires a distance from Weber's work and an attitude toward it quite different from that of official sociology; for the latter naturally enough wishes first to inquire into the accuracy of Weber's descriptions and the validity of the hypotheses he proposes to account for them. In the present study, however, we must from the outset suspend such judgments, which bear on the "referent" of these texts, in order the more clearly to disengage the latter's internal structure.

Surely, in the case of a theoretically sophisticated scholar who in his own writings explicitly discusses the use and functions of models or, as he calls them, "ideal types" in the practice of historiography, there can be no room for the reactions of a scandalized positivism to an approach that, like our own, seems to assimilate sociology and discursive prose to the various other forms of overt or disguised fantasy or storytelling. Still, one can admit the paradox inherent in a search for personal or unconscious, somehow "psychological," structures in the work of a man who aimed at the establishment of sociology as a "value-free" discipline and who struggled to provide a methodological foundation for a genuinely objective and scientific analysis of social institutions. But a growing literature reevaluating Weber from a radical point of view[1] has made it plain that Weber's *Wertfreiheit* was itself a passionate value judgment that has nothing in common with that positivistic and academic type of objectivity to which it has so often been assimilated by Weber's American interpreters. We must therefore initially determine the meaning of this concept, before proceeding to an analysis of the practical work that Weber executed in its name.

I

It cannot be doubted that Weber first evolved the doctrine of *Wertfreiheit* as a weapon in his polemic struggle against politically oriented teaching not so much on the Left as on the far Right and that he had in mind the stridently nationalistic and anti-Semitic lectures of Treitschke in particular. Yet, a notion like that of value-free and objective research cannot but be influenced by the element in which it originates and by the use to which it is put. It is not a matter of indifference for us, therefore, that it is not the product of some neutral atmosphere of scientific research but amounts to the affirmation of one value over others.

It is scarcely surprising, then, that such an arm, such an ideologically strategic concept, could later be trained so effectively against the Left as well; and this is perhaps the moment at which to point out that Weber's anti-Marxism has frequently been misconceived and that much of the material generally supposed to amount to a repudiation of Marxism as a whole (for example, *The Protestant Ethic)* is in fact explicitly directed against vulgar Marxism and against that economism of the Second International to which Engels had himself objected.[2] I will return to Weber's view of vulgar Marxism in a later section. Here I want to point out that his work on the influence of religious factors on economic development, far from discrediting historical materialism as a theory, can just as adequately be considered a contribution to it.

In reality, Weber's most influential legacy to the anti-Marxist arsenal lay not in some idealistic reaction against a materialism he himself clearly shared with Marx but rather in the strategic substitution, in his own research and theorization, of the political for the economic realm as the principal object of study, and thus, implicitly, as the ultimately determining reality of history. Thus, Weber made of political and social history—the growth of bureaucracies, the influence of the charismatic individual and his function in political institutions—an autonomous field of study that can be examined in relative isolation from questions of economic development. Such a displacement takes the form, in our own time, of the classic strategy by which analyses of capitalism are parried by discussions of political freedom, and concepts of economic alienation and of the commodity system replaced by attacks on party bureaucracy, the "new class," and the like.

As a statesman and a political theorist, it is certain that Weber was indeed profoundly antisocialist, and his (well-founded) doubts of the capacity of the Social Democratic leadership to govern the nation were only the external and practical reinforcements of a far more deeply held position with which I will try to come to terms in what follows. In this sense Weber is a classic manifestation of all the ambiguity of liberalism in its traditional nineteenth-century sense: hostile to the Junkers and to Wilhelm II, to nationalistic apologetics of the Treitschke variety, yet himself affirming the ultimate value-giving category of the nation in the face of the class-oriented internationalism of Marxian socialism. Called both the "German Machiavelli" (Meinecke) and the "greatest German of our age" (Jaspers), Weber is a somber and enigmatic figure, whose death at the very outset of the Weimar Republic leaves his historical significance in the transition from the Wilhelminian era to that of Hitler forever in doubt.

Wertfreiheit as a scientific value is surely intimately related, in some way yet to be determined, to those political positions; and it is just as surely related to Weber's troubled emotional life. For psychoanalysis, Weber has, indeed, all the fascination of the *grand malade*, the illustrious bearer of a neurosis in which intellectual productivity is closely related to the intermittent crippling effects of unconscious forces. The facts of his biography—unusual parental conflict, a four-year period of virtual intellectual paralysis at the very height of an active career, other grave symptoms more recently revealed in Arthur Mitzman's book *The Iron Cage*—all testify to the presence in Weber of the most serious Oedipal disturbances, arousing, in the words of H. Stuart Hughes, "the paradoxical suspicion that the most probing social theory of our time was the indirect sequel of an *unresolved* neurosis of a classic Freudian type."[3]

Yet, Weber's breakdown is no mere clinical curiosity but must itself be understood in the wider context of a European (and North American) moral crisis that has not yet found its historian. Nothing is indeed quite so striking as the simultaneous appearance, within the various national situations at the end of the nineteenth century, of comparable visions of the crippling of energies, of analogous expressions of a philosophical pessimism that is itself but the intellectual exposition of some more concrete lived experience. One thinks of Flaubert or of the Tennyson of *In Memoriam;* of Hardy or Huysmans; of the "ordeal" of Mark Twain; of the self-imposed dreariness of Tolstoy's later years; of Ibsen or of Mallarmé's "sterility."

These phenomena have all been the objects of intensive study, of course, but only within the various national frameworks, each of which has seemed to dictate its own characteristic mode of interpretation. Thus, in France, the loss of energy is seen as the result of what is essentially a political dilemma: the failure of the Revolution of 1848, and the increasing disillusionment, first with the regime of the Second Empire, and finally with that of the Third Republic itself. In England, on the other hand, it has been customarily thought of in religious or philosophical terms, as a slow withdrawal of the "sea of faith," as a result of the impact of Darwin and then of triumphant positivism and of the ravages made by the development of natural science in a social milieu organized around the established Church. In Germany and in America, finally, this generalized cultural depression has most frequently been accounted for economically, by the sudden growth of a brash and uninhibited business civilization, of a "gilded age" in which the materialism and philistinism of the new industrialist find their monuments in the sprawling and unlovely cities of Chicago or Berlin, in which the opposition thus tends to take on the coloration of the aesthete, whether in Thomas Mann's artists or in the flight of American intellectuals to the older European cities. These modes of explanation are, of course, not mutually exclusive and have moreover often been accompanied by yet a fourth diagnosis, at least for the Protestant countries, namely, that of Victorianism in sexual matters, which gives the age its name and which expressses itself in the triple guise of the authoritarian patriarchal family, the taboo on sexual expression, and the obligatory frigidity of "respectable" women.

No doubt all these factors played their part, but it would seem essential, before evaluating any of them, to look more closely at the nature of the concrete experience they are invoked to explain, which is generally known under its contemporary designation as "spleen," or "ennui." To have a complete picture of what happened to Weber, in other words, we would need a thorough phenomenological description of this psychic condition, and to put it this way is to realize that ennui is itself a historical phenomenon, one that does not necessarily have any equivalent in other cultures or indeed at other stages of our own. We must, for instance, make a structural distinction between this late nineteenth-century condition and the Romantic dispair of the early years of the century. In the latter, the sufferer withdraws completely from the world, to sit apart in a post of Byronic malediction or to return in the guise of the Satanic outcast and enemy of society. To such a state, the essential gesture of which is *refusal,* either heroic or dejected, the description as well as the diagnosis made by Freud for the condition he called "melancholia" might most fittingly apply: "The distinguishing mental features of melancholia are a profoundly painful dejection, abrogation of interest in the outside world, loss of the capacity to love, inhibition of all activitiy, and a lowering of the self-regarding feelings to a degree that finds utterance in self-reproaches and self-revilings, and culminates in a delusional expectation of punishment."[4] For Freud, such symptoms result from the loss of an object in which the libido has been invested and which has been narcissistically associated with the self: "the testing of reality, having shown that the loved object no longer exists, requires forthwith that all the libido shall be withdrawn from its attachments to this object. Against this demand a struggle of course arises—it may be universally observed that man never willingly abandons a libido-position, not even when a substitute is already beckoning to him. This struggle can be so intense that a turning away from reality ensues, the object being clung to through the medium of a hallucinatory wish-psychosis."[5] We may perhaps overhastily suggest that the object thus mourned by the Romantics was the aristocractic world itself, which even the Restoration was unable to bring back to life.

We may thus describe Romanticism as a coming to consciousness of some fundamental loss in shock and rage, a kind of furious rattling of the bars of the prison, a helpless attempt to recuperate lost being by posing and assuming one's fatality in "interesting" ways. But by mid-century this shock is old, and the very object of the loss has been forgotten; the sufferer can no longer remember a situation qualitatively different from his own and assumes, naturally enough, that all life is thus empty. Ennui is thus not so much a form of suffering as an absence of feeling in general, one in which, in a psychic atmosphere as windless and impassive as a Victorian interior, only the passage of time itself is registered, in the absence of any real activity. The fundamental gesture of ennui is not revolt but renunciation, as in the heroes of Henry James and of Fontane: it does not withdraw from the world but remains within it, gazing at its activities with all the narcotic indifference of Alice's Caterpillar, and finds characteristic expression in those lengthy catalogs of the objects of human enterprise through which Flaubert recites the litany of earthly vanities. (In this sense, the triumphant catalogs of a Whitman would be understood as a second-degree recuperation, as the attempt, not unlike that of Nietzsche, to repossess the dead world through an effort of the will, in a kind of manic joy.)

It is equally important, however, to distinguish ennui from that affect most characteristic of our own time, namely, *anxiety*, for the latter is an active principle, and the classic descriptions of Heidegger and Sartre make it clear that anxiety is intimately related to praxis itself and results from a sudden awareness of the self as the unjustified source of all values and of all action, an awareness that can arise only in the moment of choice and not in a situation of generalized inactivity. In this sense, we might schematically understand Romantic despair, ennui, and anxiety as three moments in the same historical process: in which the soul, having first registered its shock and distress at the new and barren world in which it finds itself, begins with a kind of paralyzed detachment to take an inventory of its surroundings, before at length coming to the conclusion that it is itself the very ground of the latter's bustling agitation and the source and foundation of the values on which, as in a void, those activities depend. Such a historical pathology would therefore illustrate the psychic adaptation of man to an increasingly humanized world.

Paradoxically, however, one of the classic descriptions of ennui is not a modern one at all, and Thomas Aquinas' characterization of what he called "acedia" as a "kind of sadness, whereby a man becomes sluggish in spiritual exercises because they weary the body"[6] may illuminate another essential component of the experience in question. For Aquinas' terms suggest that ennui, or acedia, is not a primitive but rather a very sophisticated reaction, a disease of clerics: "Acedia, according to Damascene, is 'an oppressive sorrow,' which, namely, so weighs upon man's mind that he wants to do nothing (thus acid things [acida] are also cold). Hence acedia implies a certain weariness of work, as appears from a gloss on Psalms 106, 18, *Their soul abhorred all manner of meat,* and from the definition of some who say that acedia is a sluggishness of the mind which neglects to begin good."[7] Acedia is thus something that happens to intellectuals, and its relationship to the monastic environment takes on renewed significance for us if we recall that, for Weber, monasticism is one of the early forms of rationalization itself. Not the panic of peasants in the fact of a new technology, therefore, but rather the weariness of the intellectual specialist, who knows the *how* so well that he comes to doubt the *why:* such is the picture of ennui that emerges from these early accounts, and it may help us make the transition from a phenomenological description of the experience itself to the ways in which traditional philosophical thought has conceptualized it.

The principal form such conceptualization has taken seems to me to be the separation of means from ends, and if such a separation is thought to be a universal characteristic of human beings as plan-making animals, it suffices to relate it to the various forms of human society to realize that they have always been aware of it as such. In a tradition-oriented society, indeed, where tasks are assigned by birth or by ritual, the internal temporal dissociation within the act itself that characterizes the lag between an aim and its execution is not yet present. The techniques for achieving a given end are themselves sacred, are therefore performed for their own sake and in their own right. Such societies, therefore, lack the abstract concept of an "act" as such, a concept that subsumes under itself the most heterogeneous forms of human exertion; and the latter are felt to be as autonomous and as intrinsically meaningful as the various totemic animals or the various castes according to which their performers are organized.

It is worth noting that even when we reach the birth of philosophical abstraction in classical Greece, the elaborate Aristotelian system of the four causes (material, effective, formal, and final)[8] implies a somewhat different orientation toward activity than our own stark opposition between means and ends. The Aristotelian concept reflects an artisanal culture and makes a greater place for the concrete situation itself, for the act of making and of handicraft, which, with its inherited techniques, may be seen as a kind of halfway house between tradition-oriented societies and our own technological one. Thus, for Aristotle, the clay (material cause) still demands to be formed into the pot; the métier still has a kind of inner logic, a voice of its own; and the preexisting forms and patterns do not yet have the stark independence of the modern notion of an "end." Obviously, the modern notion is implicit in the Aristotelian scheme, but it does not yet function with the abstract and depersonalized force it has come to have in the modern secular market culture, in the world of desacralized technique.

Surely the emergence of the modern dichotomous view of action is related to the secularization of action in the modern world in general, to the twin affranchisement from the bonds of tradition that is the result of the French Revolution and the development of the market system. Now for the first time in human history the realm of values becomes itself problematical and can be isolated and contemplated independently; now in the new middle-class culture for the first time people weigh the various activities against each other; what we call private life or individualistic subjectivity, indeed, is precisely the distance that permits them to do so and to hold their professional enterprises at arm's length. Hence, for instance, the originality in the realm of the novel of the "Quel métier prendre?" of a Stendhal, whose works explore as it were the atomic weights of the various professionals and political regimes as alternate life forms. Yet, such an exploration already implies the existence of a certain ennui: what René Girard has termed the "Romantic lie" of innate passions and inborn vocations has vanished, and to wonder what to do with your life is already to commit yourself in advance to a certain ontological dissatisfaction with any of the ultimate possibilities. Finally, with Stendhal's admirer Nietzsche, this essential distance from all values permits a theory of Value to come into existence for the first time; but a theory that takes value itself as its object and for which all values are thus from this point of view equivalent, if not interchangeable, implies the existence of a vantage point beyond all values, one that permits the transcendence or the "transvaluation" of all value as such. This is, indeed, the profound relevance of Nietzsche for Weber, for whom, at the same time, ironically, Nietzsche's diagnosis remains valid:

> He who wishes to create new values must be capable of destroying existent values remorselessly: creation passes through destruction, good and evil go hand in hand. But since this creation lies beyond good and evil, the existing moral norms are of no use and only his will to truth can guide the creator in his titanic struggle. *For the will to truth is also a form of the "will to power,"—perhaps even its supreme form* [italics mine]. The task of the true seeker for wisdom is *to valorize values themselves,* a task that prevents him from participating effectively in the material struggle of men among each other. Yet this nonintervention is no sign of weakness. On the Contrary.[9]

Fleischmann's account of Weber's essential Nietzscheanism thus confirms the interpretation of *Wertfreiheit,* suggested above, as an active and polemic weapon, as a mode of self-affirmation and of intellectual conquest in the sense of the Nietzschean "will to power."[10]

Once ends have been thus sundered from means, in lived experience and in the theory that reflects it, it is impossible to put the two back together again, to restore the "naive" and primitive, unself-conscious unity of action in the older tradition-oriented cultures; and the emphasis of contemporary philosophy on restoring the concrete, on being in the world, on praxis as a total process, may best be understood against the background of this dissociation. Ennui, which is, as we have said, one of the most characteristic and emblematic experiences of the modern world, can now be seen to presuppose the rift between intention and act as a precondition of its own existence: to know spleen, the sufferer must be able to see activity as pure technical performance without intrinsic purpose or value.

What is paradoxical about such an experience is indeed that it is contemporaneous with one of the most active periods in human history, with all the mechanical animation of late Victorian city life, with all the smoke and conveyance inherent in new living conditions and in the rapid development of business and industry, with the experimental triumphs of positivistic science and its conquest of the university system, with all the bustling parliamentary and bureaucratic activity of the new middle-class regimes, the spread of the press, the diffusion of literacy and culture, the ready accessibility of the newly mass-produced commodities of a consumer civilization. Thus, we are faced with the peculiar impression that life becomes meaningless in direct proportion to people's control of their environment and that a humanization of the world goes hand in hand with a spreading philosophic and existential despair. It is as though the meaningfulness of the world remained intact only so long as some portion of that world—an imperfectly dominated Nature, a blindly theocratic and hierarchical social tradition—hung beyond human reach; as though it were only at the point at which middle-class man was free to make or remake his own world from top to bottom that its fundamental absurdity came home to him.

In this situation, the most original thinkers are clearly enough not those who have not yet glimpsed the new meaninglessness of life; nor yet again those who, having been granted such alarming insight, then set about divising some "philosophy of as if" to paper over the void. Indeed, it can be said that the most interesting artists and thinkers of this period choose and will the very experience of meaninglessness itself, and cling to it as to some ultimate reality, some ultimate truth of existence of which they do not wish to be cheated: "lieber will noch der Mensch *das Nichts* wollen," cried Nietzsche, "als *nicht* wollen." In this sense Weber's *Wertfreiheit* is a passionate refusal of the illusions of meaning itself, a repudiation of all philosophies which—the Hegelian world spirit and the Marxist dialectic just as much as Christian Providence—seek to convince us that some teleological movement is immanent in the otherwise chaotic and random agitation of empirical life. "Wherever rational empiricism has been able to complete with any consequence the process of the desacralization of the world and its transformation into a causal mechanism, the definitive result is a tension with the demands of that ethical postulate that the world be seen as a divinely ordered cosmos in some way oriented towards an ethical meaning." And having quoted this passage from Weber's *Sociology of Religion*, Wolfgang J. Mommsen goes on to observe: "This is the conviction in which Max Weber resolutely combats all the variously devised philosophies of history of his day....And it is particularly noteworthy and striking with what sometimes wholly unbridled passion Weber waged this struggle."[11] This attitude, which we may term "heroic cynicism," is evidently something rather different from mere scientific objectivity, and constitutes one of the most interesting aspects of a genuinely consequent conservative position. It is one for which the existent, the status quo, amounts somehow to Being itself, so that revolutionary project as well as naive and nostalgic illusion come to seem equally "unrealistic." It is this vested interest in Being that is in general responsible for the reactionary political views of the majority of the great realistic novelists, and much the same might be said for the sociologist of Weber's stamp: the functional study of society requires you to presuppose that the entire social mechanism is complete and present before your very eyes; the visionaries who want to tinker with it risk invalidating the carefully recorded results of your experimental measurements.

Yet, the pluralism suggested by Weber's (and Nietzsche's) suspension of all values is as far from that tolerant coexistence ritually invoked by modern liberal apologists as was *Wertfreiheit* itself from the dominant fetish of positivistic objectivity. Pluralism for Weber means *pantheism*, not peaceful coexistence but a Homeric battlefield, in which "different gods struggle with one another, now and for all times to come. We live as did the ancients when their world was not yet disenchanted of its gods and demons, only we live in a different sense. As Hellenic man at times sacrificed to Aphrodite and at other times to Apollo, and, above all, as everybody scarificed to the gods of his city, so do we still nowadays, only the bearing of man has been disenchanted and denuded of its mystical but inwardly genuine plasticity. Fate, and certanly not 'science,' holds sway over these gods and their struggles. One can only understand what the godhead is in the one or in the other order."[12] These various gods are not only the various Weltanschauungen, the competing ideologies of the modern marketplace, but also, and above all, the various and unrelated zones and dimensions into which individual life is shattered in the modern world, and which make of the process of living a kind of random sacrificing, now to public, now to private, deities of all shapes and conceptions. This irreconcilable struggle between the heterogeneous values of modern life has the practical result, described at the close of Weber's other great lecture, "Politics as a Vocation," of dividing the realm of *Realpolitik* as irrevocably from the preoccupations of ethics as at the end of the *Baghavad-Gita*, where Arjuna is admonished, in spite of his horror of killing, to return to the battle and "do what must be done."

It now becomes perhaps a little clearer why the "religiously unmusical" Weber was so fascinated by religion itself. The metaphorical language of pantheism used above underscores the way in which, for Weber, the religious phenomenon is the very hypostasis of value in general, value seen from the outside by the man who no longer believes in any values and for whom such living belief has thus become a kind of mystery in the older ritualistic sense. In this Weber takes his place in that modern tradition of an *aesthetic* valorization of religion that may be said to have been inaugurated by Chauteaubriand in *Le Génie du christianisme* and prolonged in our own time by such works as Malraux's *Voix du silence*. It is a curious attitude, one that combines something of the allure of a religiously fellow-traveling agnosticism with the secret inferiority longings of the impotent in matters of belief, and it furnishes as striking a symbol as any other of Weber's concept of scientific research, that uncomfortable ascesis and renunciation that permits Value to become visible as an object of study and that results in the characteristic conclusion to the passage quoted above from "Science as a Vocation": "With this understanding, however [the vision of life as a struggle between the gods], the matter has reached its limit so far as it can be discussed in a lecture-room and by a professor."

We may therefore conclude that Weber's attitude toward values preeminently constitutes a value in its own right, and that it is the difficulty of maintaining such an inner contradiction that imposes on him that attitude of paralysis, of suspended action and judgment, which is so frequently mistaken for objectivity in the usual academic sense of the term. That *Wertfreiheit* should with Weber's followers resolve itself into simple objectivity is scarcely surprising, for Weber's own tortured and Nietzschean solution could not be maintained for long, or without the greatest personal cost. But this means that we are as fully entitled to inquire into the ideological content of Weber's system as into its scientific validity or the accuracy of its research. Indeed, the mythic structure of that system, or worldview, would seem to call for methods that overflow the limits of a purely semantic or cognitive investigation. For the historian and the social scientist are called on, henceforth, to tell the story of the various "gods" and of their struggles with each other, a story that sometimes like those told by Nietzsche, involves the mystery of a god's death. What more fitting object, then, for narrative analysis?

II

Max Weber's thinking offers a privileged object for what must initially be a purely logical or conceptual analysis, inasmuch as it is explicitly organized into pairs of binary oppositions, albeit of a rare complexity. "When one comes to try to isolate the main *logical* outline of Weber's analysis," Talcott Parsons tells us, "the prominence of the pattern of dichotomization is striking."[13] As a kind of checklist of such oppositions in Weber, we might recall the most famous of all, that of bureaucracy versus charisma, but also asceticism versus mysticism, *Berufmensch* versus *Fachmensch*, *Realpolitik* versus ethics, politics versus science, and so forth.

At the same time, the extraordinary intricacies attained by combinations between these various terms—particularly in late Weber, where, as Herbert Marcuse has said, "the method of formal definitions, classifications and typologies celebrates true orgies"[14]—suggests that to try to read Weber term by term, to comprehend each semantic phenomenon in isolation or even in combination with its conceptual opposite number, is an agonizing and in the long run sterile enterprise. At best, we can hope to transcend the bewildering results of this thinking by isolating those simpler and more central mechanisms from which the types and definitions themselves emerge; and to do so, the accompanying permutational mechanism or "semantic rectangle" developed by A. J. Greimas would seem to offer the most useful instrument for sorting out the basic elements that make up Weber's system:

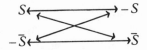

The premise of this schema, which distinguishes between the contrary of a given term S ($-S$, or what we may term "anti-S") and its simple negative or contradictory ($\bar{S}$, or "not-S"), holds that all concepts are implicitly or explicitly defined in terms of conceptual oppositions. Its advantage lies in the possibility it suggests of generating other supplementary and related elements out of that initial pair of contrary terms. Thus, for example, we observe that the contrary of S, or $-S$ (anti-S), logically possesses a contradictory of its own in not-anti-S (or $\bar{S}$). Moreover, it should be noted that each side of the rectangle constitutes the possibility of a synthetic term (S united with $-S$ is termed a "complex" term, whereas the union of $-\bar{S}$ and $\bar{S}$ is a "neutral" one) that marks out as it were the closure or outer limits of the thought system in question.[15]

That such an approach is scarcely alien to the spirit of Weber's thought may be judged by reference to one of the most fundamental Weberian classification schemes, namely, that of the four types of social behavior: "Like all action, social action can also be determined in the following ways: (1) as *end-rational* [*zweckrational*]: through expectations about the behavior of external objects and of other people where such expectations are utilized as 'conditions' or 'means' toward rationally pursued and conceived success-oriented individual *ends;* (2) as *value-rational* [*wertrational*]: through conscious belief in the unconditional value of a given type of conduct as such—whether that value be ethical, aesthetic, religous, or of whatever character—and irrespective of the ultimate success of the conduct in question; (3) as *affective* [*affektuell*], and in particular emotional: through the immediate experience of affects and states of feeling; (4) as *traditional:* through habit become instinctive.''[16]

The Greimas scheme allows us to articulate as a set of logically limited conceptual possibilities what we might otherwise be tempted to see as a relatively unsystematic list of empirically observed and classified types of actions:

$$S \longleftrightarrow -S$$

S	$-S$
END-RATIONAL	VALUE-RATIONAL
(business or commercial activity)	(ethics)
$\overline{-S}$	$\overline{S}$
TRADITIONAL	EMOTIONAL

Such a logical restructuration accounts for an impression that must more or less obscurely strike every reader of Weber at one time or another, namely, that there is a qualitative difference between the terms of the initial opposition (end- or *value*-rationality) and those of the second (tradition or emotion). It now becomes clear that the latter are not positive explanations in their own right, but are rather privative ones, simple negations of the positive terms and thus in some sense catchalls for material that does not fit into the official analytic system. Examples that fit the categories S and $-S$ are by definition interpretable by the social scientist (are in other words, in Weber's terminology, "rational"!) inasmuch as in either type of conduct so designated we are able to detect the presence of an ends-means structure (the end is immanent to the means in S—here misnamed "end-rational" when Weber means to stress the predominance of means and technique—while it is transcendent to them in $-S$). But in the so-called emotional category $\overline{S}$ we are concerned with material that amounts to a simple disorder of S itself: some end is clearly sought, although it is not thematized as a value in its own right, but the agent has lost control of his means and his technical equipment for achieving that end. And in the even more interesting case of tradition-oriented behavior, collective, rather than, as in $\overline{S}$, individual, we find examples of conduct that do not seem to be governed by any visible end or value, although they present observable regularities and may thus be supposed to be intelligible or "rational" in some way. Tradition-oriented conduct is in fact institutionalized behavior whose original aim—endowed by the charismatic act of some leader or value-giver—has been gradually lost from view. It is thus value-rationality gone stale, transformed into something unrecognizable, and proves meaningful or rational in the past only, in the light of that original and obliterated charismatic gesture of which it is the trace and the ruined memorial. Indeed, it would seem that such a term must if anything be understood in a purely formal manner, as one that serves as the beginning of a genuine historical transformation and that thus falls outside the full intelligibility of the elements of the latter. It has within it the arbitrariness of all starting points and may for want of a better expression be described as "sham-cognitive," as having the appearance only of an explanation or of an intellectual category (for it is clear that, if we had set the frame, the temporal coordinates, at an earlier point in time, what is here called "tradition-orientation" would then become something like the institutionalization of charisma, in other words, a phenomenon closely linked to the later notion of bureaucratization itself, and as such fully comprehensible in rational terms). The next step in an analysis of this kind would evidently be an investigation into the origins of the binary opposition on which this entire conceptual system is based. We have already sketched the historical evolution of the ends-means dichotomy in our opening section; an explanation of Weber's own personal attraction to such a conceptual opposition is offered in the concluding section of this chapter.

But the very presence, within an apparently static and logical schema, of what amounts to a genuine historical change (in other words, the lapse of what was originally value-oriented action into tradition-oriented action) suggests that Weberian typology, even at its most abstract, as here, conceals a kind of narrative behind its classificatory appearance. We may give, as an example of this, Weber's sociology of religion, in which the operative sociological distinction is that between cults organized around the person of the magician and those conducted by a priesthood: "those professional functionaries who influence the gods by means of worship" are thus explicitly contrasted with "magicians who coerce demons by magical means."[17] The student of Weber here recognizes one of his great themes, namely, the contrast between charismatic and irrational forms of life and those rational and collective arrangements of which the modern bureaucracy is the supreme, but not the only, example. At the same time, it would seem clear that what is at issue in such a distinction is not the mere classification of given religious phenomena into one or the other category, but rather the problem of explaining the historical transition from one form to the other.

The distinction between magician and priest is in fact not the primary one, and when we resolve it into the basic conceptual terms and operations of which it is composed, Weber's ability to construct a historical explanation out of a system of apparently static, classificatory terms will become clearer. The power of the magician is, for Weber, based on the way he combines some uniquely personal or charismatic prestige with the use of magical powers for immediate and individual gain, whether of a spiritual type (salvation) or a material one (rain). To juxtapose the magician with the priest in these terms is to understand that the magician's personal prestige amounts to a claim to a purely individual revelation, whereas the sacramental power of the priesthood is based on its participation in what is given as a universal doctrine. The bureaucratic organization of the priesthood may then be read as the negation of the purely personal and individual power of the magician, and we may tentatively formalize the relationship of these various characteristics to each other as follows:

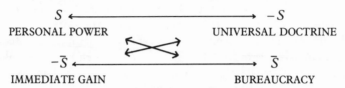

$$S \longleftrightarrow -S$$

PERSONAL POWER   UNIVERSAL DOCTRINE

$$-\bar{S} \longleftrightarrow \bar{S}$$

IMMEDIATE GAIN   BUREAUCRACY

In such a schema, each historical agent would appear to recapitulate the opposite side of a rectangle, or what Greimas designates as its "deictic" axis: thus the figure of the magician amounts to the synthesis of the two left-hand terms, S and $-\bar{S}$ (or "personal power" and "immediate gain"), whereas the priesthood unites the two right-hand attributes $-S$ and $\bar{S}$ (or "universal doctrine" and "bureaucracy").

But a visual inspection of the semantic rectangle makes it clear that two further logical possibilities remain unfilled, namely, those of the "complex" and "neutral" terms, in other words, the syntheses of S and $-S$, and $-\bar{S}$ and $\bar{S}$, respectively.

These additional conceptual possibilities, indeed, are what permits Weber to explain the historical transformation of religion from its early, magical origins to its later codified and bureaucratic structure: for the complex term logically provided by the system may now serve as the mediator between the two forms. For a realization of this complex term, which unites the characteristics of personal authority with the claim to a universal doctrine, we must turn to the figure of the prophet, one that has a crucial significance for Weber's reading of history. For the prophet (and Weber sees the Old Testament prophecy as the archetype of this sociological function) is essentially the bearer of rationalization itself: "In all times there has been but one means of breaking down the power of magic and establishing a rational conduct of life: this means is great rational prophecy. Not every prophecy by any means destroys the power of magic; but it is possible for a prophet who furnishes credentials in the shape of miracles and otherwise, to break down the traditional sacred rules. Prophecies have released the world from magic and in doing so have created the basis for our modern science and technology, and for capitalism."[18]

Thus, the prophet is able to mediate the basic contradiction between the two social forms or moments of religious practice and to provide a historical transition from one to the other by assimilating traits selected from the opposing forms and by repudiating others. He thereby serves as the means of liquidating the magician's concern with immediate gain and of preparing a situation in which may ultimately appear a bureaucracy that will eclipse his own historical function as well and render it henceforth unnecessary.

In the light of this transformation of an apparently static and classificatory logical schema into a historical and essentially narrative process, it does not seem too farfetched to suggest that the sunken neutral term at the base of the rectangle, which unites bureaucracy with immediate gain, may designate a historical form that will in its turn replace the priesthood and indeed supplant organized religion in general; for such a description characterizes nothing quite so well as that anonymous "organization man" of the modern bureaucratic and capitalist state who was the ultimate desacralized product of the prophet's historic mission. Our rectangle would thus be completed as follows:

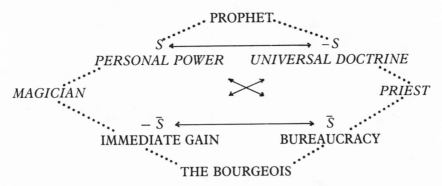

At this point, therefore, we find ourselves confronting a theoretical problem that may alternately be characterized as that of history or that of narrative, depending on whether we raise it in connection with the object of our study or our own method of analyzing that object, respectively. Both the interpretation of historical change and the analysis of narrative structure require us to come to grips with what in structural terminology is known as the "diachronic"; the problem arises, however, from the apparent necessity of the mind to grasp diachrony in what are essentially "synchronic," or static and systematic, terms. Thus, it would seem that to "understand" history involves a translation of flux or change into some relatively fixed relationship between two states or moments—the "before" and the "after" of the historical transformation. "Every apprehension of meaning," Greimas tells us, "has as its consequence the transformation of history into permanencies of various kinds: whether we have to do with the inquiry into the meaning of an individual life or into the meaning of a story (or of history itself [both designated by the French word *histoire*]), the inquiry, in other words, the fact that we assume a message-receiving attitude before a linguistic manifestation, has the result that the historical algorisms are felt as states, which is to say as static structures."[19] In a sense, then, the problem of narrative analysis may be seen as the reverse of that of history; for where history involves some basic conceptual breakthrough to the realities of change and of the diachronic in general, narrative already presupposes some fundamental feeling of change which we are then called on to account for in synchronic and analytic terms. Narrative analysis, in other words, requires us to explain the imaginative illusion of change, of time, or of history itself, by reference to basic components of the narrative line that are bound to be static ones.

We have already seen one way in which this transformational process may be conceived in the mediations provided for by the various combinations inherent in the semantic rectangle. It would seem useful, however, to consider a model explicitly devised to account for narrative transformations as such: a model of this kind, indeed, would seem, more appropriate for the analysis of those works of Weber, such as *The Protestant Ethic and the Spirit of Capitalism*, that deal with historical material similar to that involved in the discussion of the prophet (in other words, the changeover from older to newer religious forms, and beyond them, to a wholly secularized worldview), but that deal with it in an explicitly narrative rather than classificatory and expository manner.

Such a model is available to us in Claude Lévi-Strauss' much debated formalization of the structure of myth, which he proposes in the following fashion: "it would seem henceforth evident that every myth (taken as the totality of its variants) can be reduced to a formula of the following type:

$$F_x(a) : F_y(b) \cong F_x(b) : F_{-a}(y)$$

where, the two terms a and b being given along with their functions, a relationship of equivalence is affirmed between two situations respectively defined by an inversion of *terms* and of *relations*, under two conditions: (1) that one of the the terms be replaced by its contrary (in the above formalization a and $-a$); (2) that a correlative inversion be made between the *function value* and the *term value* of two elements (above y and a)."[20] It should be pointed out that if this formula is taken in a purely semantic sense, as the basic mechanism of the "deep structure" of myth, then no surface narrative movement is implied, and we are dealing simply with an antinomy in which the primitive mind poses the equivalence ($\cong$) of two apparently contradictory cognitive systems (in Lévi-Strauss' analysis of the Oedipus myth, kinship and cosmology). If, on the other hand, we use it to deal with narrative events, its advantage is to suggest the ways in which, without the addition of any new terms, some illusion of change and transformation may nonetheless be generated; and this is accomplished by a shifting of valance from positive to negative (transformation of a to $-a$) and an inversion of what was formerly a term into a function and vice versa. I should add that a good deal of experimentation with this use of the forumla has led me to specify the following two additional rules of operation, namely: (3) in spite of their designations (x

would not seem to have to be related to y in any way), in practice the two functions must always be felt to be opposites of each other; and (4) in the assignment of terms to functions, there must be a kind of asymmetrical harmony between x and b on the one hand, and y and a on the other (such dissymmetry is necessary to generate the illusion of change, inasmuch as the left-hand side of the equation must be felt to be a precarious and unstable situation from which some type of sudden restructuration is bound to emerge).

Let us now try to rewrite, in terms of the formula in question, Weber's major work on Protestantism, a work that, as is well known, undertakes to give at least a partial explanation of the preparation of the tradition-oriented mentalities of the inhabitants of a feudal peasant Europe for an eventual accommodation to the discipline and delayed gratification inherent in modern industrial labor. The problem is familiar to us from the industrialization in our own time of the Third World, as well as from the stereotypical colonial image of a precapitalist "native" population as lazy, untrustworthy, alcohol-prone, and in general innocent of the European sense of linear time and of the performance principle.[21] Such a contemporary reference, however, helps us glimpse the metaphysical overtones in Weber's treatment, for whom "rationalization" is not some mere local and historic stage in the development of European capitalism, but rather a kind of impending doom, foretelling the descent of that "iron cage" of ascetic rationalism in which we moderns are condemned to imprisonment for the rest of civilized time.[22] Such a vision of history is doubtless what lends these dry pages, interlarded with dead theology and the most unbearable scholarly apparatus, their emotional impact: *de te fabula narratur!* Weber's monograph has about it some of the dizzying pessimism of Freud's *Civilization and Its Discontents* or of the early novels of H. G. Wells, which, contemporaneous with it, offer the same remorseless gaze into a dwindling future.

The Protestant Ethic aims at demonstrating the intimate relationship between the rationalization of modern life (with its resultant *Entzauberung*, or desacralization, its transformation into an organized and disciplined market system) and the development of the Lutheran or Calvinistic notion of a *Beruf*, or religiously sanctioned vocation to live ascetically *within* the world itself. The forces of religious sanction and of secularization govern those constitutive elements of human activity that are ends and means, respectively, so that, following the procedure outlined above, we may distribute the basic terms and functions in Weber's thesis as follows:

x = rationalization
y = "religionalization," or the conversion
    into a purely religious value or sanction
a = ends
b = means.

But before showing how these components are combined into a narrative, it is perhaps worth suggesting the way in which narrative analysis can deal with the patently polemic character of Weber's essay. For, like all historical theses, Weber is writing *against* another position; his text is designated to correct some widespread misapprehension of the nature of Protestantism and of its relationship to the business ethic: that misapprehension is, clearly enough, the vulgar or economistic Marxist view that the new religious forms are to be seen merely as "reflections" of changes in the infrastructure, in other words, of the newly developing economic forms of market capitalism.[23]

That Weber's critique of this view involved something a little more complicated than a mere defense, in the face of vulgar Marxist materialism, of some "idealistic" worldview, that *The Protestant Ethic* amounts to something a little more substantive than some idle affirmation of the shaping power of spirit (for example, religious values and concepts) over social history, may be judged by the warning with which his book concludes: "It is, of course, not my aim to substitute for a one-sided materialistic an equally one-sided spiritualistic causal interpretation of culture and of history."[24]

What third position it is that Weber stakes out for himself we will be able to evaluate shortly. I suggest here, however, that what he objects to in the vulgar Marxist account of the rise of capitalism is not its materialism, but rather the naive linearity of the story it has to tell. In terms of narrative analysis, in other words, we here confront the phenomenon of what is currently termed "intertextuality," in which the text under study must be seen in a relationship of tension and superposition to some older text without which the first cannot properly be understood. Thus, the so-called realistic novel is written against some older dominant narrative form, which it has the function of correcting: *Don Quixote* is to be understood against the background of the romance, Flaubert against that of Balzac and romanticism, and so forth. There is, therefore, where narration is concerned, no such thing as "naive realism," or rather, the latter always entails an internal and structural repudiation of the narrative conventions, which with its "common sense" it undercuts and structurally subverts (in the history of the novel there is often a class content to such devaluation, the older form connoting the aristocratic paradigm, the "realistic" one embodying the new bourgeois values of materialism, common sense, and money).

Lévi-Strauss' formula provides us with a useful way of dramatizing the type of story against which *The Protestant Ethic* is directed. For the vulgar Marxist narrative of the development of Protestantism may be seen as one in which, with the increasing rationalization of the infrastructure, with the increasing economic organization, first of ends and then of the means themselves, there takes place a corresponding shift in the superstructure: thus the older religion of ends and other worldly values gives way to a new rationalization of the innerworldly means, in other words, to the new religious ideology of Calvinism. To accommodate this historical narrative, we must rewrite Lévi-Strauss' formula as follows:

$$F_x(a) : F_x(b) \cong F_{-y}(a) : F_{-y}(b)$$

where the rationalization of ends is to the rationalization of means as the secularization of ends (in other words, Protestant, as opposed to medieval, theology) is to the secularization of means, or to the development of the modern secular and bureaucratic state in general. What strikes us about such a formalization is that it lacks that inversion of terms and functions with which Lévi-Strauss sought to convey some sense of a genuine historical leap and of the emergence of something historically and qualitatively new and unexpected. In this sense, then, we may characterize Weber's objection to the vulgar Marxist position as an aesthetic one, one that detects the weakness of the earlier explanation through flaws in the latter's narrative construction (and it may be suggested in passing that all historical "revision," all the "great debates" about historical interpretation, whether of the class basis of the English civil war, or of origins of the Cold War, or whatever, may be understood in narrative terms in precisely this way).

Returning to the original formula, we are now in a better position to judge the adequacy with which Weber himself conveys the qualitative transformation at stake in this moment of historical change. Thus articulated, Weber's thesis would find expression as follows: the rationalization of ends [$F_x(a)$] is to the religionalization of means [$F_y(b)$] as the rationalization of means [$F_x(b)$] is to the "nonfinalization" of religion [$F_{-a}(y)$], where the reversals of this concluding expression open up a perspective in which religion, now taken as a term rather than a function, ceases to be felt as an ultimate end or value in its own right. Thus, the prolongation of this historical event into the secular waste of modern times is inherent in the initial thesis.

Even more crucial is the operative emphasis placed here upon what we have had to call the "religionalization" of means, which is, it seems to me, the central and most original aspect of Weber's argument. This moment of the formula [$F_y(b)$] does more than to suggest that religion is not, as the vulgar Marxist analysis had it, some mere reflex of infrastructural change. Indeed, it shifts the emphasis from the relationship between religion and "ends," or conscious, superstructural values, and draws our attention to the effect of religious change on the organization of the means themselves; the position of this moment in the formula suggests that it is precisely this effect that triggers the historical restructuration at issue. Thus, paradoxically religionalization becomes itself the principal agent in the process of secularization as a whole.

How this is to be understood in more traditional Weberian language may be conveyed by the following recapitulation of Weber's argument: by destroying the monastic order, Luther made it impossible to pursue otherworldly ends, for there now no longer exist institutions that sanction withdrawal from the daily world of work. Yet, the result of such an institutional transformation is not, as the vulgar Marxist version would have it, the immediate secularization of means, in other words, of the organization of daily life. Rather, with Calvinism we have to do with a new and more thoroughgoing integration of precisely those means into a religious framework. For Calvin, faced with a separation of ends from means so absolute that the ultimate end or value of life was thrust into otherworldliness and the unknowable, found that only the means, in other words, earthly existence itself, remain as a testing place, as a trial and preparation. For the drama of salvation: innerworldly life thus undergoes "a systematic rational ordering of the moral life as a whole."[25] "The process of sanctifying life," Weber tells us, "could thus almost take on the character of a business enterprise. A thoroughgoing Christianization of the whole of life was the consequence of this methodical quality of ethical conduct into which Calvinism as distinct from Lutheranism forced men."[26] This was indeed the view of its contemporaries, such as Sebastian Franck, who "saw the significance of the Reformation in the fact that now every Christian had to be a monk all his life."[27] Thus, we witness here a dialectical reinforcement between what appeared to be the two antithetical positions of rationalization of ends $[F_x(a)]$ and a "religionalization" of means $[F_y(b)]$: something which leads us to a result quite different from what could have been predicted from the linear, vulgar Marxist narrative, the means now becoming *more* rather than less religious, even while the ends grow ever more secularized.

On the right-hand side of the equation the peculiar tension or disequilibrium thus generated is just as unexpectedly resolved; for Calvinism's increasing rationalization of means, or earthly conduct $[F_x(b)]$, results in the sudden permutation of the final term, in other words, in the disappearance of religion itself as an ultimate value from the henceforth totally rationalized and desacralized world of the capitalist marketplace.

Let us now open a methodological parenthesis in order to evaluate the adequacy of the Lévi-Strauss formula in reaching these conclusions. Its advantage over Greimas' schema lay in its claim to deal with diachrony, or, in other words, with the *irreversible* character of narrative and historical change. In fact, however, its principal strength turns out to have been the possibility of comparison that it affords with other narrative versions of the same events, and the way in which it permitted us to dramatize the "intertextuality" of Weber's thesis. What Greimas' relatively static and logical scheme is on the other hand able to demonstrate, what is absent from Lévi-Strauss' formula as it is here worked out,[28] is the hypothesis of some central mediatory figure or institution that can account for the passage from one temporal and historical state to another one. In other words, Lévi-Strauss' formula, operating as it does with something like a deep structure of narrative, shows us the various conceptual elements or data at work as they combine and interact with each other, but does not give us a very adequate picture of their articulation into those basic surface units of narrative that are the latter's *characters* (in history, of course, these are often groups or movements, such as "Protestantism").

If we now seek to evolve some more adequate scheme that will combine the twin requirements of narrative irreversibility, and of figuration or articulation into agents or characters, it becomes obvious that in one way or another Protestantism will itself serve as a kind of mediation between the traditional medieval world from which it emerged and the modern secularized one that it in its turn prepared. In the case of the vulgar Marxist narrative against which Weber's is to be understood, this mediation would take the rather banal form of a transitional state in which life is made less religious by a new theological doctrine (Protestantism) that systematically dismantles the traditional medieval religious structures and allows wholly secular ones to take their place.

As against this, Weber's hypothesis recovers something of its original and paradoxical willfullness: the transition from religion to *Entzauberung*, from the medieval to the modern moment, is effected, he tells us, not by making life less religious but by making it *more* so. Calvin did not desacralize the world; on the contrary, he turned the *entire* world into a monastery. We must therefore devise some notation for the difference between this explicit and self-conscious religious investment of life by Calvin and the relatively unthematized and traditionalistic religious framework of medieval life in general (something I have tried to convey by the brackets in the graph that follows). The basic and constitutive terms of the three overall stages in this historical progression may now be articulated:

	MEDIEVAL	PROTESTANT	MODERN
RELIGIOUS ENDS OR MEANING	[+]	+	−
RATIONAL ORGANIZATION OF MEANS	−	+	+

It would, therefore, appear that the crucial transformation on the level of means from a traditional and nonrationalistic organization to a rational and quantified one in modern times has been effectuated within the framework, or better still, beneath the cover, of an intensified "religionalization" of ends, in other words, by a new thematization of religion on the level of ends or values, by a removal of the brackets.

But we have not yet taken full advantage of the superiority, in the present context, of this scheme over the formula proposed by Lévi-Strauss; for another indication of the inherent structural limitations of the latter may be seen in the way in which it obliged us to telescope into the single term "religionalization of means" what were in fact two distinct moments of Protestantism, the theology of Luther and that of Calvin. In reality, Weber's text proposes not three, but rather four historical stages, which amount to a virtual *combinatoire* of all the possible logical permutations between ends and means, on the one hand, and innerworldly or otherworldly stances, on the other.

In this light, Weber's portrayal of Luther, for him still an essentially medieval figure, may be understood in terms of narrative strategy: the importance of Luther lies not in his having brought new content to theology as Calvin will, but rather in his having actualized or thematized what was already implicit in the medieval system, in other words, in his having—in terms of our schematic representation—removed the brackets from medieval religious thought. This is the moment, indeed, to recall Weber's view of the medieval monastery as an enclave of rationalization within a tradition-oriented world: "In that epoch the monk is the first human being who lives rationally, who works methodically and by rational means toward a goal, namely the future life. Only for him did the clock strike, only for him were the hours of the day divided—for prayer. The economic life of the monastic communities was also rational."[29]

It is because Luther represents a conscious and indeed agonized renewal of the habituated religious thinking of the Middle Ages that he strikes down the artificial isolation of monastic life. His aim is thus a regeneration of religious value or end-orientation; but in so doing, without realizing it, he liberates the nascent rationalism of the monasteries, which are now able to spread to all domains of life. To use another set of Weberian oppositions, we may describe the medieval situation before which Luther found himself as one in which innerworldly otherworldliness (the institutional sanction of otherworldliness, in other words, the monasteries) and innerworldly thisworldliness (in other words, ordinary daily secular life in general) coexisted. Luther does not bring anything new to this situation; yet by closing off one of its terms, by destroying the institutional possibility of an innerworldly practice of otherworldliness, he prepares the way for Calvin's more decisive permutation, in which a new otherworldly thisworldliness or, if you prefer, an innerworldly asceticism, comes into being. So it is that the intimate relationship that existed between rationalization of means and religionalization of ends within the monasteries now leaps beyond the containment of the monastic institution into the general conduct of life in the outside world itself, allowing us to rearticulate our basic scheme as follows:

		PROTESTANT		
	MEDIEVAL	LUTHER	CALVIN	MODERN
RELIGIOUS ENDS	+	+	+	−
RATIONAL MEANS	−	−	+	+

There remains to be characterized the final transition to the situation of modern capitalism, and it is here more than anywhere else that Protestantism assumes its function as a "vanishing mediator." For what happens here is essentially that once Protestantism has accomplished the task of allowing a rationalization of innerworldly life to take place, it has no further reason for being and disappears from the historical scene. It is thus in the strictest sense of the word a catalytic agent that permits an exchange of energies between two otherwise mutually exclusive terms; and we may say that with the removal of the brackets, the whole institution of religion itself (in other words, what is here designated as "Protestantism") serves in its turn as a kind of overall bracket or framework within which change takes place and which can be dismantled and removed when its usefulness is over.

Such a picture of historical change—however irreconcilable it may be with vulgar Marxism—is in reality perfectly consistent with genuine Marxist thinking and is, indeed, at one with the model proposed by Marx himself for the revolutions of 1789 and 1848: in 1789 Jacobinism played the role of the vanishing mediator, functioning as the conscious and almost Calvinistic guardian of revolutionary morality, of bourgeois universalistic and democratic ideals, a guardianship that could be done away with in Thermidor, when the practical victory of the bourgeoisie was assured and an explicitly monetary and market system could come into being; and in that parody of 1789 which was the revolution of 1848, it was similarly under the cloak of the traditions and values of the great revolution, and of the empire that followed it, that the new commercial society of the Second Empire emerged.

This suggests that we may associate what our chart designates as the realm of ends with the Marxian concept of the superstructure, while that of means constitutes the infrastructure as such. Thus, in both Weber and Marx, the superstructure may be said to find its essential function in the mediation of changes in the infrastructure along the lines we have characterized; and to understand it in this way, as a "vanishing mediator," is to escape the false problems of priority or of cause and effect in which both vulgar Marxist and the idealist positions imprison us.

But the purpose of the present study is more extensive than this, for its hypothesis is nothing less than that the concept of the vanishing mediator characterizes all of Weber's sociological and historical thinking and may be seen as the dominant structure of his imagination. Within the material limits of the present essay, however, I cannot illustrate the full range of Weber's applications of such a concept to the most varying historical materials, from his analysis of the role of Bismarck in the unification of modern Germany to his discussion of the importance of Roman law in the evolution of the modern legal system. I must therefore be content to return to the earlier example of the prophet to demonstrate that the notion of a vanishing mediator articulates the material we discussed there in a more adequate way as well.

For above and beyond his transitional position between the stage of magic and that of the essentially rational religious organization of the priesthood, the prophet may be understood in the present context as a kind of debracketing of the charismatic authority implicit in the traditional institution of the magician. For the prophet, like the magician, requires "charismatic authentication, which in practice meant magic. . . .[But] the typical prophet propagates ideas for their own sake and not for fees, at least not in any obvious or regulated form. . . .Thus developed the carefully cultivated postulate that the apostle, prophet, or teacher of ancient Christianity must not professionalize his religious proclamations."[30] What is this to say but that the prophet claims more for himself than the magician? Such a noninstitutionalized affirmation of his own personal powers and vocation is thus at one with the intensification of charisma as a social force:

	MAGICIAN	PROPHET	PRIEST
CHARISMATIC POWER	[+]	+	−
RATIONAL RELIGIOUS ORGANIZATION	−	+	+

Yet, what such a historical narrative describes is the "cooling off" or solidification of charisma itself, as the latter—a vanishing mediator in the truest sense of the expression—serves as a bearer of change and social transformation, only to be forgotten once that change has ratified the reality of the institutions.

III

It will be observed that if a single explanational pattern seems to return again and again throughout Weber's works, this recurrence can most adequately be accounted for by the fact that, in a sense, Weber dealt over and over again, and in the most varied forms, with only a single sociological phenomenon; or, if you prefer the language of the present essay, he told a single story again and again under the most varying disguises and behind the most disparate appearances. The story is of course that of rationalization, a process Weber finds to be at work in ancient prophecy just as much as in modern bureaucracy, in Prussian agriculture just as much as in Protestant theology. But such an observation merely displaces the problem, for rationalization, surely, is a model rather than an empirical fact, an "ideal type" rather than an observable social institution; and the question of Max Weber's fascination with this process, which he saw at work everywhere, poses itself anew.

I have already, in the opening section, sketched the cultural and historical context of that experience of the divorce of means from ends that has its objective embodiment in rationalization just as it finds its subjective expression in ennui. Yet, it is certain that the uniquely structured themes of a life and of a work are not simply lifted from the thin air of the social and cultural environment: Sartre is only the most recent to have insisted on the crucial significance of childhood as the moment in which the "ideas in the air," the culturally available roles and themes, are reinvented, as though for the first time, through the unique medium of an individual existence. For Sartre, the function of psychoanalysis is to provide an instrument of social and historical investigation, one that takes as its privileged object the formation of an individual from out of the contents and materials of that determinate historic family structure within which he develops: "existentialism. . .believes that it can integrate the psychoanalytic method which discovers the point of insertion for man and his class—that is, the particular family—as a mediation between the universal class and the individual. The family in fact is constituted by and in the general movement of History, but is experienced, on the other hand, as an absolute in the depth and opaqueness of childhood."[31] Sartre's analysis of the way in which the personality patterns of Flaubert (and the obsessive themes of his work) emerge from an opposition between the personality structures of his parents (personality structures the content of which is essentially sociological) may serve as a model for our present task, which is that of an *interpretation* of the structural description we have arrived at.

As a nuclear unit, however, the family is a relatively recent institution: the manor or household, Charles Morazé tells us,

> had still been a vast collective group at the end of the old regime, and still opened its doors to newly married couples. They had their place at the common table. Several generations and innumerable families of cousins lived happily together under one and the same roof. . . . The change of habits which took place in the last decade of the eighteenth century led young married couples to set up their own homes. They wished to live in their own houses and to keep themselves. The large number of well-paid jobs opened to them by the widening of social life encouraged this process. The new family broke away from its own folk. It now consisted of the limited group—father, mother, child. . . . Responsibility fell more and more on the individual. . . . Each man felt master of his own destiny and responsible for his own children.[32]

Such a shrinkage in the primal "scene" of childhood, such a sharp reduction in its vital cast of characters, could not but affect the mechanisms that shape the psyche as well as the symbolism through which the latter deciphers the outside world.

At the same time, the external environment of the bourgeois family is alter-
ing no less dramatically: for with the political and socioeconomic triumph of
the new class, that class Other in reaction against which the very structures of
middle-class identity had come into being—the aristocracy—weakens or disappears altogether, so that the hitherto external aggression of middle-class individuals must now find a new object and be reoriented within the relative
autonomy and closure of the new bourgeois nuclear family. In a striking page,
Arthur Mitzman draws the consequences of such a reorientation:

> I would argue that in the generations before the 1860s it was the
> archrepressiveness of the Victorian superego that inspired both the
> economic triumphs of the European bourgeoisie and its demands for
> social status and political power. As long as the bourgeoisie remained
> politically unsuccessful, there was a certain equilibrium created by
> the continued deflection of the aggressiveness that was not absorbed
> by the conquest of nature into the concealed *Ressentiment*, conscious
> hostility or open struggle against traditional powers. In other words,
> there was a rationally defensive political outlet for the psychic bile
> accumulating in the souls of those energetic Victorians, and because
> the struggle of bourgeois against aristocrat seemed to make sense, the
> oedipal hostilities and the struggle for release of the shackled, built-
> in aggressions of the nineteenth-century bourgeois could be ration-
> alized in the name of Progress and Reason. But when the last
> generation of rebellious bourgeois achieved success in the 1860s and
> early '70s their descendants, no less repressed and hostile than
> themselves, were deprived of those glorious visions of terminal con-
> quest by means of which the earlier generations had sublimated their
> hostilities. Aggressions masquerading as political passions had
> formerly been unleashed against the aristocracy. But now the older
> generation of bourgeois politicians ruled either in place of or
> alongside the conservative aristocracy: revolt against the generation
> in power no longer permitted the early transference of patricidal ag-
> gressions to enemies condemned by Reason and History.[33]

These changes in the external situation of the bourgeois family are not
without their repercussions on its internal structure as well, and in particular
on the development of the role of the mother. The mother or wife was, of
course, even in the larger traditional households, the object of an exchange
with another bourgeois family, but such an exchange functioned hitherto as
alliance between such families against the class enemy. Now, however, and to
say so is simply to reinterpret the increasing freedom and status of the
bourgeois woman, the wife comes to represent an alternate lifestyle *within* the
bourgeois family itself, a different familial tradition, a mode of life that calls
the hitherto unquestioned values of the father into question. So the older
struggle between the bourgeois patriarch and the oppressive aristocracy tends
to reorganize itself into a structural opposition between the two middle-class

parents themselves. And it is characteristic of the children of this generation of *grands bourgeois* to take inventory of the antithetical parental traits and to think of themselves as problematical or dialectical combinations of the latter (think, for example, of André Gide's appeal to the coexistence of Normandy and the Midi, of Protestantism and Catholicism, within himself, or Thomas Mann's analogous evocations of the contact between the Hanseatic North and the culture of the Mediterranean).

Such was, at any rate, the way in which Max Weber thought about parental influences, for Marianne Weber could only have had her authority for reflections of the following kind from her husband himself:

> In those years [of adolescence] it was uncertain whether [Max] would settle for the character type of his father or that of his mother. He already had the obscure feeling that some such choice would lay before him as soon as he took himself in hand and began consciously to work out a personality of his own. On the one hand the mother, in whom the forces of the gospel held sway, in whom loving service and self-sacrifice had become a second nature, yet who lived by uncomfortably heroic principles and mastered her excessive daily chores in a constant ethical tension, punctilious to a fault and relating every meaningful occurrence calmly to the eternal itself. She is so heartily decisive and fresh in the way she masters everyday existence, so joyously open to all the beauty of life—how liberating is her laughter!—but daily she descends into the deeps and is anchored in the otherworldly. By comparison, the father, honorable through and through, wholly disinterested in politics and in the exercise of his office, and clever besides, of an even disposition, warm and friendly when things go according to his wishes, is nonetheless a typical bourgeois, satisfied with himself and with the world. He categorically rejects any acknowledgement of the problematical sides of life. In later years he loved his domestic comfort and withdrew from all suffering and pity. His liberal political ideals could not be realized, and new ideologies, which might have demanded sacrifices of him in the service of this or that cause, failed to attract him.[34]

Between the respectfully retouched lines of Marianne Weber's portrait, one can sense the presence of that Oedipal clash which resulted in Max Weber's nervous breakdown and of which Mitzman is able, for the first time, to give us a complete account.[35] But Marianne's pages provide rich materials for an analysis of the complex interaction of parental traits in Weber's background. In one sense, the father, as a successful politician, would appear to stand for action, in opposition to the tradition of Protestant inwardness perpetuated by the mother. The lifestyle of the father, as it emerges from the old patrician mercantile class, is one of nonchalance and accommodation and has nothing of that driven, compulsive quality which the mother's sense of conscience and duty enforce. From this point of view, then, the father's activity may be compared to those "bracketed" and tradition-oriented types of behavior in which aims are pursued without any thematization of the values or absolutes involved—in this case, political pursuits for the tradition-sanctioned motives of personal ambition and social prestige. Paradoxically it is the mother, with her family origins in the Prussian bureaucracy, who unites in herself both rationalized work and a religious sense of values. Thus, the "choice" from which Max Weber's own personality may be expected to evolve is far from a simple option between two relatively univocal symbols; and it is perhaps not too farfetched to see the origins of Weber's often exasperating habit of dichotomization in this childhood situation in which, with every clash, he must estimate the configuration of parental values involved. In the present context, however, what interests us is that the three positions fit very neatly into the scheme we have devised for the analysis of Weberian narrative:

	FATHER	MOTHER	MAX WEBER
ULTIMATE PURPOSEFULNESS OR MEANING	[+]	+	−
COMPULSIVE WORK	−	+	+

Obviously such an equivalence cannot be expected to prove anything or seal an argument for a skeptical reader, for my reading of Weber's family situation is as little empirical, is as fully prestructured, as that of any other kind of text. But I think that I can best anticipate misunderstanding and possible abuse of the present hypothesis by suggesting that the operation I have in mind here is something other and more complicated than what has come to be known, following Goldman, as the discovery of *homologies* between phenomena of different orders and levels—in the present instance, between the texts of Weber, his biographical experience, and the social structure of the Germany of his time.

Rather, I would argue that we have to do here with a process, one that finds its most fundamental *genetic* expression on the biographical level. This process can be defined as one of self-definition, or it can be described in the more classic terminology of the Oedipus complex; and our formalization of it is designated to articulate the way in which Weber goes about solving the problem that it poses, namely, the requirement for the male child to identify with the father and thus to reproduce the latter's character structure. What the present hypothesis suggests is that this identification is achieved at the price of a transformation of the paternal value system so thoroughgoing as to make the latter virtually unrecognizable. In this appropriation and restructuration it is clearly the mother's value system that serves as catalyst and mediator: the intense and inward sense of values of his mother allowed Weber to see his father's existence as an antithesis, as mere opportunism, routine action in a mechanical and unexamined scheme of things. At this point, then, the hostility and resistance to the father acquires the social meaning of a defense of individualistic "spirituality" and inwardness against bureaucratic routine.

On the other hand, we will understand nothing about this process if we do not grasp the fact that Weber's relationship to his mother was no less ambivalent. Indeed, to attack the father is implicitly to defend what the mother herself stands for, namely value, but also compulsion, enforced work, and obligatory activity dialectically related to the unrealizable and ideal character of the otherworldly ethical values of which she is the emissary. Of the father's heritage Weber rejected the unthematized, tradition-oriented kinds of activity which he felt essentially to lack value or ethical content; but paradoxically —and this paradox is the very heart not only of Weber's personal development, but of his work as well—he had to reject the mother's insistence on ethics as well, or rather, he had to come to terms with what she represented— pure value—in some other fashion than a personal conversion and commitment to it. An early intellectual distrust of ethical programs such as that of Channing—a favorite thinker of Helene Weber[36]—suggests that it was the mother who was associated in Weber's mind with unpractical "idealism" of the type of socialism itself that Weber's heroic cynicism later decisively rejected. For what accompanies such idealism, as a kind of psychic punishment, is precisely compulsive work; and Weber's subsequent breakdown and long psychic paralysis may in this context be seen, not only as self-punishment and guilt for the attack on the father, but equally well as an aggressive act directed against the maternal principle, as a symbolic refusal of the system of values represented by the mother. At any rate, it is clear from Helene Weber's skeptical attitude toward her son's illness that she understood it in precisely this way.[37]

So we are to read the scheme outlined above as the way in which Weber used his maternal heritage to transform that of the father, subsequently discarding the mother's values in their turn when their mediatory function had been fulfilled. The mother's values permitted Weber to achieve at length a scholarly existence of backbreaking and compulsive labor, but only when they had themselves been liquidated: this was accomplished by their thematization as an object of study in their own right. Thus, it is no accident that Weber is the sociologist of religion *par excellence*, even though remaining "religiously unmusical"; for he could not separate himself from the mother while he was himself personally committed to her religious beliefs. Nor, on the other hand, could he simply liquidate this feature without a trace, given the crucial function of the mother as a mediation in his own development. So the solution is that classic one described by Freud under the term "sublimation": the fascination with religion remains, but transposed to a "higher" level, in which the type of relationship entertained with the object is no longer that of belief, but rather that of scientific interest.

This is, however, not the only, nor even the principal, way in which the process of Weber's psychic development enters and influences his work; to suggest one way in which such influence may be conceived, I return briefly to Lévi-Strauss' interpretation of those mythological structures the descriptive analysis of which has already furnished some of our analytical instruments and procedures. In his well-known treatment of the Oedipus myth from which I borrowed the narrative formula discussed above, Lévi-Strauss suggests that the mythic narrative results from a conceptual hesitation betwen two theories of birth, such theories themselves being the reflection of various irreconcilable modes of tribal or familial organization, which are then projected into a series of episodes that offer the primitive mind the semblance of a solution to the underlying social contradiction or conceptual antinomy.[38] In the later volumes of his *Mythologiques,* he offers what seems to be a somewhat different description of the nature and function of myths: the latter, he tells us rather elliptically, "signify the spirit that elaborates them by means of the world of which it is itself a part."[39] What this means in the general context of Lévi-Strauss' thinking is that myths take as their deepest subject the emergence of Culture (and thus of mythic storytelling as well) from Nature, or, to put it even more succinctly, that all myths are myths about *origins*, stories designed to provide answers to such questions as, How did the leopard get his spots? Where did fire come from? and so forth. For our present purpose, we may telescope these two definitions and suggest that a myth is the attempt, in the form of a story about origins, to resolve some underlying and apparently irreconcilable contradiction.

In the case of Max Weber, the contradiction in question is evidently enough that between the two parental systems, but it is a contradiction of which he himself is the resolution! The fascination with the mystery of origins then logically takes the form of an inquiry—conscious or unconscious—into the formation of his own personality, into the incomprehensible emergence of something called Max Weber from the massive and apparently timeless parental antinomies. But to be interested in this process is *the same* as being interested in the process of rationalization in general; for Weber's personality, his espousal—not to say invention—of the very institution of "scientific objectivity," amounts to the disengagement of rationalized inquiry from the older forms of the two parental activities. It is therefore no accident that Weber's attention goes in every historical age and in every type of sociological material toward precisely those phenomena that may be considered signs or traces of the rationalization process, for this is the form taken by his own unconscious obsession with his own origins; to put it another way, the very theme of rationalization constitutes the autoreferentiality of Weber's scientific inquiry, the way in which the historical or sociological narrative designates itself, or, to use Lévi-Strauss' expression, "signifies" its own powers. Therefore, I do not need to propose a homology between Weber's character structure and those "external" realities of history and modern social development: it is he himself who links the two in his work, or rather, who uses the first as a way of reading the second. Thus he grasps the social and historical fact of *Entzauberung* by giving it the genetic form of his own personal experience of the same phenomenon; in other words, he objectifies his own private situation by projecting it into that of modern alienation in a purely technical universe, that of the disappearance of the older traditionalistic and charismatic forms of social life. The question, How did I become what I am? thus becomes enriched and thematized, "sublimated," when in the realm of "objective" historical investigation it takes on the form, How did rationalization come about? What are the origins of the modern desacralized world?

We may now conclude by recapitulating the process through which Weber's basic themes are generated. An expanded version of Greimas' rectangle allows us to see them as a series of progressive and cumulative negations, each of which projects the previous material as it were onto a different thematic level while at the same time preserving its fundamental unity:

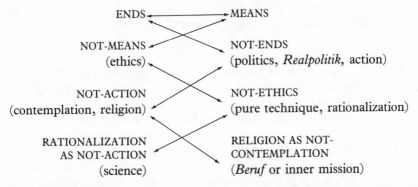

Such a self-generating mechanism dramatizes the agonizing rift in Weber's life and work between contemplation and action, between meaning and activity, between the fascination with ethics and religion and the theory and practice of politics and organization. But we must not give the impression that these interests are to be understood in any purely personal or clinical way. For it was the basic hypothesis of this concluding section of our study that the fundamental mode of existence of such "themes" is social: the means-ends dichotomy, indeed, we associated with the personality clash between Max Weber's parents. But this clash merely reflects and dramatizes, embodies on the level of individual existence, a tension that originates on the scale of the social classes themselves. In this sense, each parent can be seen to represent and to individualize a distinct faction in the bourgeoisie of mid-nineteenth-century Germany: for the mother was formed in the values and lifestyle of the Prussian bureaucracy, with its emphasis on service and on a severely interiorized sense of duty; while the father incarnated those older preindustrial mercantile traditions of the type familiar in literature from the *Buddenbrooks* of Thomas Mann. On the level of the social classes themselves, then, the problem of the integration of these two distinct bourgeois traditions is at one with the very unification of modern Germany and its transformation into an industrial worldpower. The solution of Max Weber, therefore, on the level of individual psychology and the private life, is emblematic of the possible options of a resolution on the plane of social history.

That apparently purely personal solution becomes of even more consequence to the student of German history when we realize that our manipulation of the semantic rectangle, even in such expanded form, is not yet complete, for we have not yet generated the ultimate agents or characterological categories of Weber's thought—the complex and the neutral terms, respectively. The latter, that ultimate combination of the privative terms of this chain of negations, some final union of "science" on the one hand and a sense of *Beruf*, or "inner mission," on the other, must surely be what is embodied in Weber's own personal life choice, in what he described so eloquently as "science as a vocation"; and we have already been able to sense the profound ambiguity and tension that invests Weberian *Wertfreiheit*.

But this neutral term is itself dialectically linked to the other combinational possibility available in the Weberian system, to the complex term that would be a synthesis of ends and means, if such a thing were possible, and in which the original rift between the two would be transcended and forgotten. Such a state is to be found in only one moment of Weber's sociology, namely, that of the appearance of the charismatic hero: the nostalgia for the bearer of charisma is surely more than the projection of the ideal father into past and future; it is also and no doubt most fundamentally a vision of the liberated self as well, a self integrated beyond the contingencies of the fallen world of the historical present, in a realm in which meaningful action is once more possible, in which means and ends are at one and henceforth never to be disjoined. Like all wish-fulfillments that have never been fully raised to consciousness, however, such a vision was fraught with terrible risks and could never be wholly benign in influence: the subsequent destiny of Germany itself is there to testify to it.

But the charismatic hero remains, for Weber, an ideal. Of the reality, both of his own life and of the historical phenomena he was able to make us see, there survives *The Protestant Ethic*, that ambivalent elegy to the potency of the maternal principle, its introspective structure projected outward until it becomes at length indistinguishable from the dreary bureaucratic landscape of the disenchanted modern world itself.

Winter/Spring 1974

Chapter 2
Architecture and the Critique of Ideology

How can space be "ideological"? Only if such a question is possible and meaningful—leaving aside the problem of meaningful *answers* to is—can any conceptions or ideals of nonideological, transfigured, Utopian space be developed. The question has itself tended to be absorbed by naturalistic or anthropological perspectives, predominantly based on conceptions of the human body itself, most notably in phenomenology. The body's limits but also its needs are then appealed to as ultimate standards against which to measure the relative alienation either of older commercial or industrial space of the overweening sculptural monuments of the International Style or of the postmodernist "megastructure." Yet arguments based on the human body are fundamentally ahistorical and involve premises about some eternal "human nature" concealed within the seemingly "verifiable" and scientific data of physiological analysis. If the body is in reality a social body, if therefore there exists no pregiven human body as such, but rather the whole historical range of social experiences of the body, the whole variety of bodily norms projected by a series of distinct historical "modes of production" or social formations, then the "return" to some more "natural" vision of the body in space projected by phenomenology comes to seem ideological, if not nostalgic. But does this mean that there are no limits to what the body, socially and historically, can become, or to the kind of space to which it can be asked to "adapt"?

Yet if the "body" ceases to be the fundamental unit of spatial analysis, the very concept of space itself becomes problematized: What space? The space of rooms or individual buildings, or the space of the very city fabric itself, in which those buildings are inserted, and against whose perceptual background my experience of this or that local segment is organized? Yet the city, however

35

it is construed, is space-in-totalization; it is not given in advance as an object of study or analysis, after the fashion of the constructed building. (Perhaps even the latter is not given in this way either, except to the already abstract sense of sight: individual buildings are then "objects" only in photographs.)

It is important to recognize (or to admit) that this second series of questions or problems *remains* essentially phenomenological in its orientation; indeed, it is possible that the vice of our initial question lies there, that it still insists on posing the problem of the relationship of the individual subject and of the subject's "lived experience" to the architectural or urban, spatial object, however the latter is to be construed. What is loosely called "structuralism" is now generally understood as the repudiation of this phenomenological "problematic," of such presuppositions as "experience"; it has generated a whole new counterproblematic of its own, in which space—the individual building or the city itself—is taken as a text in which a whole range of "signs" and "codes" are combined, whether in the organic unity of a shared code, or in "collage" systems of various kinds, in structures of allusion to the past, or of ironic commentary on the present, or of radical disjunctures, in which some radically new sign (the Seagram's Building or the Radiant City) *criticizes* the older sign system into which it dramatically erupts. Yet in another perspective it is precisely this last possibility that has been called back into question, and which can be seen as a replication, in more modern "structuralist" language, of our initial question. In all the arts, the new "textual" strategies stubbornly smuggled back into their new problematic the coordinates of the older political question, and of the older unexamined opposition between "authentic" and "inauthentic." For a time, the new mediations produced seemingly new versions of the older (false?) problem, in the form of concepts of "subversion," the breaking of codes, their radical interruption or contestation (along with their predictable dialectical opposite, the notion of "cooptation"). It is the viability of these new solutions that is today generally in doubt: they now are taken to be more Utopianism, only of a negative or "critical" variety. They seemed at first to have repudiated the older positive and nostalgic ideals of a new Utopian—authentic, nonalienated—space or art; yet their claim to punctual negativity—far more modest at first glance—now seems equally Utopian in the bad sense. For even the project of criticizing, subverting, delegitimating, strategically interrupting, the established codes of a repressive social and spatial order has ultimately come to be understood as appealing to some conception of critical "self-consciousness," of critical distance, which today seems problematic; whereas on a more empirical level, it has been observed that the most subversive gesture itself hardens into yet another form of being or positivity in its turn (just as the most negative *critical* stance loses its therapeutic and destructive shock value and slowly turns back into yet another critical ideology in its own right).

Is some third term beyond these two moments—the phenomenological and the strucutral—conceivable? Pierre Bourdieu, in his *Outline of a Theory of Practice*, explicitly attempts such a dialectical move beyond these two "moments," both of which are for him indispensable, yet insufficient: the concept of "practice"—the social body's programming by its spatial text, not taken to be the "bottom line" both of everyday experience and of the legitimation of the social structure itself—while offered as just such a solution, has only been "tested" on the much simpler materials and problems of precapitalist space in the Kabyl village. Meanwhile, Henri Lefebvre's conception of "space" as the fundamental category of politics and of the dialectic itself—the one great prophetic vision of these last years of discouragement and renunciation—has yet to be grasped in all its pathbreaking implications, let alone to be explored and implemented; while Lefebvre's influential role as an ideologist and a critic of French architecture today must be noted and meditated upon.

It is precisely a role of this kind that yet another logically possible position—faced with the dilemmas we have outlined above—explicitly repudiates: this is the position of Manfredo Tafuri, which in at least some of its more preemptory expressions has the merit of stark and absolute simplicity. The position is stated most baldly in the "Note" to the second Italian edition of *Theories and History of Architecture:* "one cannot 'anticipate' a class architecture (an architecture 'for a liberated society'); what is possible is the introduction of class criticism into architecture."[1] Although Tafuri's working judgments—in texts written over a number of years—are in fact far more nuanced and ambiguous than such a proposition might suggest, certain key elements can at once be isolated: (1) The architectural critic has no business being an "ideologist," that is, a visionary proponent of architectural styles of the future, "revolutionary" architecture, and the like; her role must be resolutely negative, the vigilant denunciation of existent or historical architectural ideologies. This position then tends to slip into a somewhat different one: (2) The practicing architect, in *this* society and within the closure of capitalism as a system, cannot hope to devise a radically different, a revolutionary, or a "Utopian" architecture or space either. (3) Without any conceivable normative conception of architectural space, of a space of radical difference from this one, the criticism of buildings tends to be conflated with the criticism of the ideologies of such buildings; the history and criticism of architecture thus tends to fold back into the history and criticism of the various ideologies of architecture, the manifestos and the verbal expressions of the great architects themselves. (4) Political action is not renounced in such a position, or not *necessarily* (although more "pessimistic" readings of Tafuri are certainly possible). What is, however, affirmed here is consonant with the Althusserian tradition of the "semi-autonomy" of the levels and practices of

social life: politics is radically disjoined from aesthetic (in this case architectural) practice. The former is still possible, but only on *its* level, and architectural or aesthetic production can never be immediately political; it takes place
somewhere else. Architects can therefore be political, like other individuals,
but their architecture today cannot be political (a restatement of proposition
2, above). It follows, then, that: (5) An architecture of the future will be concretely and practically possible only when the future has arrived, that is to
say, after a total social revolution, a systemic transformation of this mode of
production into something else.

This position, which inevitably has something of the fascination of uncom-
promising intransigence and of all absolutes, must be understood, as I will try
to show below in more detail, first of all within the history of contemporary
Marxism, as a repudiation of what the Althusserians called Marxist "humanism" (including very specifically its "Utopian" component as symbolically
represented by Marcuse or by Henri Lefebvre himself). Its refusal to entertain the possibility of some properly Marxian "ideology" (which would seek
to project alternate futures), its commitment to a resolutely critical and
analytical Marxian "science"—by way of a restriction to the operation of de-
nouncing the ideologies of the past and of a closed present—all these features
betray some kinship with T. W. Adorno's late and desperate concept of a
purely "negative dialectic." The ambiguity of such a position lies in its very
instability, and the way in which it can imperceptibly pass over into a post-
Marxism of the type endorsed by the French *nouveaux philosophes* or by
Tafuri's collaborator, Massimo Cacciari. This is to suggest that Tafuri's position is *also* an ideology, and that one does not get out of ideology by refusing
it or by commiting one's self to negative and critical "ideological analysis."

Yet at this stage, such an evaluation remains at the level of mere opinion
and in that form has little if any interest. In what follows I will try to give it
more content by examining Tafuri's work—and most notably his short, widely read, but dense and provocative *Architecture and Utopia*[2]—in three distinct
perspectives. The first must be that of the Marxist context in which it was
first produced, a context in which a series of significant but implicit moves
may go unrecognized by the non-Marxist or American reader for want of the
appropriate background. The second perspective (in no special order) will be
that of the discursive form in which Tafuri works, namely historiography
itself, and most particularly narrative history, whose formal dilemmas and
problems today may be seen as determining (or at least overdetermining) certain of Tafuri's organizing concepts. Finally, it will be appropriate to recon-
sider this considerable body of work (now largely available in English) in the
context of a vaster contemporary event, which has its own specifically
American equivalents (and which is by no means limited to the field of architecture, although the battle lines have been drawn more dramatically there
than in any other art)—namely the critique of high modernism, the increas-

ingly omnipresent feeling that the modern movement itself is henceforth extinct; this feeling has often been accompanied by the sense that we may therefore now be in something else, sometimes called postmodernism. It is incidentally a matter of no small significance, to which we will return, that this second theme—the dawning of some new postmodernist moment or even "age"—is utterly alien to Tafuri himself and plays no role in his periodizing framework or in his historical narrative.

I want to deal first with the second of my three topics, namely that which has to do with historiography, with the problem of writing history, and in this case of writing the history of a discipline, an art, a medium. That there has been a crisis in narrative or storytelling history since the end of the nineteenth century is well known, as is the relationship between this crisis and that other crisis in the realistic novel itself: narrative history and the realistic novel are indeed closely related and in the greatest nineteenth-century texts virtually interchangeable. In our own time, this ongoing crisis has been rethematized in terms of the critique of representation, one of the fundamental slogans of poststructuralism: briefly, the narrative representation of history necessarily tends to suggest that history is something you can see, be a witness to, be present at—an obviously inadmissible proposition. On the other hand, as the word itself suggests, history is always fundamentally storytelling, must always be narrative in its very structure.

This dilemma will not bother those for whom history-writing is not an essential task; if you are satisfied to do small-scale semiotic analyses of discrete or individual text or buildings, presumably the problem of the writing of history, the telling of a historical story, will not unduly preoccupy you. I say "presumably" because I think that this problem also leaves its traces on such static analyses, and indeed it seems to be an empirical fact that the issues of history are returning everywhere today, not least within semiotics itself (the history of semiotics, the turn of semiotic analysis to the problem of genres, the problem of a semiotic of historical representation).

However, leaving other people to their concerns, it will be clear that no issue is more central or more acute than for those with some commitment to a dialectical tradition, since the dialectic has always for better or for worse been associated with some form or other of historical vision. For myself, I am much attracted by Louis Althusser's solution, which consists in proposing, in the midst of the crisis of historical representation and of narrative history, that the historian should conceive her task not as that of producing a representation of history, but rather as that of producing the *concept* of history, a very different matter indeed.

But how is this to be done? Or rather, to be more modest about it, how has this actually been done in practice? From this perspective, it will be of interest to read *Architecture and Utopia* with a view toward determining the way in which it suggestively "produces the concept" of a dialectical history of architecture. But this is a rare enough achievement for one to want, initially, to juxtapose Tafuri's text with those very rare other realizations of this particular genre or form. I can think of only two contemporary dialectical histories of comparable intensity and intellectual energy: T. W. Adorno's *Philosophy of Modern Music* (a seminal text, on which Thomas Mann drew for his musical materials in *Doktor Faustus*), and in the area of the history of literature, Roland Barthes' early and unequalled *Le Degré zéro de l'écriture (Writing Degree Zero)*. You will understand that this limited choice does not imply a lack of interest in the contributions that a Lukács, a Sartre, an Asor Rosa, a Raymond Williams, among others, have made to the restructuration of traditional paradigms of literary history. What the three books I have mentioned have in common is not merely a new set of dialectical insights into literature, but the practice of a peculiar, condensed, allusive discursive form, a kind of textual *genre*, still exceedingly rare, which I will call dialectical history.

Let me first single out a fundamental organizational feature that these three works share, and which I am tempted to see as the ultimate precondition to which they must painfully submit in order to practice dialectical thinking: this is the sense of Necessity, of necessary failure, of closure, of ultimate unresolvable contradictions and the impossibility of the future, which cannot have failed to oppress any reader of these texts, particularly readers who as practicing artists—whether architects, composers, or writers—come to them for suggestions and encouragement as to the possibility of future cultural production.

Adorno's discussion of musical history culminates, for instance, in Schoenberg's extraordinary "solution"—the twelve-tone system—which solves all the dilemmas outstanding in previous musical history so completely as to make all musical composition after Schoenberg superfluous (or at least regressive) from Adorno's perspective, yet which at the same time ends up as a baleful replication or mirror image of that very totalitarian socioeconomic system from which it sought to escape in the first place. In Barthes' *Writing Degree Zero*, the well-known ideal of "white writing"—far from being what it often looks like today, namely a rather complacent account of postmodernist trends—stood in its initial historical context and situation as an equally impossible solution to a dilemma that rendered all earlier practices of writing or style ideological and intolerable. Tafuri's account, finally, of the increasing closure of late capitalism (beginning in 1931 and intensifying dialectically after the war), systematically shutting off one aesthetic possibility after another, ends up conveying a paralyzing and asphyxiating sense of the futility of any kind of architectural or urbanistic innovation on this side of that equally inconceivable watershed, a total social revolution.

It would be silly, or even worse, frivolous, to discuss these positions in terms of optimism or pessimism. I will later make some remarks about the political presuppositions that account for (or at least overdetermine) some of Tafuri's attitudes here; what I prefer to stress now is the formal origin of these somber visions of the total system, which, far worse than Max Weber's iron cage, here descends upon human life and human creature praxis. The strengths of the readings and insights of Adorno, Barthes, and Tafuri in these works is for one thing inextricably bound up with their vision of history as an increasingly total or closed system: in other words, their ability to interpret a given work of art as a provisional "solution" is absolutely dependent on a perspective that reads the artwork against a context reconstructed or rewritten as a situation and a contraction.

More than this, I find confirmation in these books for an intuition I have expressed elsewhere, namely that the dialectic, or powerful dialectical history, must somehow always involve a vision of Necessity or, if you prefer, must always tell the story of failure. "The owl of Minerva takes its flight at dusk": dialectical interpretation is always retrospective, always tells the necessity of an event, why it *had* to happen the way it did; and to do that, the event must already have happened, the story must already have come to an end. While this may sound like an indictment of the dialectic (or as yet one more post-Marxist "proof" of its irrecuperably Hegelian character), it is important to add that such histories of necessity and of determinate failure are equally inseparable from some ultimate historical perspective of reconciliation, of achieved socialism, of the "end of prehistory" in Marx's sense.

The restructuration of the history of an art in terms of a series of situations, dilemmas, contradictions, in terms of which individual works, styles, and forms can be seen as so many responses or determinate symbolic acts—this is, then, a first key feature of dialectical historiography. But there is another no less essential one that springs to mind, at least when one thinks in terms of historical materialism, and that is the reversal associated with the term "materialism" itself, the anti-idealistic thrust, the rebuke and therapeutic humiliation of consciousness forced to reground itself in a painful awareness of what Marx called its "social determination." This second requirement is of course what sets off the present texts sharply from old-fashioned Hegelian spiritual historiography, but which in turn threatens to undermine the historiographic project altogether, as in Marx's grim reminder in the *German Ideology:*

> We do not set out from what people say, imagine or conceive, nor from people as narrated, thought of, imagined, conceived, in order to arrive at people in the flesh. We set out from real, active human beings, and on the basis of their real life-process we demonstrate the development of the ideological reflexes and echoes of this life-process. The phantoms formed in the human brain are also, necessarily, sublimates of their material life-process, which is empirically verifiable and bound to material premises. Morality,

religion, metaphysics, all the rest of ideology and their corresponding forms of consciousness, thus no longer retain their semblance of independence. They have no history, no development, in their own right; but it is rather human beings who, developing their material production and relationships, alter, along with this their real existence, their thinking and the products of their thinking. Life is not determined by consciousness, but consciousness by life.[3]

Now the slogan of "materialism" has again become a very popular euphemism for Marxism. I have my own reasons for objecting to this particular ideological fashion on the Left today: facile and dishonest as a kind of popular-front solution to the very real tensions between Marxism and feminism, the slogan also seems to be extraordinarily misleading as a synonym for "historical materialism" itself, since the very concept of "materialism" is a bourgeois Enlightenment (later positivist) one and fatally conveys the impression of a "determinism by the body" rather than, as in genuine dialectical Marxism, a "determination by the mode of production." At any rate, in the context that concerns us here—the description of "dialectical historiography"—the drawback of the word "materialism" is that it tends to suggest that only one form of dialectical reversal—the overthrow of idealism by materialism or a recall to matter—is at work in such books.

Actually, however, the dialectical shock, the reversal of our habits of idealism, can take many forms: and it is evident that in the dialectical history of an art its privileged targets will be the idealistic habits we have inherited in thinking about such matters, and in particular Hegelian notions of the history of forms and styles, but also empiricist or structuralist notions of isolated texts. Still, it is best to see how these reversal-effects have been achieved in practice, rather than deducing them a priori in some dogmatic matter. And since none of these works every raises one key issue of concern to everyone today, it is appropriate to preface a discussion of them with the indication of a fundamental form of contemporary "reversal" which may not leave them unscathed either: namely the way in which contemporary feminist critiques cut across the whole inherited system of the histories of art and culture by demonstrating the glaring absence from them, not merely of women as such, but, in the architectural area, of any consideration of the relationship between women's work and interior space, and between the domination of women and the city plan itself. For male intellectuals, this is the most stunning materialist reversal of all, since it calls *us* effectively into question at the same time that it disturbingly seems to discredit the very foundations and institutional presuppositions of the disciplines in question.

Indeed, the lesson for us in criticism of this kind may well be, among other things, precisely this: that a materialist or dialectical historiography does its work ultimately by undermining the very foundations, framework, constitutive presuppositons of the specialized disciplines themselves—by unexpectedly demonstrating the existence, not necessarily of "matter" in that limited sense, but rather in general of an *Other* of the discipline, an outside, a limit, the revelation of the *extrinsic*, which it is believed to be scandalous and unscholarly to introduce into a carefully regulated traditional debate.

Adorno's book perhaps goes least far in this direction: the *Philosophy of Modern Music* operates its particular reversal by shifting from the subject (the great composers and their styles and works) to the object, the raw material, the tonal system itself, which as a peculiar "logic of content" has its own dynamics and generates fresh problems with every solution, setting absolute limits to the freedom of the composer at every historical moment, its objective contradictions increasing in intensity and complexity with each of those new moments until Schoenberg's "final solution"—the unification of vertical and horizontal, of harmony and counterpoint—seems to produce an absolute that is a full stop, beyond which composition cannot go: a success which is also, in genuine dialectical fashion, an absolute failure.

Barthes' reversal is useful because his problematic (which is essentially that of the Sartre of *What Is Literature?*) is the most distant from the rhetoric of materialism and materiality and consists rather in a vision of the nightmare of history as blood guilt and as that necessary and inevitable violence of the relationship of any group to the others which we call class struggle. Both writers—Sartre and Barthes himself—reverse our placid conceptions of literary history by demonstrating how every individual text, by its institutionalized signals, necessarily selects a particular readership for itself and thereby symbolically endorses the inevitable blood guilt of that particular group or class. Only, where Sartre proposed the full Utopian solution of a literature of praxis that would address itself to a classless society, Barthes ingeniously imagines a different way of escaping from the "nightmare of history," a kind of neutral or zero term, the projection of a kind of work from which all group or class signals have been eliminated: white or bleached writing, an escape from group blood guilt on the other side of group formation (which in later Barthes will be reoriented around reception rather than production and become the escape from class struggle into an equally nonindividual kind of *jouissance* or punctual schizophrenic or perverse ecstasy, in *The Pleasure of the Text*).

This is the moment to observe the temptation of the "zero degree" solution in Tafuri himself, where it constitutes one, but *only* one, of the provisional working possibilities very sparsely detectable in his pages. A Barthesian reading of Tafuri's account of Mies and the Seagram's Building seems more plausible, as well as more historical, than a Heideggerian one, particularly if we attend to the content of Tafuri's pro-Mallarmean celebration of the glacial silence of this building, rather than to its rather Germanic language:

The "almost nothing" has become a "big glass" . . . reflecting im-

ages of the urban chaos that surrounds the timeless Miesian
purity. . . . It accepts [the shift and flux of phenomena], absorbs
them to themselves in a perverse multi-duplication, like a Pop Art
sculpture that obliges the American metropolis to look at itself
reflected . . . in the neutral mirror that breaks the city web. In this,
architecture arrives at the ultimate limits of its own possibilities.
Like the last notes sounded by the Doctor Faustus of Thomas
Mann, alienation, having become absolute, testifies uniquely to its
own presence, separating itself from the world to declare the world's
incurable malady.[4]

This is, however, less the endorsement of a Miesian aesthetic than a way of
closing the historical narrative, and, as we will see in a moment, of endowing
the implacable and contradictory historical *situation* with an absolute power
that such desperate nonsolutions as Barthesian "bleached writing" or Miesian silence can only enhance.

Returning for the moment to the strategies of the materialist reversal, we
see that Tafuri's use of such strategies is original in that it includes an
apologia for the primacy of architecture over all the other arts (and thereby of
architectural theory and criticism as well); but the apologia is distinctly un-
traditional and, one would think, not terribly reassuring for people profes-
sionally committed to this field of specialization. Architecture is for Tafuri
supreme among the arts simply because its Other or exterior is coeval with
History and society itself, and it is susceptible therefore to the most fundamental materialist or dialectical reversal of all. To put it most dramatically,
if the outer limit of the individual building is the material city itself, with its
opacity, complexity, and resistance, then the outer limit of some expanded
conception of the architectural vocation as including urbanism and city plan-
ing is the economic itself, or capitalism in the most overt and naked expression of its implacable power. So the great centra-European urbanistic projects
of the 1920s (the Siedlungen, or workers', housing in Berlin, Frankfurt, and
Vienna) touch their Other in the seemingly "extrinsic" obstacle of financial
speculation and the rise in land and property values that causes their absolute
failure and spells an end to their Utopian vocation. But whereas for some
traditional history of forms this is an extrinsic and somehow accidental, ex-
traneous fact, which essentially has "nothing to do" with the purely formal
values of these designs, in Tafuri's practice of the dialectic, this seemingly extrinsic situation is then drawn back into the dialectical spiral itself and passes
an absolute judgment of History proper upon such Utopian forms.

These two dialectical reversals—the judgment on the project of an individual building, text, or "work of art" by the preexisting reality of the city
itself—the subsequent judgment on aesthetics of urban planning and
ensembles by that vaster "totality" which is capitalism itself—these are only
two of the modes of reversal among many in Tafuri's little book; and it is this

very richness of the forms of an anti-idealist turn, the dialectical suppleness of Tafuri's use of varied thematic oppositions, which makes his text both so fascinating and exemplary, and so bewilderingly dense and difficult to read. Other modes of reversal could be enumerated: most notably the unpleasant reminder of the professional status of intellectuals themselves and the ideological and idealistic distortions that result from such status; as well as the thematics of a Keynesian management of the "future"—a kind of credit and planning system of human life—which is one of the more novel sub-themes of this work and of its staging of the critique of modernist Utopianism.

What must be stressed at this point, however, is the way in which the principal "event" of such dialectical histories—the contradiction itself, the fatal reversal of this or that aesthetic solution as it comes to grief against its own material underside—necessarily determines the form of their narrative closure and the kind of "ending" they are led to project. In all three, the present is ultimately projected as the final and most absolute contradiction, the "situation" that has become a blank wall, beyond which History cannot pass. Such an "end of history," or abolition of the future, is most obvious in Adorno, where it is paid for by the tragic "blind spot" of the philosopher-composer, who must on the one hand systematically reject the "other" of his culture (including the movement of popular or mass culture—contemptuously dismissed by Adorno under the all-purpose term "jazz" or "easy music," and that whole movement of Third World history and culture, which is the "repressed" of his Eurocentrism); at the same time he must refuse even the development of advanced music beyond his "final stage," repudiating Stockhausen, electronic music, all the developments of the 1950s and 1960s, with the same stubborn passion that leads him to bracket any conceivable *political* future in *Negative Dialectics*.

We have already examined the more ingenious conception of a "negative way" in Barthes' ideal of a zero degree of writing or in Tafuri's passing hommage to Mies. What must now be underscored is the constitutive relationship between Tafuri's possibility of constructing dialectical history and his systemic refusal of what, in *Theories and History of Architecture*, is called "operative criticism." This type of criticism, most strikingly employed in classical works like Giedion's *Space, Time and Architecture*, reads the past selectively and places an illusory historical analysis, the *appearance* of some "objective" historical narrative, in the service of what is in reality an architectural *manifesto*, the "normative" projection of some new style, the *project* of future work and future possibilities: "the planning of a precise poetical tendency, anticipated in its structures and derived from historical analyses programmatically distorted and finalised" *(T & A*, p. 141)—in short, "ideological criticism [which] substitutes ready-made judgments of value (prepared for immediate use) for analytical rigor" (p. 153). But this judg-

ment on the spurious appropriation of the past in the service of an endorsement of aesthetic action in the present implies that "rigorous" analytical
history must in turn be bought by a stoic renunciation of action and of value,
and a well-nigh Hegelian renunciation of all possible futures, so that the owl
of Minerva can wing its flight into the past. Tafuri's "pessimism" is thus to
be seen as a formal necessity of the generic structure of his text—dialectical
historiography—rather than as an "opinion" or a "position" in its own right.

Unfortunately, it must *also* be read as just such an opinion or position; and
at this point a purely formal and textual necessity intersects with and is overdetermined by ideology, and becomes the vehicle for a whole set of ideological messages and signals which have real content and which can best be appreciated by way of the Marxian traditions in which they emerge.

It seems to me most convenient to decode these signals in the context of a
current and general Left appropriation of the older right-wing "end of
ideology" slogans of the late 1950s. In that period, the period of the
Eisenhower era and the great American celebration, the "end of ideology"
meant not merely the death of Marxism, but also the good news of the end of
the classical capitalism anatomized by Marx, and the apparition of some new
social order whose dymanics was no longer based on production and
associated with social classes and their struggle, but rather on a new principle, which was therefore to be seen in all those senses as "beyond ideology."
This new social system will then be named, by the ex-Marxist right-wing
theorists of an "end of ideology," most notably Daniel Bell, as "postindustrial society"[5] (others will call it consumer society, media society, consumer capitalism, and so forth); and its dynamic will be characterized by the
primacy of knowledge, of scientific and technological know-how, and by the
primacy of a new social group (no longer a class in the Marxian sense), namely the technocrats.

For obvious reasons, the Left repudiated this kind of analysis for a number
of years, remaining intent on demonstrating that the classical analyses and
concepts of Marx's *Capital* were still valid for the period that Bell and others
were intent on describing as the dialectical mutation of "postindustrial society." It is clear that something of the force of Bell's theory derived from the
optimism of the Eisenhower era, the period of American empire and a global
pax americana; and that History itself, better than any left countertheories or
critiques, undertakes to pronounce judgment on the "end of ideology," "post
industrial society" thesis and to lay it to rest in our own moment of the return
of more classical global economic crisis, worldwide depression, unemploy-
ment, and the like.

Paradoxically, however, it was precisely in the intervening years that the
Left itself caught up with the thesis of a new historical moment, a radical
historical break, and produced its own version of the "end of ideology"
thesis. This also had something to do with changes in social atmosphere and

temperature, and with the alteration of the quality of life in the advanced world, that is to say, with mutations in the appearance or surface of social life. It became clear to everyone, in other words, that with consumerism, with the enormous penetration and colonization of the apparatus of the media, with the release of new nonclass social forces in the 1960s—forces associated with race and gender, with nationalism and religion, with marginality (as with students or the permanently unemployed—something decisive had changed in the very "reality of the appearnce" of capitalism. The new Marxian version of the "state" will explain the originality of the features of so-called postindustrial society as a new stage of capitalism proper, in which the old contradictions of capital are still at work, but in unexpectedly new forms. The features enumerated by people like Bell—for example, the primacy of science, the role of bureaucracy—will be retained, but interpreted very differently in the light of a new moment which can be called "late capitalism" or the multinational world system (in the traditional Marxian periodization this would be a third moment of capitalism, after those of classical market capitalism, and the stage of imperialism and monopoly, and could be dated from the immediate postwar period in the United States and the late 1950s in Europe).[6] Although we do not have time for a detailed discussion of this extremely important new Marxian theory of the contemporary world, we must, before returning to Tafuri, underscore two significant features of that theory.

First, it is the theory of something like a total system, marked by a global deployment of capital around the world (even, on many accounts, reaching into the still far from autonomous economic dynamics of the nascent socialist countries), and effectively destroying the older coherence of the various national situations. The total system also is marked by the dynamism with which it now penetrates and colonizes the two last surviving enclaves of Nature within the older capitalism: the Unconscious and the precapitalist agriculture of the Third World—the latter is now systematically undermined and reorganized by the Green Revolution, whereas the former is effectively mastered by what the Frankfurt School used to call the Culture Industry, that is, the media, mass culture, and the various other techniques of the commodification of the mind. I should also add that this enormous new quantum leap of capital now menaces that other precapitalist enclave within older capitalism, namely the nonpaid labor of the older interior or home or family, thereby in contradictory fashion unbinding and liberating that enormous new social force of women, who immediately then post an uncomfortable new threat to the new social order.

On the other hand, if the new expansion of multinational or late capitalism at once triggers various new forms of struggle and resistance, as in the great revolts of the 1960s, it also tends to be accompanied by a mood of pessimism and hopelessness that must naturally enough accompany the sense of a total system, with nothing outside itself, within which local revolts and resistances come to be seen, not as the emergence of new forces and a new logic of a radically different future, but rather as mere inversions within the system, punctual reversals of this or that systemic feature—no longer dialectical in their force, but merely structural(ist). The Marxist response to this increasing windless closure of the system will be varied: it can take the form of a substitution of the time-scale of the prognosis of the *Grundrisse*, for that, far more imminent, of *Capital* proper. In the *Grundrisse*, indeed, Marx seems to project a far greater resiliency for capitalism than in *Capital* itself, one which better accommodates the unexpected new vitality and dynamism of the system after World War II. The key feature of this position will be the insistence on what is, after all, a classical notion of Marx, namely that a socialist revolution and a socialist society are not possible until capitalism has somehow exhausted all its possibilities, but also not until capitalism has become a worldwide and global fact, in which universal commodification is combined with a global proletarianization of the work force, a transformation of all humanity (including the peasants of the Third World) into wage-workers. In that case, the chances for socialism are relegated into some far future, while the ominous nature of the current "total system" becomes rather positive again, since it marks precisely the quantum progression toward that final global state. But this means, in addition, that not only can there not be socialism in one country, there cannot be anything like socialism in one bloc of countries: socialist revolution is here by definition global revolution or it is nothing. And equally obviously, there can be no emergence of a different social system within the interstices of the old, within this or that sector of capitalism proper. Here, I think, you will have already recognized the perspective that is characteristic of Tafuri's work: there can be no qualitatve change in any element of the older capitalist system—as, for instance, in architecture or urbanism—without beforehand a total revolutionary and systemic transformation.

(Total-systems theory can of course also be explained in terms of the kind of textual determinism already evoked above: the purpose of the theorist is to build as powerful a model of capital as possible, and as all-embracing, systemic, seamless, and self-perpetuating. Thus, if the theorist succeeds, he fails: since the more powerful the model constructed, the less possibility will be foreseen in it for any form of human resistance, any chance of structural transformation.)

Yet the meaning of this stark and absolute position, this diagnosis of the total system of late or multinational capital, cannot fully be grasped without taking into account the alternative position of which it is the symbolic repudiation; this is what may be called neo-Gramscianism, the more "optimistic" assessment of some possible "long march through the institutions," which counterposes a new conception of some gradualist "war of position" for the classical Leninist model of the "war of maneuver," the all-or-nothing seizure of power. There are, of course, many reasons why radical Italian intellectuals today should have become fatigued with the Gramscian vision, paradoxically at the very moment when it has come to seem reinvigorating for the Left in other national situations in Europe and elsewhere. The most obvious of these reasons is the thirty-year institutionalization of Gramsci's thought within the Italian Communist party (and the assimilation of Gramsci, in the Italian context, to that classical form of dialectical thought which is everywhere systematically repudiated by a Nietzschean post-Marxism). Nor should we forget to underscore the structural ambiguity or polysemousness of the basic Gramscian texts, written in a coded language beneath the eyes of the Fascist censor, these texts either can be "translated back" into classical Leninism or, on the contrary, can be read as a novel *inflection* of Leninism in a new direction, as post-Leninism or stimulating new form of *neo*-Marxism. There are therefore "objectively" many distinct Gramscis, between which it would be frivolous to attempt to decide which is the "true" one. I want, however, to suggest that with some Gramscian alternative, the possibility of a very different perspective on architecture and urbanism today is also given, so that the implications of this further digression are not a matter of Marxist scholastics, nor are they limited to purely political consequences.

At least two plausible yet distinct readings of the Gramscian slogan, the struggle for "hegemony," must be proposed at this point. What is at stake is the meaning of that "counterhegemony" which oppositional forces are called upon to construct within the ongoing dominance of the "hegemony" of capital; and the interpretive dilemma here turns on the (false) problem of a materialist or an idealist reading. If the Gramscian struggle, in other words, aims essentially at the *preparation* of the working class for some eventual seizure of power, "counterhegemony" is to be understood in purely superstructural terms, as the elaboration of a set of ideas, countervalues, cultural styles, which are virtual or *anticipatory*, in the sense that they "correspond" to a material, institutional base that has not yet "in reality" been secured by political revolution itself.

The temptation is therefore to argue for a "materialist" reading of Gramsci on the basis of certain key figures or tropes in the classical Marxian texts. One recalls, for example, the "organic" formulations of the 1859 Preface to the *Critique of Political Economy:* "new, higher relations of production never appear before the material conditions of their existence have matured within the womb of the old society"; "productive forces developing in the womb of bourgeois society create the material conditions for the solution of the antagonism [of all previous history as class conflict] ."[7] One must also note the celebrated figure with which, in passing, the Marx of *Capital* characterizes the status of "commerce" within the quite different logic of the "ancient" mode of production: "existing in the interstices of the ancient world, like the gods of Epicurus in the *intermundia* or the Jews in the pores of Polish society."[8]

Such figures suggest something like an *enclave* theory of social transition, according to which the emergent future, the new and still nascent social relations that announce a mode of production that will ultimately displace and subsume the as yet still dominant one, is theorized in terms of small yet strategic pockets or beachheads within the older system. The essentially *spatial* nature of the characterization is no accident and conveys something like a historical tension between two radically different types of space, in which the emergent yet more powerful kind will gradually extend its influence and dynamism over the older form, fanning out from its initial implantations and gradually "colonizing" what persists around it. Nor is this some mere poetic vision. The political realities that have been taken as the "verification" and the concrete embodiment of "enclave theory" in contemporary society are the legendary "red communes" of Italy today, most notably Bologna, whose administration by the Communist party has seemed to demarcate them radically from the corruption and inefficiency of the capitalist nation-state within which, like so many foreign bodies, they are embedded. Tafuri's assessment of such communes is particularly instructive:

> The debate over the historical centers and the experience of Bologna have shown that architectural and urbanistic proposals cannot be put to the test outside definite political situations, and then only within improved public structures for control. This has effected a substantial modification in the role of the architectural profession, even further redimensioned and characterized by an increasing change in the traditional forms of patronage and commissioning. . . .Although what [the new left city administrations] have inherited is in a desperate state and the financial difficulties are staggering, one can hope that from this new situation may come the realization of the reforms sought for decades. It is on this terrain that the Italian workers' movements are summoned to a historical test whose repercussions may prove to be enormous, even outside Italy. (*MA*, p. 322)

These lines (written, to be sure, in the more favorable atmosphere of 1976) betray a rather different Tafuri than the somber historiographer of some "end of history" who has predominated in the preceding pages.

What complicates this picture, however, is the discovery that it is precisely some such "enclave theory" which on Tafuri's analysis constitutes the "Utopianism" of the modern movement in architecture; that, in other words, Tafuri's critique of the international style, the informing center of all his works, is first and foremost a critique of the latter's enclave theory itself. Le Corbusier, for example, spoke of avoiding political revolutions, not because he was not committed to "revolution," but rather because he saw the construction and the constitution of new space as the most revolutionary act, one that could "replace" the narrowly political revolution of the mere seizure of power (and if the experience of a new space is associated with a whole transformation of everyday life itself, Le Corbusier's seemingly antipolitical stance can be reread as an *enlargement* of the very conception of the political, and as having an anticipatory kinship with conceptions of "cultural revolution" that are far more congenial to the spirit of the contemporary Left). Still, the demiurgic hubris of high modernism is fatefully dramatized by such visions of the towers of the Plan Voisin, which stride across a fallen landscape like H. G. Wells' triumphant Martians, or of the gigantic symbolic structures of the Unités d'habitation, the Algiers plan, or Chandigarh, which are apocalyptically to sound the knell of the cramped and unsalubrious hovels that lie dwarfed beneath their prophetic shadow. We will shortly enter into the terms of Tafuri's critique of modernism itself. Suffice it to say for the moment that its cardinal sin is precisely to identify (or conflate) the political and the aesthetic, and to foresee a political and social transformation that is henceforth at one with the formal processes of architectural production itself. All of this is easier to demonstrate on the level of empirical history, where the new enclaves of the international style manifestly failed to regenerate anything around them; or where, when they did have the dynamic and radiating influence predicted for them by the Masters, the results, if anything, were even more depressing, generating a whole series of dismal glass boxes in their own image, or a multiplication of pseudo-Corbusian towers in the desolation of parks which have become the battleground of an unending daily war of race and class. Even the great emblem of the "red communes" can, from this perspective, be read differently: for it can equally well be argued that they are not enclaves at all—not laboratories in which original social relations of the future are being worked out, but rather simply the administration of inherited capitalistic relations, albeit conducted in a different spirit of social commitment than that of the Christian Democrats.

This uninspiring balance sheet would settle the fate of the Gramscian alternative if the "enclave theory" were its only plausible interpretation. The latter may, however, be seen as an overly reductive and rather defensively "materialist" conception of the politics of space. But it can equally well be argued that Gramsci's notion of "hegemony" (along with the later and related idea of "cultural revolution") attempts rather to displace the whole distinction of materialism versus idealism (and, along with it, of the traditional concept of base and superstructure). It would therefore no longer be "idealist" in the bad old sense to suggest that "counterhegemony" means producing and keeping alive a certain alternate "idea" of space, the urban, daily life, and the like. It would then no longer be so immediately significant (or so practically and historically crippling) that architects in the West (with the possible exception of France)—owing to the private property system—do not have the opportunity of projecting and constructing collective ensembles that express and articulate original new social relations (and needs and demands) of a collective type. The essential would rather be that they are able to form conceptions and Utopian images of such projects, against which to develop a self-consciousness of their concrete activities in this society (it being understood, in Tafuri's spirit, that such collective projects would only practically and materially be possible after a systemic transformation of society). But such Utopian "ideas" are as "objective" as material buildings: their possibilities—the possibility of conceiving such new space—have conditions of possibility as rigorous as any material artifact. Those conditions of possibility are to be found, first and foremost, in the uneven development of world history and in the existence, elsewhere, in the second and Third Worlds, of projects and constructions that are not possible in the First; this concrete existence of radically different spaces elsewhere (of whatever unequal realization) is what objectively opens the possibility for the coming into being and development of "counterhegemonic values" here. A role is thereby secured for a more "positive" and Gramscian architectural criticism, over against Tafuri's stubbornly (and therapeutically) negative variety, his critical refusal of Utopian speculation on what is not possible within the closure of the multinational system. In reality, both of these critical strategies are productive alternatively according to the situation itself, and the public to which the ideological critic must address herself; and there is no particular reason to lay down either of these useful weapons. It is at any rate worth quoting yet another appreciation of Tafuri—this one, unexpectedly, of the Stalinallee (now the Karl Marx-Allee) in East Berlin—in order to show that his practical criticism is often a good deal more ambivalent than his theoretical slogans (and also further to dispel the feeling that the celebration of Mies' negative mysticism, quoted above, amounts to anything like a definitive position):

> However, in the case [of the Stalinallee, in East Berlin] it would be wrong to regard what resulted as purely ideological or propagandistic; in reality, the Stalinallee is the fulcrum of a project of urban reorganization affecting an entire district, establishing an axis of development toward the Tiergarten different from that developed historically. In addition, this plan inverts the logical manner in which a bourgeois city expands by introducing into the heart of the metropolis the residence as a decisive factor. The monumental bombast of the Stalinallee—now renamed Karl Marx-Allee—was conceived to put in a heroic light an urbanistic project that set out to be different. In fact, it succeeds perfectly in expressing the presupposition for the construction of the new socialist city, which rejects divisions between architecture and urbanism and aspires to impose itself as a unitary structure.[13] (MA, pp. 332, 326)

Such a text can evidently be used to support either position: the negative one—that such a collective project, with its transcendence of the opposition building/city, is only possible *after* a revolutionary transformation of social relations as a whole; or the more Gramscian one outlined above, that the very existence of such an ensemble in some other space of the world creates a new force field which cannot but have its influence even over those architects for whom such a project is scarcely a "realistic" possibility.

Still, until now we have not considered what kind of "total system" sets limits to the practical transformation of space in our time; nor have we drawn the other obvious consequence from the neo-Marxian theorization of "consumer society" or of the new moment of late capitalism, namely that to such a new moment there may very well correspond a new type of culture or cultural dynamic. This is therefore the time to introduce our third theme or problem, namely that of postmodernism and of the critique of classical or high modernism itself. For the economic periodization of capital into three rather than two stages (that of "late" or multinational capitalism being now added to the more traditional moments of "classical" capitalism and of the "monopoly stage" or "stage of imperialism") suggests the possibility of a new periodization on the level of culture as well. From this perspective, the moment of "high" modernism, of the International Style and of the classical modern movement in all the arts—with their great *auteurs* and their "Utopian" monuments, Mallarmean "Books of the World" fully as much as Corbusean Radiant Cities—would "correspond" to that second stage of monopoly and imperialist capitalism which came to an end with the Second World War. Its "critique" therefore coincides with its extinction, its passing into history, as well as with the emergence, in the third stage of "consumer capital," with some properly postmodernist practice of pastiche, of a new free play of styles and historicist allusions now willing to "learn from Las Vegas," a moment of surface rather than of depth, of the "death" of the old individual subject or bourgeois ego, and of the schizophrenic celebration of the commodity fetishism of the image, of a now "delirious New York" and a countercultural California, a moment when the logic of media capitalism penetrates the logic of advanced cultural production itself and transforms the latter to the point where such distinctions as those between high and mass culture lose their significance (and where the older notions of a "critical" or "negative" value of advanced or modernist art may also no longer be appropriate or operative).

As I have observed, Tafuri refuses this periodization and we will observe him positioning his critique of the "postmoderns" beneath the general category of a still high modernist Utopianism, of which they are seen merely as so many epigones. Still, in this country and for this public, the thrust of his critique of Utopian architecture will inevitably be associated with the generalized reaction here against the older hegemonic values and norms of the International Style, about which we must attempt to take an ambivalent and nuanced position. It is certain, for instance—as books like Tom Wolfe's recent *From the Bauhaus to Our House* readily testify—that the critique of high modernism can spring from reactionary and "philistine" impulses (in both the aesthetic and the political sense) and can be belatedly nourished by all the old middle-class resistances which the modern movement met and aroused in its first freshness. Nor does it seem implausible that in certain national situations, most notably in those of the former fascist countries, the antimodernist position is still essentially and unambiguously at one with political reaction, as Habermas has suggested,[9] If so, this would explain Tafuri's decision to uncouple a reasoned critique of modernism from the adoption or exposition of any more "positive" aesthetic ideology. In the United States, however, whatever the ultimate wisdom of applying a similar strategy, the cultural pull and attractiveness of the concept of postmodernism clearly complicates the situation in ways that need to be clarified.

It will therefore be useful to retrace our steps for the moment, and however briefly to work through the terms of Tafuri's critique of modernism as he outlines it for us in *Architecture and Utopia*, where we meet a left-wing version of the "end of ideology" roughly consistent with the periodizations of some new stage of capital that have just been evoked. On this view, ideas as such—ideology in the more formal sense of a whole system of legitimizing beliefs—are no longer significant elements in the social reproduction of late capitalism, something that was obviously not the case in its earlier stages. Thus the great bourgeois revolutionary ideology of "freedom, equality, and fraternity" was supremely important in securing the universal consent of a variety of social classes to the new political and economic order; this ideology was thus also, in Tafuri's use of the term, a Utopia, or rather, its ideologizing and legitimizing function was concealed behind a universalizing and Utopian rhetoric. In the late nineteenth century—particularly in the French Third Republic (the "Republic of the Professors")—the rise of positivism, with its militant anticlericalism and its ideal of a lay or secular education, suggests the degree to which official philosophy was still thought to be a crucial terrain of ideological struggle and a supreme weapon for securing the unity of the state; whereas in our own time, until recently, what is generally called New Deal Liberalism (or in Europe, the social democracy of the welfare states) performed an analogous function.

All of this would seem to be in question today. We will want, Adorno says somewhere, to take into account the possibility that in our time the commodity is its own ideology: the practices of consumption and consumerism, on that view, themselves are enough to reproduce and legitimate the system, no matter what "ideology" you happen to be committed to. In that case, not abstract ideas, beliefs, ideologies, or philosophical systems, but rather the immanent practices of daily life now occupy the functional position of "ideology" in its other larger systemic sense. And if so, this development can clearly serve as one explanation for the waning power of the Utopian ideologies of high modernism as well. Indeed, Tafuri explicitly associates the demiurgic value of architectural planning in the modern masters with the Keynesian ideal of the control of the *future*. In both versions, "Utopia" is the dream of "a 'rational' domination of the future, the elimination of the *risk* it brings with it" *(A&U*, p. 52): "Even for Le Corbusier the absolute of form is the complete realization of a constant victory over the uncertainty of the future" (p. 129). It is therefore logical enough that both these ultimate middle-class ideologies or Utopias—Keynesianism *and* high modernism— should disappear together, and that their concrete "critique" should be less a matter of intellectual self-consciousness than simply a working out of history itself.

But "ideology" has a somewhat different focus in Tafuri's schematic over-view of bourgeois architectural thinking from the dissolution of the Baroque to our own time, where these varied aesthetic Utopias are analyzed in terms of something closer to a Hegelian "ruse of reason" or of History itself. Their Utopian form thus proves to be an instrument in the edification of a business system and the new dynamism of capital; whatever content they claimed in themselves, their concrete effects, their more fundamental function, lay in the systematic destruction of the past. Thus the emergence of secular conceptions of the city in the eighteenth century is primarily to be read as a way of clearing away the older culture: "the deliberate abstraction of Enlightenment theories of the city served . . .to destroy baroque schemes of city planning and development" (p. 8). In much the same way, the dawn of modernism proper—the moment when ideology is overtly transformed into Utopia, when "ideology had to negate itself as such, break its own crystallized forms and throw itself entirely into the 'construction of the future'" (p. 50)—this supreme moment of Freud and Nietzsche, of Weber and Simmel, and of the birth of high modernism in all the arts, was in reality for Tafuri a purely destructive operation in which residual ideologies and archaic social forms were systematically dissolved. The new Utopianism of high modernism thus unwittingly and against the very spirit of its own revolutionary and Utopian affirmations prepared the terrain for the omnipotence of the fully "rational-ized" technocratic plan, for the universal planification of what was to become the total system of multinational capital: "the unmasking of the idols that obstructed the way to a global rationalization of the productive universe and its social dominion became the new historical task of the intellectual" (p. 51). It also became the historic mission of the various cultural avant-gardes them-selves, for which, in reality although not according to their own manifestos, "the autonomy of formal construction" has as its deepest practical function "to plan the disappearance of the subject, to cancel the anguish caused by the pathetic (or ridiculous) resistance of the individual to the structures of domination that close in upon him or her" (p. 73). Whatever avant-garde or architectural aesthetic Utopias thought they were intent on achieving, therefore, in the real world of capital and in their effective practice, those ends are dialectically reversed and serve essentially to reinforce the techno-cratic total control of the new system of the bureaucratic society of planned consumption.

We may now return to the beginnings of Tafuri's story in the eighteenth century. The Enlightenment attempt to think urbanism in some new and more fully rational way generates two irreconcilable alternatives: one path is that of architecture as the "instrument of social equilibrium," and "geometric silence of Durand's formally codified building types," "the uniformity en-sured by preconstituted formal systems" (p. 13); the other is that of a "science of sensations" (p. 11), a kind of "excessive symbolism" (p. 13) which we may interpret as the conception of a libidinal resistance within the system, the breakthrough of Desire into the grids of power and control. These two great Utopian antitheses—Saint-Simon versus Fourier, if you like, or Lenin versus Marcuse—are, then, for Tafuri the ideological double-bind of a thinking imprisoned in capitalist relations. They are at once unmasked in Piranesi's contemporaneous nightmarish synthesis of the Camp Marzio and are also, unexpectedly, given a longer lease on life in the New World, where, with the open frontier and in the absence of feudalism, the new urban syn-thesis of Washington, D.C., retains a vitality henceforth forbidden to Euro-pean efforts.

Interestingly enough, in our present context, these two alternatives also roughly correspond to the analyses of Adorno and Barthes respectively. The first Utopian alternative, that of rationalization, will little by little formulate its program in terms of overcoming the opposition between whole and part, between urban plan and individual architectural monument, between the molar and the molecular, between the "urban organism as a whole" and the "elementary cell" or building blocks of the individual building (Hilberseimer). But it is precisely this "unified field theory" of the macro and the micro, toward which the urbanistic work of a Corbusier strives, which is projected, in Adorno's book, by Schoenberg's twelve-tone system, the ultimate abolu-tion of the gap between counterpoint and harmony, between overall form and the dynamics of the individual musical "parole" or theme. But Schoenberg's extraordinary synthesis is sterile, and in architecture the "unified field theory" destroys the individual work or building as such: "the single building is no longer an 'object'; it is only the place in which the elementary assemblage of single cells assumes physical form; since these cells are elements reproducible ad infinitum, they conceptually embody the prime structure of a production line that excludes the old concepts of 'place' or 'space'" (p. 105). This Utopian impulse has then ended up rationalizing the object world more extensively and ferociously than anything Ford or Taylor might have done on their own momentum.

Yet the second, or libidinal, strategy is no less "ideological" in its ultimate results: Barthes' intellectual trajectory is complicated, and I will not take the time here to insert him neatly back into this scheme (although I think something like this could be done). Suffice it to observe that, following Benjamin, Tafuri sees this second, libidinal strategy in its emergence in Baudelaire as having unexpected subjective consequences which harmonize with the objective external planification achieved above: "Baudelaire had discovered that the commercialization of the poetic product can be accentuated by the poet's very attempt to free himself from his objective conditions" (p. 92). The new vanguard subjectivity, in other words, ends up training the consumer for life in the industrial city, teaching "the ideology of the correct use of the city" (p. 84), freeing the aesthetic consumer from "objects that were offered to judgment" and substituting "a process to be lived and used as such" (p. 101). This particular strategy now prolongs itself into, and revitalizes itself in, the postmodernist ideologies and aesthetics of the present period, denounced by Tafuri in a memorable passage:

Thus the city is considered in terms of a suprastructure. Indeed art is now called upon to give the city a suprastructural guise. Pop art, op art, analysis of the urban "imageability," and the "prospective aesthetic" converge in this objective. The contradictions of the contemporary city are resolved in multivalent images, and by figuratively exalting that formal complexity they are dissimulated. If read with adequate standards of judgment this formal complexity is nothing other than the explosion of the irremediable dissonances that escape the plan of advanced capital. The recovery of the concept of *art* thus serves this new cover-up role. It is true that whereas industrial design takes a lead position in technological production and conditions its quality in view of an increase in consumption, pop art, reutilizing the residues and castoffs of that production, takes its place in the rear guard. But this is the exact reflection of the twofold request now made to the techniques of visual communication. Art which refuses to take its place in the vanguard of the production cycle, actually demonstrates that the process of consumption tends to the infinite. Indeed, even the rejects, sublimated into useless or nihilist objects which bear a new *value of use*, enter into the production-consumption cycle, if only through the back door.

This art that deliberately places itself in the rear guard is also indicative of the refusal to come to terms with the contradictions of the city and resolve them completely; to transform the city into a totally organized machine without useless squanderings of an archaic character or generalized dysfunction.

In this phase it is necessary to persuade the public that the contradictions, imbalances, and chaos typical of the contemporary city are inevitable. Indeed the public must be convinced that this chaos contains an unexplored richness, unlimited utilizable possibilities, and qualities of the "game" now made into new fetishes for society. (pp. 137, 139)

The power of such negative critiques of ideology (which construe ideology exclusively in terms of "false consciousness") lies in the assumption that everything that does not effectively disrupt the social reproduction of the system may be considered as part and parcel of the reproduction of that system. The anxieties provoked in almost everyone by such an implacable and absolute position are probably healthy and therapeutic in one way or another. As I have begun to suggest before, however, the real problem in such an analysis lies elsewhere, in the assumption that "social reproduction" in late capitalism takes much the same form as in the earlier period of high modernism, and that what some of us call the "postmoderns" simply replicate the old modernist solutions at lower levels of intensity and originality. Thus Philip Johnson's "ambiguous eclecticism ends up as mere jugglery" *(MA, p. 397)*; "the work of Louis Kahn and the British architect James Stirling represent two opposite attempts to breathe life into a seemingly moribund art" *(MA, p. 400)*; Robert Venturi's *Complexity and Contradiction in Architecture* flattens out the new-critical concepts of ambiguity and contradiction, dehistoricizing them and emptying them of all their tragic (and properly high modernist) tension, with a view toward "justifying personal planning choices rather more equivocal than ambiguous" *(T&H, p. 213)*.

Yet there would seem to be a certain inconsistency in the reproach that the newer architects fail to achieve even that tragic tension which was itself considered to be Utopian and ideological in the masters. The other fact of this inconsistency can then be detected in the consonance and profound historical kinship between Tafuri's analysis of modernism and the onslaughts of the postmodernists, most notably Venturi himself, a critique which goes well beyond the usual themes of the hubris of central planning,[10] the single-function conception of space and the puritanism of the streamlining abhorrence of ornament. Venturi's analysis, particularly in *Learning from Las Vegas* (1972), centers specifically on the dialectic (and the contradiction) between the building and the city, between architecture and urbanism, which forms one of the major strands in the historiography of the Italian theorist. The monumental duck of the international style—like Mallarme's *Livre*, like Bayreuth, like *Finnegans Wake*, or like Kandinsky's mystical painting—proposes itself, as we have already suggested, as a radically different, revolutionary or subversive enclave from which little by little the whole surrounding fabric of fallen social relations is to be regenerated and transformed. Yet in order to stage itself as a *foyer* of this kind, the "duck" must first radically separate itself from that environment in which it stands; it thereby slowly comes to be, by virture of that very inaugural disjunction, that constitutive self-definition and isolation, not a building but a *sculpture*. After the fashion of Barthes' concept of connotation, the duck ends up—far from emitting a message with a radically new content—simply designating itself and signifying itself, celebrating its own disconnection as a message in its own right.

Whatever else may be said about the architecture of postmodernism—and however it is to be judged politically and historically—it seems important to recognize that it does not seek to do *that* but rather something very different. It may no longer embody the Utopian ideology of high modernism, may indeed in that sense be vacuous of any Utopian or protopolitical impulse, while still, as the suspicious prefix "post" suggests, remaining in some kind of parasitic relationship with the extinct high modernism it repudiates; yet what must be explored is the possibility that with postmodernism a whole new *aesthetic* is in the process of emerging, an aesthetic significantly distinct from that of the previous era.

The latter—high modernism—can perhaps most effectively be characterized (following Althusser's notion of "expressive causality") as an aesthetic of identity or of organic unification. To demarcate the postmodernist aesthetic from this one, two familiar themes may serve as points of reference: the dialectic of inside and outside and the question of ornament or decoration. For Le Corbusier, as is well known, "the plan proceeds from within to without" in such a way that the outside of the building expresses its interior; stylistic homogeneity is thus here achieved by unifying these two opposites, or, better still, by assimilating one of them—the exterior—to the other. As for ornament, its "contradiction" with the reality of the wall itself is overcome by the hygienic *exclusion* of the offending term.[11] What may now briefly be observed is that Robert Venturi's conception of the "decorated shed" seeks, on the contrary, to reinforce these oppositions and thereby to valorize *contradiction* itself (in a stronger way than his earlier terminology of "complexity" or "ambiguity" might suggest). The philosophical formulation of this very different aesthetic move might be found in the (properly poststructural or postmodernist) idea that "difference relates": an aesthetic of homogeneity is here displaced, less in the name of a random heterogeneity, a set of inert differences randomly coexisting, than in the service of a new kind of perception for which tension, contradiction, the registering of the incompatible and the clashing, is in and of itself a strong mode of relating two incommensurable elements, poles, or realities. If, as I believe, something like this characterizes the specific internal logic of postmodernism, it must be seen at the very least as constituting an original aesthetic and one quite distinct from the high modernism from which it seeks to disengage itself.

It will no doubt be observed that the symbolic act of high modernism, which seeks to resolve contradiction by stylistic fiat (even though its resolution may remain merely symbolic), is of a very different order and quality from that of a postmodernism that simply ratifies the contradictions and fragmented chaos all around it by way of an intensified perception of, a mesmerized and well-nigh hallucinogenic fascination with, those very contradictions themselves (contenting itself with eliminating the affective charge of pathos, of the tragic, or of anxiety, which characterized the modern movement). In this sense, no doubt, Marx's early critique of Hegel's theory of religion retains its force for postmodernism: "self-conscious man, insofar as he has recognized and superseded the spiritual world. . .then confirms it again in this alienated form and presented it as his true existence; he reestablishes it and claims to *be at home in his other being.*"[12]

I must add, to this juxtaposition, my feeling that *moralizing* judgments on either of these aesthetics are always the most unsatisfactory way to reach some ultimate evaluation of them; my own perspective here is a historicist one, for which any position on postmodernism must begin by being a self-critique and a judgment on *ourselves,* since this is the moment when we find ourselves and, like it or not, this aesthetic is a part of us.

That is, however, not the most important point to be made in the present context. One of the more annoying and scandalous habits of dialectical thought is indeed its identification of opposites, and its tendency to send off back to back seemingly opposed positions on the grounds that both share and are determined and limited by a common problematic, or, to use a more familiar language, represent the two intolerable options of a single double-bind. One is tempted to see something of the sort at work here, in the opposition between Tafuri's cultural pessimism, with all its rigor and ideological asceticism, and the complacent free play of a postmodernism content to juggle the pregiven tokens of contemporary social reality, from which even the nostalgic memory of earlier commitments to radical change has vanished without a trace.

It is possible that these two positions are in fact the same, and that as different as they may at first seem, both rest on the conviction that nothing new can be done, no fundamental changes can be made, within the massive being of late capitalism? What is different is that Tafuri's thought lives this situation in a rigorous and self-conscious stoicism, whereas the practitioners and ideologues of postmodernism relax within it, inventing modes of perception in order to "be at home" in the same impossible extremity: changes of valence, the substitution of a plus sign for a minus, on the same equation.

Perhaps, in that case, something is to be said for Lefebvre's call for a politics of space and for the search for a properly Gramscian architecture after all.

1985

Chapter 3
Pleasure
A Political Issue

*Something on the order of a subject can be discerned on the
recording surface: a strange subject, with no fixed identity,
wandering about over the body without organs, yet always remaining peripheral to the desiring-machines, being defined by the
share of the product it takes for itself, garnering here, there and
everywhere a reward, in the form of a becoming or an avatar,
being born of the states that it consumes and being reborn with
each new state: "c'est donc moi, c'est donc à moi!. . . The
subject is produced as a mere residue alongside the desiring
machines: a conjunctive synthesis of consumption in the form of a
wonderstruck: "c'était donc ça!" [wow!]*
Gilles Deleuze and Félix Guattari, *Anti-Oedipus*

*At Yekaterina Peshkova's in Moscow one evening, listening to
Isaiah Dobrovein playing Beethoven's sonatas, Lenin said:*
   *"I don't know of anything better than the
'Appassionata.' I can listen to it every day. Amazing,
superhuman music! I always think with a pride that may be
naive: look what miracles people can perform!"*
   *And screwing up his eyes and chuckling he
added without mirth:*
   *"But I can't listen to music often, it affects my
nerves, it makes me want to say sweet nothings and pat the
heads of people who, living in a filthy hell, can create such
beauty. But today we mustn't pat anyone on the head or we'll
get our hand bitten off: we've got to hit them on the heads, hit*

61

them without mercy, though in the ideal we are against doing
any violence to people. Hm-hm—it's a hellishly difficult office!"
　　　　　　　　　Maxim Gorski, *Reminiscences of Lenin*

So pleasure, we are told, like happiness or interest, can never be fixed directly by the naked eye—let alone pursued as an end, or conceptualized—but only experienced laterally, or after the fact, as something like the by-product of
something else. When taken as an end in its own right, pleasure ceases to be
that and imperceptibly transforms itself into something quite different, a passion, one of those great inhuman metaphysical "choices of being," celebrated in his own peculiar way by Sade, and crystallized in great archetypal
figures such as those of Don Juan or Herr Jakob Schmidt—no longer
hedonists at all, these last, but subjects possessed.

I pause here to register another dimension of our topic—namely, history
itself, the historicity of our own conjuncture. I am suddenly struck by the
fact that no one has mentioned these archetypal (male) quest-figures lately, or
any of their accompanying cortege from the portrait gallery of bourgeois individualism, such as the Adventurer. Is it possible that they have disappeared
altogether from consumer society, and that their former passions have been
reduced or expanded, either into psychopathology—as in the former "glut-
tony"—or into the badge and sign of microgroup behavior—as in gay pro-
miscuity? At any rate, it becomes clear that the question of the originality of
our own situation—consumer capitalism, postindustrial society, or, better
still, what Ernest Mandel calls "late capitalism"—will have to be reckoned
into any discussion of the relationship between pleasure and politics.

So no pleasure in its own right, only pleasurable activities, or something
like a fading effect of pleasure after the fact. Yet the word continues to exist,
and this suggests yet another qualification in the topic. Will it focus on the
experience of the pleasurable, and what that might mean for politics or do to
political activity? Or is something else at stake, namely, the *idea* of pleasure,
the ideologies of pleasure, the political value of slogans that raise the banner
of that abstract idea, about which the familiar question might be debated
regarding its subversive power as a revolutionary "demand"? New needs,
new demands: at once an influential political ideology from our own immediate past takes shape again in the mind's eye—the New Left or Marcusean one. According to this, the cultural contradiction of late capitalism is to
be grasped in the way in which the consumption system stimulates new needs
and new demands, many of them false or spurious to be sure, yet whose
dynamic and pressure can no longer be accommodated within the system,
whose very mass therefore threatens to blow it sky-high. This politicocultural analysis is part of a larger one, for which, more recently, Rudolph
Bahro's conception of "surplus consciousness" might serve as a motto, signifying the general surplus cultural overproduction of a system that in a new,

yet classical, way generates its own Other and negation from within itself. We believed this yesterday: do we still do so? If not, why not? What has changed all around us since the 1960s to render this particular political strategy—for it was that too—archaic and outmoded?

The reminder at least usefully suggests something else at the same time: that there has been a whole series of Left political or ideological positions on pleasure and hedonism in our recent past, and that we need to confront a few more of those before "deciding" what we really think ourselves. (What we really think may simply be a residue of one of those older ideologies, in fact). Oddly, the Marcusean position emerges from its own opposite, that other even more influential tradition in Frankfurt School thought which insists on the determinate relationship between commodification and what we may have been tempted to think of as pleasure. How do we distinguish, in other words, between real pleasure and mere diversion—the degradation of free time into that very different commodity called "leisure," the form of commodity consumption stamped on the most intimate former pleasures from sexuality to reading? This analysis rests on the more general systemic description of a prodigious expansion of late capitalism, which now, in the guise of what has variously been called the "culture industry" or the "consciousness industry," penetrates one of the two surviving precapitalist enclaves of Nature within the system—namely, the unconscious. (The other one is the precapitalist agriculture and village cultures of the Third World.)

The commodification approach raises two questions. The first is an immediately practical-political one: if what people today imagine to be pleasure is nothing but a commodity fix, how to deal with that addiction? Who is to break the news to them that their conscious experience of leisure products—their conscious "pleasure" in consumption—is in reality nothing but false consciousness? Indeed, even further, who has the authority—and in the name of what?—to make such an assessment? What was scandalous about Marcuse's solution could already be measured by the volume of liberal outrage that greeted *Repressive Tolerance*. From out of the cultural baggage of their own "great tradition," liberals were horrified to glimpse the outlines of Plato's Philosopher-King alive and well in consumer society and offering to lay hands on the media and their rights to free speech. For an antiauthoritarian Left, however, which had begun to raise its own questions about the place of truth and the privileges of interpretation, the Marcusean version of Frankfurt School analysis could also at best awaken the proverbial mixed feelings, since in the traditions of the Left the Platonic sage generally bears the rather different name of the revolutionary party.

It is at any rate clear that the problematic of new revolutionary needs and demands and that of the commodification of desires and pleasures are dialectically at one with each other. If the former is an ideological mirage, it is a mirage generated by the correspondingly ideological conception of "degraded" consciousness and of commodified consumption. From a more populist view, indeed, the question might be raised as to whether all that mindless consumption of television images, that self-perpetuating ingestion of the advertising images of things rather than the things themselves, is really all that pleasurable—whether the consumer's consciousness is really so false and so little reflexive as it dutifully treads the rotating mill of its civic responsibility to consume.

The way to tell the difference between a pleasure and a fix, a therapist once said, is that you can do without the former. But this is surely something the subject is somewhere naggingly aware of, in her heart of hearts. Indeed, the pronoun suggests that the conception of the mindless consumer, the ultimate commodified false consciousness of shopping-center capitalism, is a conception of otherness; that degraded consumption is assigned to women, to what used to be called "Mrs. American Housewife." The genealogy goes all the way back to the first collective fantasies about suburban life in the 1950s, Philip Wylie's "Momism," for instance, and the psychoanalytic terror of a consuming Mom, who not only presided possessively over all the new postwar products but also threatened to eat *you* up as well—a consumption fantasy with teeth in it, according to all the archaic textbooks. As for the exhausted male worker or businessman, according to this stereotype, he has presumably always been more lucid about the worthlessness of the evening images that flicker across his face. But in the raw anti-intellectualism of American capitalism from the outset, was not culture always something worthless and "feminine" in all its forms, from European "high" culture all the way to the substitute gratifications of the pulps and comic books?

What the Frankfurt School theorized in revulsion and historical anxiety as the degradation of culture and the fetishization of the mind has more recently been celebrated, in positive forms, on this side of the Rhine. It is well known that the theorists of a French poststructuralism simply change the valences on the old descriptions of Adorno, Horkheimer, and Marcuse, so that what used to be denounced as commodification is now offered by Deleuze and Guattari as the consciousness of the ideal schizophrenic, the "true hero of desire." Behind this peculiar shift lies something more than mere national or generational difference. Both accounts share a secret referent, whose identity they rarely blurt out as such; both aim implicitly to come to terms with the same troubling and preemptory reality. This we can now identify as *American* capitalism, whose historical modifications are, one would think, the determinant of those secondary theoretical ones. From the Manhattan or Hollywood or nascent consumerism and modernization, in which the German refugee intellectuals with some bewilderment retained their central European cultural pride and dialectical self-consciousness, to the "delirious New York" and countercultural California of the 1960s superstate, with its very different gravitational pull over the intellectuals of a diminished Western Europe—much has changed, including pleasure itself and its images and functions.

The most consequent and influential French counterposition on pleasure is, however, associated with another name, that of the late Roland Barthes, about whom some remarks are unavoidably in order. What Barthes was, and what he became, is a complicated and interesting subject, only a little of which can be developed here. But as the trajectory is inscribed in *Le Plaisir du texte* in surcharged fashion, the symbolic meaning of that pamphlet cannot, I think, really be grasped without something being said about it. The very date of that influential, fragmentary statement—1973—is in retrospect charged with significance. Marking a break dramatized by the emergence of the oil weapon and the onset of a global economic crisis that is still with us (and expressed politically in such different events as the Chilean Coup and in France the "common program" of the Left), the general moment from 1972 to 1974 can be seen as the definitive end of whatever, worldwide, came to be known as the 60s. In the area of culture and theory this moment was also the occasion for a range of statements and disguised manifestos that all in one way or another repealed that period and its values and urgencies. They called a halt, often in the form of a return to the very moral values the 60s had called into question, as in Lionel Trilling's very different, yet equally symptomatic *Sincerity and Authenticity* (1972). Nothing seems so distant from the moralizing of this last, with its defense of tradition and the canon, and its obligatory great books format, as Barthesian hedonism and Barthes' own complacent, stubborn commitment to the *instant*, whether of reading or writing, his self-indulgence (here, self-indulgently, transformed into a very *theory* of self-indulgence), his blissful renunciation of the "high seriousness" of the Anglo-American critic's sense of the moral vocation of criticism itself—"nothing to *say* about the *texte de jouissance;* . . . you can't talk *about it,* you can't only talk 'within' it, on its own terms, abandoning yourself to a voluptuous plagiarism, hysterically reaffirming *jouissance* in its essential void."[1]

Although it is an attractive alternative to the pieties of Anglo-Saxon cultural elitism—not least because the latter still forms *our* particular institutional horizon—on rereading today, *Le Plaisir du texte* does strike one as oddly defensive. Its polemic targets are no doubt textual puritans rather than the polymorphous and hallucinogenizing partisans of a 60s' "authenticity," against whom Trilling is concerned to draw the line. The more significant feature here is that for both writers, in their very different national situations, these seemingly antithetical adversaries are both fantasized as images and representations of a dominant *Left*—only where for Trilling, that Left is embodied in the rising tide of the barbarism of a student and black radicalism, for Barthes it takes the form of the *Marxist gendarme,* the more traditional puritanism of the French Communist party and of some orthodox Leninism. In both discussions, then, the ostensible subjects of individual gratification (aesthetic, on the one hand; self-expression or "authenticity," on the other) prove to be vehicles for some deeper political and ideological position, in which the values of "decorum," on the one hand, and physical pleasure, on the other, are stimulated and appealed to for confirmation of a repudiation of Left politics by two writers whose theoretical methods have had some historical relationship to Left philosophical traditions.

Whether the Left has historically been puritanical, or indeed whether there is something in the very essence of revolutionary mentality that somehow forever dooms it to a puritanical stance, are questions central to the present topic but quite impossible to answer empirically. The Lenin story, for instance, shows *his* puritanism to have been tactical: he obviously *liked* Beethoven (on the other hand, that line of inquiry opens up the troubled matter of the refusal of modernism and *its* peculiar pleasures by the orthodox Left). Whoever says pleasure, however, generally means sex, and it is generally around the end of a properly Soviet cultural revolution in the late 1920s (dramatized among other things, in the early 1930s, by the exclusion of Wilhelm Reich and the halt to his experiments with a properly "sexual politics") that the discussion of Left puritanism turns. Whatever the contributions of a Freudian habit of analysis may be in this area (the deeper unconscious attitudes of Bolshevik leaders themselves, for example), it may not be inappropriate to recall the strategic and tactical dimensions of such turns, which have to do with the very different matter of the key issues and slogans susceptible of mobilizing (or alienating) working-class people. Although this line of discussion does not need to take the condescending framework of some stages theory of consciousness, or to be staged around analysis of the relative backwardness of working-class consciousness on sexual matters— "they're not ready for women's or gay liberation or abortion"; "they need further cultural reeducation"—note that precisely those analyses, however condescending, are central to any real discussion of cultural revolution itself, of the programmed habits of subalternity, obedience, and the like, which cultural revolution seeks to dissolve.

But there is a different way of understanding working-class resistance to slogans of a sexual politics (always assuming that such resistance exists "empirically" and is a crucial factor in the construction of political and ideological strategies). That is the class symbolism of such questions. The conception of the primacy of class issues and class consciousness suggests that from a working-class perspective, issues of sexual liberation may be grasped , not on their own terms, but rather as so many class ideologies and as the collective expression of groups (such as middle-class youth) that working-class people identify as the class enemy. This should at least alert us to the possibility that the discussion of pleasure as a phenomenon may not have much to do at all with the rather different discussion of pleasure, sexual liberation, or the Utopian or libidinal body, as a political slogan or value.

It is at least certain that one of the historical merits of Barthes' booklet was to have legitimized the overt discussion of pleasure as a theme on the Left (along with other somewhat less influential discussions such as Sebastiano Timpanaro's notion of a "pessimistic hedonism"). Indeed, the interest in such matters is clearly part of a more general feeling which emerged from the 60s that traditional Marxism had failed to address itself to a whole range of essentially existential issues—death and the meaning of life; the whole realm of the unconscious; religion, the Utopian; the whole area of daily life and its qualities or modes of alienation, and whether a politics of daily life is conceivable; Nature finally and the ecological.

I have, however, omitted from this list that political issue in which the most powerful restatement of a Left puritanism for our time has been made; it seems to me frivolous to describe this as an existential issue, although the temptation to do so tells us something about the limits of the existential corrections or completions of Marxism, and about the relationship of existential categories to purely individual experience. The result would seem to be that while feminism may seem an existential issue to *men*, it is a matter of group struggle for women, which is something quite different. At any event, paradoxically, the reintroduction of the "problem" of pleasure on the Left (thematized by Barthes out of a whole French theoretical culture, most notably marked by Lacanian psychoanalysis) now paves the way for an interesting reversal, and for the kind of radical political argument *against* pleasure of which Laura Mulvey's "Visual Pleasure and Narrative Cinema" is one of the more influential statements.[2] Her program—"the destruction of pleasure as a radical weapon"—is based on the theoretical identification of traditional filmic viewing pleasure with the symbolic expression of male power in the "right to look," a right whose ultimate object becomes the woman's body, or rather, the woman *as* body. Something of the politics of the article could still, I think, be argued in the older class terms evoked above; the right to look the defense of sexual liberation, including pornography and the whole culture of the libidinal image as such—these would be slogans attractive to males, but symbolically marked (now in gender, rather than class ways) for women as the practices of the other, of the oppressor, of a form of domination analogous to that of the class enemy. The more theoretical basis for the argument—which rests on the Lacanian account of the constitution of the male subject (in particular the problem of the "mother's phallus," the fetish, and so forth)—is menaced by the ahistorical framework of most psychoanalytic approaches, insofar as it may project a perspective in which men's sexuality will somehow always be formed in this way and always associated with just such scoptocratic, fetishizing impulses: Amazonianism or lesbian separatism would then be the only consequent "solution." For males of good will, meanwhile, the depth-psychological part of the argument may well serve mainly to reinforce that tendency to ideological *examen de conscience*, morbid introspection and *autocritique*, and the guilt trip, which, in an unusual mutation of older religious practices, is so often an attractive way for the isolated Left intellectual to "work out his personal salvation." (Paradoxically, this last is also the promise of Barthesian hedonism.)

At any rate, if it begins to turn out that the value of "pleasure" as a political slogan is not merely unattractive to working-class people but also to women, then its ideological effectivity is evidently a rather diminished one. As for Barthes himself, returning to him one last time, the concept of "pleasure"—or more properly of *jouissance*—had a more complicated function, which may be made clearer if we grasp *Le Plaisir du texte* as a return to the issues that had preoccupied him years earlier in *Writing Degree Zero* (1953). The earlier book was still situated within an essentially Sartrean problematic, that of *What Is Literature?* (1947), a problematic to which Barthes gave a very different solution from that of Sartre himself, but which shares the latter's vision of history as a nightmare of blood guilt. Sartre had shown in his book that the necessary restrictions of all literary languages to the "signals" of local or limited (nonuniversal) groups or publics made all literary practices, in the world as we know it, the symbolic endorsement of the class violence of this or that group against the others. Sartre's orthodox solution—the endorsement of the proletariat as the last class, as the only possibility for the emergence for the first time in history of a genuinely universal public—is explicitly designated as a Utopian one. Barthes then ingeniously imagined a rather different way of escaping from the "nightmare of history," namely the projection of a kind of writing from which all group or class signals had been eliminated: white or bleached writing, the practice of a kind of Utopian neutrality, which would enable an escape on this side *(en deçá)* from the collective guilt inherent in the practice of any of the literary signs as such. Ironically, the whitest writing always slowly turned into a literary institution and a practice of literary signs in its own right, over time: Barthes' contemporaneous example, Camus, no longer looks very neutral to us today, nor do the later practitioners of the then *nouveau roman*.

So it is that in *Le Plaisir du texte*, the operation is staged in a rather different way. It is now through reception rather than production that History may be suspended, and the social function of that fragmentary, punctual *jouissance* which can break through any text will then be more effectively to achieve that freedom from all ideologies and all commitment (of the Left as much as of the Right) that the zero degree of literary signs had once seemed to promise. *Atopie* rather than *utopie:* such is the nonplace of Barthes' *jouissance*, where the dominant ideology of the sentence and of the institution of literature is to be undermined. Unlike the seemingly related *Tel Quel* or Kristevan formulations, however, where such undermining is saluted as a revolutionary act in itself, Barthes is too wisely cynical to wish to describe such moments in more glamorous terms than those of the local resistance of perversion and in the perverse (leitmotifs of his essay) to the contaminations of power. In any case, even the flight from history and politics is a reaction to those realities and a way of registering their omnipresence, and the immense merit of Barthes' essay is to restore a certain politically symbolic value to the experience of *jouissance*, making it impossible to read the latter except as a response to a political and historical dilemma, whatever position one chooses (puritanism/hedonism) to take about that response itself.

But one cannot conclude all this without some final evaluation of Barthes himself, so ambiguous a figure. Is it necessary to recall that the early Barthes *was* political, and that he furnished (and books like *Mythologies* continue to furnish) us with critical instruments and weapons of an overtly political capability? What the later Barthes meant, however, can perhaps be formulated as follows (the lesson was really there all along, but became more univocal in the later texts): he taught us to read with our bodies—and often to write with them as well. Whence, if one likes, the unavoidable sense of self-indulgence and corruption that Barthes' work can project when viewed from certain limited angles. The libidinal body, as a field and instrument of perception all at once, cannot but be self-indulgent in that sense. To discipline it, to give it the proper tasks and ask it to repress its other random impulses, is at once to limit its effectiveness, or, even worse, to damage it irretrievably. Lazy, shot through with fits of boredom or enthusiasm, reading the world and its texts with nausea or with *jouissance*, listening for the fainter vibrations of a sensorium largely numbed by civilization and rationalization, sensitive to the messages of throbs too immediate, too recognizable as pain or pleasure—maybe all this bodily disposition is not to be described as self-indulgence after all. Maybe it requires a discipline and a responsiveness of a rare yet different sort, something like free association (outsmarting the instant defenses of the ego or the rationalizing intellect) or boating, sensing and riding with a minimal current. Maybe indeed the deeper subject is here: not pleasure (against whose comfort and banalities everyone from Barthes to Edmund Burke is united in warning us), but the libidinal body itself, and *its* peculiar politics, which may well move in a realm largely beyond the pleasurable in that narrow, culinary, bourgeois sense.

So gradually the word "materialism" begins to impose itself. I have my own reasons for objecting to the current fashionable Left use of this term as an omnibus slogan. Facile and dishonest as a kind of popular-front solution to the very real tensions between Marxism and feminism, it also seems to me extraordinarily misleading and inadequate as an ideological synonym for "historical materialism" itself. "Materialism" as a term and as a concept is booby-trapped by its functional association with the eighteenth-century bourgeois Enlightenment and with nineteenth-century positivism. Whatever precautions are taken, it always fatally ends up projecting a determinism by matter (that is to say, the individual body or organism in isolation) rather than—as in historical materialism—a determination by the mode of production. It would be better to grasp Marxism and the dialectic as an attempt to overcome not idealism by itself, but that very ideological opposition between idealism and materialism in the first place. The work of both Sartre and Gramsci is there to argue for some position "beyond idealism *and* materialism," and if one does not like the projected new solution—called "praxis"— then at least it would be desirable to search for something more adequate.

Still, as far as pleasure is concerned, it may readily be admitted that it is materialist: whether or not consciousness (the psychological subject) is always and in all moments of history and modes of production constitutionally and irrecuperably idealistic, the generalization is probably safe *for us*. (At the very least, it renders the ideal of a materialist thinking problematical, professions of materialism being not at all incompatible with idealist habits of mind— quite the contrary!) So the bourgeois monad ceaselessly continues to convert things into the ideas of things, into their images, into their names, until, at a break in the process, suddenly that taboo and unimaginable "outside" breaks the thread for an instant: this fresh, wet air of spring on my face, the sheer metal taste of a musical phrase that is no longer just its own idea but the material vibration and timbre of a physical instrument itself, this "green so delicious it hurts" (Baudelaire), the irreducible mystery of flavor itself, as of roots in the earth, or the flush and comfortable fever of what the great Sartrean description of sexuality calls "in-carnation." Pleasure is finally the consent of life in the body, the reconciliation—momentary as it may be—with the necessity of physical existence in a physical world. (And then at that point, the materialization of what had formerly been idealistic as well—the materiality of words, once again, and of images; hardest of all, perhaps, of the thinking process itself, of whatever the "mind" is as an activity: the *jouissance* of the great scientific intuitions, perhaps, or of the great "deductions" of the mystery story. . . .)

Still, all this remains comfort, and comfortable, in Barthes' pejorative sense—"house, province, the meal, the lamp, the family in its appropriate place, neither too close nor too far. . . this extraordinary reinforcement of the ego (by fantasy); a padded unconscious."[3] For Barthes, this was still a privatized and Bierdermeier middle-class experience, a guilty evasion. Yet we have other class images—Bloch's celebration of the peasant household, Brecht's plebeian materialism of the worker's soup and cigar, and even Marcuse's "erotization of the work process," with its reinvention of the old material pleasure of handicraft in an advanced technological age. What can be said of *this* vision of bodily pleasure is not that it is not political, not a Utopian vision of another way of living, but rather that what it solves is my individual relationship with my own body—which is to say with Earth (Heidegger) or with what used to be called Nature—and not that very different relationship between myself or my body and other people—or, in other words, with History, with the political in the stricter sense.

Whence the troublesome unruliness of the sexual question. Is it only that comfortable material question, or is it more irredeemably scandalous—as in sexual "ecstasy" (the strongest translation of the Barthesian *jouissance)*, or in that even more somber matter of the will to power in sexual domination? These are harder "pleasures" to domesticate, their political content more easily assimilable to religions, or fascism—yet another "pleasure," this last! Therapeutic puritanism thus seems to impose itself again; yet before embracing it, it may be desirable to see what happens if we try to historicize these dilemmas, and the experiences that produced them. Is not, for example, the aesthetics of ecstasy, Barthesian *jouissance*, a properly 60s' experience? And if so, would it not be desirable for another moment to explore the historical relations between this new experience—what I will call the "pleasure of the simulacrum"—and its aesthetic objects—henceforth called "postmodernism"—as well as its socially and historically original situation—"consumer society," media society, multinational or "late" capitalism, the "society of the spectacle"?

Or is the experience so new, and without any historical antecedents or analogies whatsoever? Personally, I have found defamiliarization of Barthes' concepts in the *"Plaisir du texte"* of an earlier transitional age, the work of one of the most creative and permanently fascinating of the great class enemies, Edmund Burke's *Philosophical Enquiry into the Origin of Our Ideas of the Sublime and Beautiful*. Here already the great Barthesian opposition, where the pleasurable experience of the Beautiful—described as a comfortable and quasi-sexual relaxation of the organism ("that sinking, that melting, that langour, which is the characteristical effect of the beautiful as it regards every sense"[4]) is set off starkly against the "fearful" experience of the Sublime, which, springing according to Burke from the instinct of self-preservation, causes the body tone to draw together in reaction like a fist, in "exercise or *labour;* and labour is a surmounting of *difficulties,* and exertion of the contracting power of the muscles; and as such resembles pain, which consists in tension or contraction, in everything but degree" (p. 135). This last, however, with its train of predictable examples (great buildings or monumental colonnades, darkness, Milton, the Godhead, infinity and also "infinite" ideas including political ones, such as honor, justice, liberty"—out not yet, oddly, the inevitable "mountain" of Romantic sensibility) would not at first glance seem terribly compatible with the Barthesian ecstatic—the sudden stab of *jouissance,* the schizophrenic dissolution of the boring old bourgeois ego, *dérive,* the Neitzschean cry, scandal, break, the cleavage of the subject, the swoon, the hysterical affirmation of the ecstatic void—until one beings to note the insistent negativity of these formulations and to recall Barthes' epigraph from Hobbes, in which his own problematic and that of Edmund Burke suddenly and unexpectedly coincide: "The only true passion in my life has been *fear!"*

Fear—the aesthetic reception of fear, its artistic expression, transformation, the enjoyment of the shock and commotion fear brings to the human organism—is, on the Burkean theory of the sublime, the apprehension through a given aesthetic object of what in its awesome magnitude shrinks, threatens, diminishes, rebukes individual human life. How one could *enjoy* such an experience is suggested well enough by the grudging appearance at the end of Burke's chain of substitutions of the divine itself: "I purposely avoided, when I first considered this subject, to introduce the idea of that great and tremendous Being, as an example in an argument so light as this" (pp. 67-68). The machinery of the sacred, indeed, offers one signal method for the transformation of sheer horror (death, anxiety, the meaningless succession of the generations, the fragility and cheapness of life) into libidinal gratification. What if, for this fragile individual human *body* in Burke's scheme of things, we substituted a threatened menace to and dissolution of that other entity (whose construction on the model of the body image is signaled by the so-called mirror stage)—the psychological subject, the *ego*, the personality, the individual identity? Is it possible that the interiorization, the Nietzschean choice, the work of enjoyment, of that second type of fear might well approximate what Barthes designates, in terms that deliberately avoid any suggestion of banal pleasurability, as *jouissance?*

In that case, the analogy with Burke may have further lessons for us, since Burke's distinction between beauty and the sublime is already by way of being a structural one: immanence versus transcendence this would have been characterized, in an older philosophical language—beauty being the self-sufficient experience of small-scale objects, the small pleasures of the creation (to develop the religious theme), an experience not dialectically related to that of the sublime but rather simply *different,* distinct from it. (For Burke pleasure and pain are not opposites, but unrelated, self-sufficient experiences in something more like a triad: pleasure, pain, indifference.) The sublime, on the other hand, the pleasures of fear, the aesthetic appropriation of pain, is a rather different matter, a kind of dual or steroscopic experience, which I would in the present context prefer to call "allegorical." That is, the sublime takes its object as the pretext and the occasion for the intuition through it and beyond it of sheer unfigurable force itself, sheer power, that which stuns the imagination in the most literal sense. (The imagination finds no *figure* for that awesome power in and of itself: even Burke's "ideas of God" is a substitution.)

It then becomes a tempting speculation to specify the historical nature of this terrifying force before which the sublime, in a properly Nietzschean affirmation—choose what crushes you!—finds its gratification and its ecstatic surrender. The capital-logicians have recently made the scandalous suggestion that what Hegel called "Absolute Spirit" was simply to be read as the transpersonal, unifying, impersonal, supreme force of emergent Capital itself; one does not dare, without more wide-ranging textual evidence, and under pain of the crassest interpretive dogmatism, affirm anything of the sort for the Burkean intuition (1756). That one can do so for the Barthesian sublime, however, seems to me beyond any question. The immense culture of the simulacrum whose experience, whether we like it or not, constitutes a whole series of daily ecstasies and punctual fits of *jouissance* or schizophrenic dissolutions—"c'était donc ça! c'est donc moi! c'est donc á moi!"—may appropriately, one would think, be interpreted as so many unconscious points of contact with that equally unfigurable and unimaginable thing, the multinational apparatus, the great suprapersonal system of a late capitalist technology. It is the ecstasy of the machine once again, as in futurism, yet today without any "ideology" of the machine or any nascent representations of the excitements of its first great still physical and perceptible embodiments in the tank or the machine gun (Marinetti) or the factory itself (Diego Rivera, Léger). The idea of the computer subsumes those earlier excitements, but beyond any tangible figure or representation (the physical computer now being little more than a box with its brain wires hanging out).

That there is thus a politics and a historicity of *jouissance* seems clear, as does its fundamental ambiguity as a socially symbolic experience. The point, however, is not to awaken some scarcely dormant Left tendency to moralize such experiences, but rather to draw the lesson of what might be a radically different political use of pleasure as such. I will suggest, then, that the proper political use of pleasure must always be *allegorical* in the sense spelled out above: the thematizing of a particular pleasure as a political issue (to fight, for example, on the terrain of the aesthetics of the city; or for certain forms of sexual liberation; or for access to certain kinds of cultural activities; or for an aesthetic transformation of social relations or a politics of the body) must always involve a dual focus, in which the local issue is meaningful and desirable in and of itself, but is also *at one and the same time* taken as the *figure* for Utopia in general, and for the systemic revolutionary transformation of society as a whole. Without these simultaneous dimensions, the political demand becomes reduced to yet another local "issue" in the micropolitics of this or that limited group or its particular hobby or specialization, and a slogan that once satisfied, leads no further politically.

This dual, or "allegorical," focus is indeed what makes for both the uniqueness and the difficulties of Marxism in general as a conception of revolutionary transformation. The dialectic is in itself this dual obligation to invent ways of uniting the here-and-now of the immediate situation with the totalizing logic of the global or Utopian one. So a given economic demand must always be in some sense a figure for a more total revolutionary transformation, unless it is to fall back into economism. So also—to take an example a little more familiar to a public of Left *intellectuals*—a given piece of textual analysis must make a punctual or occasional statement about its object, but must also, at one and the same time, be graspable as a more general contribution to the Marxian problematic. And it must do so, in both instances, without the concrete local occasion turning back into some mere "example" of the "abstract" framework (which it is preferable to call the perspective of totalization). So finally the right to a specific pleasure, to a specific enjoyment of the potentialities of the material body—if it is not to remain only that, if it is to become genuinely political, if it is to evade the complacencies of hedonism—must always in one way or another also be able to stand as a figure for the transformation of social relations as a whole.

1983

Chapter 4
Of Islands and Trenches
Neutralization and the Production of Utopian Discourse

O times,
In which the meagre, stale, forbidding ways
Of custom, law and statute took at once
The Attraction of a Country in Romance...
Wordsworth

Not the least unexpected thing about the 1960s was its reinvention of the question of Utopia. "Meagre, stale, forbidding," the basic texts of the genre had been as desperately unreadable as those of obsolete forms like the masque or the mystery play, their content as irrelevant to consumer society as the draft constitutions and natural or contractual theories of the classics of political science. What had actually become obsolete, however, was a certain type of reader, whom we must imagine just as addicted to the bloodless forecasts of a Cabet or a Bellemy[1] as we ourselves may be to Tolkien, *The Godfather*, *Ragtime*, or detective stories. Such readers become extinct because the level of tolerance for fantasy is suddenly modified by a change in social relations; so in the windless closure of late capitalism it had come to seem increasingly futile and childish for people with a strong and particularly repressive reality-and-performance-principle to imagine tinkering with what exists, let alone its thoroughgoing restructuration.

Meanwhile, even among those with a commitment to social revolution, the classical polemic of Marx and Engels against Utopian socialism, which had long since stigmatized both the word and the thing itself, seemed reconfirmed by books like Charles Reich's *Greening of America* (1960), whose "critique" of capitalism (Consciousness I) proved on closer inspection to harbor the much more comfortable and reassuring conviction that the essentials of a hallucinogenic future were already latent and stirring, implicit in consumer society itself, and available at the price of one last effort—which, however, turned out merely to be an effort of "consciousness!" Meanwhile, Reich's minor premise, shared with so many of the post-1848 Utopias, had a much more serious political function, asserting, as it did, that whatever Utopia was and however it might be conceived, it was not to be construed as having anything whatsoever to do with Marxian socialism—which is to say, with any of the existing political movements for social change in the world today.

Still, compared with poor Fourier, with his unanswered ad, the immense commercial success of Charles Reich's bestseller testified to the renewal of a demand for Utopian discourse in the 1960s. It remained for the greatest Utopian thinker of that period to suggest that, given the present-day's unparalleled technological possibilities for the satisfaction of needs, "if critical theory, which remains indebted to Marx, does not wish to stop at merely improving the existing state of affairs, it must accommodate within itself the extreme possibilities for freedom. . .the scandal of qualitative difference. Marxism must risk defining freedom in such a way that people become conscious of and recognize it as something that is nowhere already in existence."[2] The history of the 60s testified to the correctness of Marcuse's strategic reassessment of the explosive political force, in that particular social and historical conjuncture, of the Utopian idea and the Utopian impulse, which are therefore not to be denounced out of hand in the name of Marx and Engels' reading of the quite different political conjuncture of the 1840s. That this was not only the opinion of the New Left may be judged by a remarkable observation of Georg Lukács himself on the "unequal rate of development" of contemporary history: "We must essentially compare our situation today with that in which people like Fourier or Sismondi found themselves at the beginning of the nineteenth century. We can only achieve effective action when we become aware that we find ourselves in that situation and when it becomes clear to us that there is a sense in which the development from Fourier to Marx remains, both theoretically and practically, a task for the future."[3] If indeed it is so that May 68, far from being our 1848, was little more than our July Revolution, we must at least allow for the possibility of some revolutionary potential in Utopian works that, like their nineteenth-century predecessors, prepare a distant and unimaginable 1848 in a situation that does not even look like a prerevolutionary one.

What is at least certain—however we ultimately decide to evaluate the Utopian impulse itself—is that anti-Utopianism constitutes a far more easily decodable and unambiguous political position: from religious arguments about the sinful hubris of an anthropocentric social order all the way to the vivid "totalitarian" dystopias of the contemporary counterrevolutionary tradition (Dostoyevsky, Orwell, etc.), Utopia is a transparent synonym for socialism itself, and the enemies of Utopia sooner or later turn out to be the enemies of socialism.

The transition from the 60s to the 70s was a passage from spontaneous practice to renewed theoretical reflection, and this is as true in the realm of Utopian discourse as it is elsewhere. It is therefore no surprise that after the reawakening of the Utopian impulse of the previous decade, we should begin to witness the maturation of a whole new generation of literary Utopias, among them the most important Utopian text since the appearance of Skinner's *Walden Two*, namely Ursula LeGuin's *The Dispossessed*. It may be more paradoxical to suggest that the theoretical fulfillment of this Utopian practice is to be located—alongside the rediscovery and renewed study of the inexhaustible anticipatory "philosophy of the future" of Ernst Bloch—in the area of narrative analysis. Such a term will seem less confining, however, when the multiple intersections of narrative analysis with the various specialized academic disciplines—literary semiotics, ethnomethodology, the anthropological study of myth and the historians' inquiry into the nature of historiography, even the dawning sense of the "narrative" structure of the experiments of natural science—are understood as blocking out the as yet empty space of a whole philosophy of narrative praxis in which the production of events and of the language that constitutes them promises to provide a more adequate conceptual framework than any of the older purely epistemological systems, as well as the newer communicational ones.

It is at any rate as a fundamental contribution to such a philosophy of narrative, as well as the most extended structural analysis of the Utopian impulse—the gesture itself as well as the genre—yet worked out, that we must read Louis Marin's *Utopiques: Jeux d'espaces*.[5] This book, exactly contemporaneous with LeGuin's novel, and elaborated in the very eye of the hurricane during Marin's Nanterre seminar in May 1968, prolongs a meditation on the Utopian event itself—"revolutionary *fête* [in which] for a few weeks historical time was suspended, institutions and the Law itself in its totality challenged in and by speech, communication circuits reopened between those who near or far were drawn within it" (p. 15/p. 3)—until that event, slowly transmuted into a text, at length becomes accessible to narrative analysis.

The text thus reconstituted is, however, Thomas More's *Utopia*,[6] one of those rare works that, whatever its precursors, inaugurates a whole genre, which it names at the same time that it exhausts its whole range of formal possibilities. It will be most convenient to see Marin's approach to More in the *Utopiques* as the inversion of Lévi-Strauss' widely known program for the "structural study of myth."[7] For Lévi-Strauss, myth is a narrative process whereby tribal society seeks an imaginary solution, a resolution by way of figural thinking, to a real social contradiction between infrastructure and superstructure (in the terms of his example of the Oedipus myth, between the tribal infrastructure of the kinship system, and the religious or cosmological systems that seem irreconcilable with it). Lévi-Strauss' relatively unsystematic essay suggests two methodological alternatives for dealing with myth, each of them informed, however, by the conviction that myth is essentially a process of mediation. In the more conventional second half of his presentation, indeed, Lévi-Strauss underscores the role of mediatory characters in the mythic narrative—ambivalent, androgynous, doubly coded figures such as the heavenly twins, the trickster, or the Cinderella/Ash-boy characters, who, by virture of the reproduction of the antithetical terms of the contradictory situation within themselves, are able to serve as the narrative occasion for the latter's seeming resolution. The originality of the first, lengthy, and largely hypothetical example of the Oedipus legend was to have transcended these more anthropomorphic categories of the individual "character" (even when that character is a mediatory one) and to have proposed a kind of impersonal chemistry of narrative events themselves which decomposes the apparent unity of the individual characters into a bundle of signifying traits just as thoroughly as it dissolves the surface units of the narrative itself. Since *Utopia* is in one sense the very prototype of the narrative without a narrative subject and without characters, the relevance of this second option will be evident.

Marin's work suggests, however, that we may now specify Lévi-Strauss' approach to myth even more sharply, for it becomes clear that the latter understands mediation essentially as an operation bearing on the two "primary" terms of the fundamental contradiction or binary opposition itself, terms we may write for convenience as S and $-S$:

$$\text{MEDIATION}$$
$$S \longleftrightarrow -S$$

But Greimas and others have taught us that this by no means exhausts the logical possibilities and permutational combinations inherent in the simplest binary opposition; not only do the logical contradictoris of S and $-S$ furnish two more independent terms, but the various axes thus generated (negative and positive deixis, implication, contradictions) suggest that even the most rudimentary "elementary structure of signification" (as Greimas calls his "semiotic rectangle"[8]) is capable of generating a number of quite distinct "mediatory" combinations alongside the one operative in Lévi-Strauss' mythic resolutions, designated in Greimas' system as the complex term C:

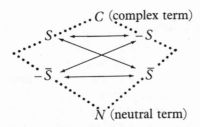

This logical schema then permits us to identify at a glance the quite different position Marin assigns the Utopian narrative; it is for him the structural inversion of myth in the following sense: where as the narrative operation of myth undertakes to mediate between the two primary terms of the opposition S and $-S$, and to produce a complex term that would be their resolution, Utopian narrative is constituted by the union of the twin contradictories of the initial opposition, the combination of $-S$ and S, a combination which, virtually a double cancellation of the initial contradiction itself, may be said to effect the latter's *neutralization* and to produce a new term, the so-called neuter or neutral term N.

In what follows we will give a good many examples of such a process, not only in order to give content to what may otherwise seem an extremely abstract proposition about the nature of Utopia, but above all to demonstrate the ways in which this hypothesis about the function of the Utopian operation may serve as a practical method for reading and analyzing the texts themselves. Before going any further, however, it is worth underscoring the polemic implications of such an approach, in particular its relationship to that debate on the nature and ideological function of representation which is one of the key problems in contemporary literary theory.

The problem of representation may be understood in its simplest form in the context of one of the most fundamental of all methodological options or alternatives that face us when we try to confront language or linguistic phenomena. Humboldt already gave striking expression to this option in the Romantic period when he evoked the twin faces of speech as *energeia* and as *ergon*, as creative power and as object created—something like a *natura naturans* and a *natura naturata* (Spinoza) in the linguistic realm itself, and two wholly different modes available to us for constructing any given individual verbal fact or entity. This alternation (which should not too hastily be assimilated to Saussure's opposition of *langue* and *parole)* has then proved to be a powerful instrument of analysis in the form given to it by present-day linguistics as a distinction between *énonciation* and *énoncé,* between the act of enunciation and the completed utterance.[9]

When we now introduce the whole question of representation into this scheme of things, and suggest that a linguistics of the *énoncé* or of the *ergon* tends essentially to grasp linguistic objects as representations, whereas a stress on the creative or processlike character of language tends to undermine representational categories, we begin to glimpse the ideological coordinates of the problem. It remained for Julia Kristeva to assimilate this linguistic distinction—better still, this distinction between two possible types of linguistics, two whole approaches to the study of verbal and literary phenomena—to the classical Marxian one between the exchange value of commodities in a market system and their use value in pre- or postcapitalist social forms. The primacy of the first of these phenomena imposes a mode of analysis in which categories of exchange are dominant, whether this be Marx's own study of the operation of surplus value and money in mature capitalism, or a linguistics ideologically related to communication theory and to the perspective of an exchange of completed "speech acts": "from the viewpoint of social distribution and consumption, and indeed, that of *communication* as well, work is always a value, whether of use or of exchange. In other words: if in communication values are always and inevitably grasped as fragments of crystallized work [from this perspective] work itself can represent nothing above and beyond that value in which it is crystallized."[10]

But as Kristeva points out, there is implicit even in the Marxian analysis of capitalism the logical and historical possibility of a very different approach to economic phenomena, an approach which suggests a quite different alternative for the study of language as well: "an other space is conceivable in which work may be apprehended independent of value as such, a space that precedes the manufacture and circulation of commodities in the circuit of communication. There, in that place [*scène*] in which work as yet *represents* no value and is not yet 'intentional' [*ne veut encore rien dire*], in other words, as yet has no *meaning*, in that other space it can only be a matter of the relationship between the *body* and systems of energy [*dépense*]" (p. 88). As is well known, Kristeva goes on to propose a "semiology" based on production to replace, or at least to coexist with, the older "semiology" of communication and representation.

This is not the place to explore the inflection given this program by the work of the *Tel Quel* and the *Screen* groups. Suffice it to say that in this society we can only fitfully break the habit of thinking in terms of finished commodities (reification)[11] along with the habit, so closely related to it, of reading according to categories of representation. Whatever the possibilities, therefore, for some genuinely postrepresentational discourse (or "textual productivity," as Kristeva calls it), we must take a keen interest in those literary or textual phenomena that reveal the tenacity of the hold of the older representational categories on our own thinking and reading; and this is the context in which Marin's *Utopiques* has a particularly striking lesson for us. To understand Utopian discourse in terms of neutralization is indeed precisely to propose to grasp it as a process, as *energeia*, enunciation, productivity, and implicitly or explicitly to repudiate that more traditional and conventional view of Utopia as sheer representation, as the "realized" vision of this or that ideal society or social ideal. Nowhere, however, does this seem more instructively difficult to manage than in the reading of a text whose tours and interminable guide-book explanations, whose static descriptions of institutions and geographical and architectural layouts, seem intent on establishing beyond any possibility of doubt or fluctuation the representation coherence and solidity of its object. Marin's book will then have as one of its fundamental tasks to convince us that it is possible to understand the Utopian text as a determinate type of *praxis,* rather than as a specific mode of representation, a praxis that has less to do with the construction and perfection of someone's "idea" of a "perfect society" than it does with a concrete set of mental operations to be performed on a determinate type of raw material given in advance, which is contemporary society itself—or, what amounts to the same thing, on those collective representations of contemporary society that inform our ideologies just as they order our experience of daily life.

Yet, the disparity still seems very great between this description of a literary text as a set of mental operations, let alone as neutralization, and our incorrigible tendency to incorporate the Utopian text back into that more conventional category of novels or narratives in which characters travel and do things and stable landscapes, kingdoms, powers, and principalities "exist." It may thus be useful to point out some of the unexpected advantages presented by this view of narrative as process, in particular a solution to that old (false) dilemma of an "extrinsic" criticism, sometimes erroneously thought of as the problem of the referent, that is, of something "real" somewhere outside the text to which the latter supposedly makes—or better still, fails to make—allusion.

If, however, we try to accustom ourselves to thinking of the narrative text as a process whereby something is done to the Real, whereby operations are performed on it and it is in one way or another "managed' (Norman Holland) or indeed "neutralized," or under other circumstances articulated and brought to heightened consciousness, then clearly we will have to begin to think of the Real, not as something outside the work, of which the latter stands as an image or makes a representation, but rather as something borne within and vehiculated by the text itself, interiorized in its very fabric in order to provide the stuff and the raw material on which the textual operation must work. In the Utopian narrative, the place of the Real—of that which must first be constituted within the work before it can be dissolved or "neutralized" by the work as process—may be identified by the obsessive references to actuality which seem part of the conventions of such texts, the perpetual play of topical allusion throughout the narrative which, intersecting the more properly diegetic interest, is constantly on the point of fragmenting the text into an anecdotal and discontinuous series of vertical indicators. Thus, for example, if it is true that Gulliver's capture of the Lilliputian fleet, along with the ensuing diplomatic negotiation, "has reference to the Treaty of Utrecht, which, effected by the Tories, ended the war with France,"[12] then Swift's text ought rightly to become an object of scandal for those of us still committed to the ideology of an "intrinsic" criticism (the practitioners of an older kind of literary history would have had no trouble with such a passage—their own difficulties lay elsewhere—while those advancing "beyond" the New Criticism have yet to confront the problem of political allegory head-on, let alone the problem of allegory in general and as such).

Still, there is reason to believe that such footnotes are not the mere cobwebs of topical and long-dead contemporary allusion to be brushed desperately away by the living reader, but rather that some such play of topical allusion is structurally indispensable in the constitution of the Utopian text as such and provides one of the distinctive traits necessary if we are to mark the Utopia off from its generic neighbors in the realm of fantasy or idyll. A regressive pastoral like W. H. Hudson's *A Crystal Age* (1887), which certainly shares Utopian features with the classical works in the genre, is distinguished from the latter primarily by the absence of any of those one-to-one allusions—generally in the form of inversions—that make the reading of Utopias a process of allegorical decipherment. So in Butler's *Erewhon*, machines are evil and illegal precisely because in Victorian England industrial progress is an ideological value presupposed in advance and uncontested; but Hudson's return to some earlier precapitalist form—whether savagery or barbarism—is an appeal to a generalized and global nostalgia, rather than to a precise set of decoding operations. This kind of idyll or fantasy, in other words, is, unlike Utopia, precisely a representation and musters its narrative resources in order to impose the fullness of an image of a different form of life, an image the fascinated contemplation of which includes both anxiety and longing within itself.

The Utopian text does not generally strive for such hallucinatory intensity and on the contrary usually merits our complaints about its transparent literalism and its unimaginative and allegorical aridity. Its topical allusions, while constituting an essential feature of the genre's structure, are nonetheless not without problems of their own, something which will then take us far in understanding the nature of Utopian production. For whereas the text requires this network or texture of topicality within itself to stand as that Real which it will underake to neutralize, it is at the same time menaced by the wealth of allusions to current events which threatens to dissolve it altogether. All genuine Utopias therefore betray a complicated apparatus which is designed to "neutralize" the topical allusion at the same time that it produces it and reinforces it. So, for instance, Ursula LeGuin's novel *The Dispossessed* seems at first glance a fairly straightforward and unproblematical transposition and fictionalization of the contemporary division of our globe today between the so-called Free World (in her book, the wealthy planet Urras) and the socialist bloc (its barren and revolutionary satellite Anarres). This identification is then further confirmed for the reader by Shevek's introduction to consumers' goods and consumerism during his visit to Urras: thus he has to learn the word for "packaging," since the practice does not exist on his own world (p. 176); his trip to the downtown luxury shopping area is a virtual nightmare (pp. 116-17); at length the very revulsion with commodities becomes a figure for Urras itself: "it is a box. . .a package, with all the beautiful wrapping of blue sky and meadows and forests and great cities. And you open the box, and what is inside of it? A black cellar full of dust, and a dead man" (pp. 305-6). No less transparently are the problems Shevek faces in his homeland—his difficulties in publishing his scientific discoveries, the conformist atmosphere of the scientific institute in which he is attacked for lack of patriotism, the attempt to prevent him from receiving a prize from "propertarian" Urras—read as stereotypical allusions to recently publicized restrictions on intellectuals in the Soviet Union. Indeed, the very conventionality of such allusions and the transparency of the novel's basic opposition between the reification of consumer capitalism and the political constraints of socialism—far from being a flaw in LeGuin's novelistic vision—actually define the very specificity of our reading of her Utopian text. To put it a different way, it is only in terms of a more conventionally novelistic and more properly representational standard of literature that her book can be reproached for the poverty of its political concepts and the naiveté of its view of present-day world history; if on the contrary we adopt Marin's view of the Utopian as process and production, we will see that it is precisely such stereotypicality, and the conventionality of LeGuin's own liberalism, that constitute the raw material upon which her Utopian praxis must do its work of transformation.

This said, we must observe that such topical reference to the contemporary situation is no sooner posited than it is undermined by a new system of topical allusions incompatible with it. We discover indeed that our initial identification of the twin planets themselves with the "Free World" and the "socialist bloc" becomes difficult to sustain in view of the fact that this division is itself reproduced all over again, but with much greater detail, within the framework of the planet of Urras alone, where, alongside the capitalist state visited by Shevek, there turns out also to be a kind of Soviet Union, represented by the centralized state socialism of Thu, and, in addition to both, an impoverished subcontinent (Benbili) in which the two great superpowers intervene and which we therefore end up identifying as our own Third World.

Nor does this particular process stop here. Soon even this system of correspondences—once set in place—is discredited by the revelation that within LeGuin's imaginary cosmography, in the intergalactic league (the Ekumen) to which the binary planets of Urras and Anarres themselves belong, the real Earth still exists, a burned-out shell, its ecology blasted by war and pollution and surviving only at the price of a regimentation qualitatively different from that of revolutionary Anarres, whose beneficent scarcity and "clean" austerity it therefore reflects back in the negative image of a baleful and toxic wasteland. At this point, clearly, it can no longer be a question of deciphering the appropriate references so much as of specifying the nature of the apparently contradictory process at work in them.

For this approach and withdrawal of LeGuin's important novel from its systems of reference, these identifications with a topical subtext that are also and simultaneously differentiations from it, betray the presence of an essential mechanism at work in all Utopias. In the original one, for instance, topical allusion takes the form of a ghostly double or phantom England that rises up behind the no-place of the island of Utopia in the text, a tangible but intermittent historical nation-state to which the scholarly footnotes, pursuing the chitinous whisper of their commentaries, make insistent reference, reconstructing it as a subtext even as they undermine the last chances of the narrative surface to achieve any "full" representation. But such "explanations"—"the island contains fifty-four city-states" because Tudor England has fifty-three counties, plus the City of London (More, p. 61, n. 7); the Andrus runs sixty miles to the sea because "the Thames 'doth twise ebbe and flowe more than 1x. miles' within twenty-four hours" (p. 64, n. 2); the butchers of Utopia work outside the cities because of "'an Acte that noe Butcher slea any maner of beast within the Walles of London'" (p. 78, n. 4), etc.—are not to be deplored as the excesses and misguided zeal of some now discredited ideal of literary-historical scholarship; but rather understood as the fitful and symptomatic expression of referential subtext which is an essential and determinate absence or Other within the structure of the Utopian text proper.

In later Utopias, it would seem that this phantom spatial superposition of More's Utopia with the Real England contemporary to him is rearticulated in time and in some sense rationally justified or "motivated" (in the meaning the Russian Formalists gave this word) by the emergence of a wholly new element, namely history itself and the new bourgeois sense of historical change and evolution. Now the Utopian text is not figuratively established across its referential subtext, but rather literally founded and edified on the latter's historical emplacement; and the narrator of *Looking Backward* finds a new and more perfect Boston on the site of the old noisy and dirty nineteenth-century industrial metropolis of the same name, whereas the visionary sleeper of *News from Nowhere* is astonished to discover that "England's green & pleasant fields" have supplanted the endless precincts of the grimy London of old. Only now Bellamy and Morris are under an obligation to provide a historical account of the transition from old to new, or rather from reality to

Utopia; and it is here that, with their denunciation of the Utopian socialists' overemphasis on sheer reason and persuasion and their failure to grasp the antagonisms of political and social dynamics, the founders of Marxism lie in wait for them.[13]

For Marin, however, the historicity of the great nineteenth-century Utopias —which might otherwise, whatever the political oversights of their authors, have seemed to mark some progress in relation to the ahistorical vision of a Thomas More—may equally be taken as a sign of mystification, and as the repression of some more genuine Utopian praxis, insofar as it strains to fill the chinks of the representational surface and to plaster over the basic structure of Utopia as a nonplace and a process of neutralization with the fuller image of some historically realizable and positively imaginable society. This is the sense in which, for Marin, after the elaboration of historical materialism as a rational mode of conceptualizing human society, Utopias as such are no longer possible, in other words, Utopian practice ceases to be an authentic mode of thought; we will return to this assertion shortly.

It is now time to introduce an initial demonstration of the central proposition of *Utopiques*, namely that the basic relationship of the Utopian text to what we have been calling its referential subtext is one of neutralization; or, in terms of More's *Utopia*, that the island of that name functions as a point-by-point negation or canceling of the historical England itself. When we remember, however, that this latter entity is to be understood as a subtext, itself constructed (and then neutralized) by the Utopian text itself, we will understand that such a proposition is not to be understood in some banal sociological sense. Rather, it is here that Greimas' semiotic rectangle has a strategic function to play, by allowing us to construe "England" (or rather "Portugal," its historical ally and surrogate in More's text and Hythloday's own country of origin) precisely as a complex term, as the combination or imaginary synthesis of the basic contradictions of More's time; to this complex term would then reply the echo of the neutral or Utopian one opposite it.

For the moment, however, we can show this only in an external, and as it were geographical, way. As a "place" on the globe, indeed, "England/Portugal" may be said to know two specific contradictories each quite distinct from the other: opposed, on the one hand, by the New World, which is *not* the old one in all the ways enumerable by the Renaissance imagination and elaborated by Renaissance hopes, and, on the other, by Asia, which is also not Europe, and very particularly not England, but that, in the terms of a very different sociohistorical conceptual system; and these two contradictory terms constitute something like a positively and a negatively charged opposite of England/Portugal respectively:

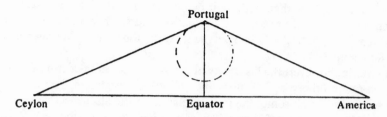

Structure of the toponyms of Raphael's voyages (Marin, p. 71/p. 47)

Hythloday's discovery of Utopia midway between the America in which he has been left during the final voyage of Amerigo Vespucci, and the Ceylon which at length he reaches on the journey home, is therefore the enactment of a complicated figure in which both of these two already negative terms are negated in their turn:

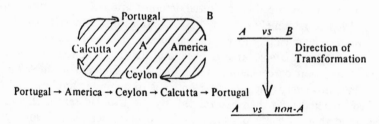

Schematic representation of Raphael's voyage (Marin, p. 66/p. 43)

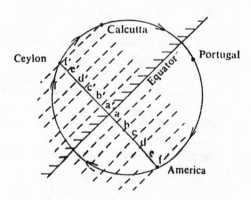

Multiple diagram of Raphael's travel narrative (Marin, p.70/p.46)

This is, however, the very fulfillment of the neuter or neutral term itself: "We know that the blessed isle is located between Ceylon and America, but also that it stands outside the toponymic circuit and outside the trajectory that runs from world to antiworld. It will thus combine—*beyond* all space—circumference and diameter, time and space, history and geography, in a place that will be neither a moment of history nor a sector of the map, a place that will be sheer discontinuity [*écart*]—a neuter—where alone the island can become manifest once the travel narrative has demonstrated the perfect equivalence of the two poles equidistant from it: homologous with Portugal and England, belonging to the same hemisphere as Ceylon and America, but distinct from all of these, neither antiworld, nor New World, but simply World other" (Marin, p. 71/p. 47).

So far we have been content to grasp neutralization as something like an objective process in its own right, as an "event" that happens to a preexisting structure, or better still, as a restructuration that takes place through the text itself. But of course this is itself only a figure of speech, and looked at more rigorously what we have been calling "neutralization" is a feature, not of the text itself, but rather of our (Marin's) model of the text. We must now therefore draw back a step and try to understand the mental operations involved in the construction of such a model. To do so, we will temporarily suspend Marin's reading of More, interpolating a simpler and somewhat more dramatic contemporary illustration drawn from a later chapter of the *Utopiques* that deals with the "Utopia of verticality" of the composer-architect Iannis Xenakis.

The reference is to the so-called cosmic vertical city imagined by Xenakis in 1965[14] in the form of a two-mile-high self-enclosed building of a type not unfamiliar in other contemporary images of the future (readers of science fiction will, for example, recall Robert Silverberg's account of daily life inside just such a vertical "utopia" in his novel *The World Inside*).

Yet to attempt a narrative exploration of such a future "society" would be to reconfirm the representational status of a verbal construction such as that of Xenakis, or, in other words, to misuse the Utopian text by shifting the focus of our reading from process to the inert end product of some static Utopian image or "vision." In this sense Marin's chapter—indeed, as we have already seen, the *Utopiques* in their entirety—is less an analysis of the Utopian text than a set of directions for the latter's "bon usage," prescriptions for reading and instructions for the appropriate application of the text to the Real. The example of Xenakis demonstrates that it is less revealing to consider Utopian discourse as a mode of narrative, comparable, say, with novel or epic, than it is to grasp it as an object of mediation, analogous to the riddles or *koan* of the various mystical traditions, or the aporias of classical philosophy, whose function is to provoke a fruitful bewilderment and to jar the mind into some heightened but unconceptualizable consciousness of its own powers, functions, aims, and structural limits. Utopian praxis "is thus, to use Kantian terminology, a schematizing activity of the social and political imagination which has not yet found its concept" (Marin, p. 211/p. 163); yet such preconceptual thinking-in-images—which has its affinities with the dream, with Lévi-Strauss' mythic thinking, and with Hegel's notion of the *Vorstellung* as a figural stage of Absolute Spirit—can only be observed in action when we construct a model in which the problems it blindly attempts to solve themselves become visible.

In the text of Xenakis, it is clear that this problem is at one with what may looosely be called the contemporary ideology of the city. But as literary analysts, we cannot commence from this starting point of the text itself, for only the text exists before us and the ideological contradiction it came into being to "solve" remains to be (re)constructed. Our first task as critics, therefore, is to project a contradiction, in other words a set of binary terms, a conceptual opposition, *such that* the literary or figurative text before us may be grasped or reread as the "resolution" (myth) or the "neutralization" (Utopia) of the hypothetical opposition thus posited. Obviously, described in this way, the interpretative process seems to break into two separate steps or stages; and it is clearly artificial and unrealistic to suppose that the interpreter has no idea where he or she is going, no preliminary intuition of the form such a reconstructed contradiction is likely to take. Still, it is useful to stress the process of reconstruction itself, as a corrective to the naive idea that the analyst or the historian can gaze into some "objective" realm of social or national or political ideology and there empirically discover the solution to his or her structural problem. Ideology does exist objectively, but not in the form of a text; like the unconscious, it is therefore not directly accessible to us, but only insofar as we have reconstructed it in what has today come to be called "textual" form, with which the literary text can then be placed in an active relationship of reaction, transformation, reflection, repression, or whatever. To omit the description of this stage—the reconstruction of the referential subtext, the hypothetical textualization of ideology—is to perpetuate the illusion that "sociological" analysis is something one can add on to a structural analysis of texts or not, as one's own temperament dictates.

In the case of Xenakis, we may feel somewhat freer in our reconstruction of that underlying, absent, social text to which his own Utopian project is a response, insofar as its basic raw materials are very precisely our own anxieties and stereotypes about the contemporary city. Our point of departure for such a reconstruction is the nature of Xenakis' u-topia itself, the fundamental features of that ultimate not-place or nonplace which he invented to neutralize the contradictions of contemporary thinking about the city. We must therefore try to reorganize the latter in such a way as to articulate our own ideology of the city, our own fuzzy stereotypes and fantasies, into a system of determinate antinomies and aporias into which the thought of Western city-dwellers about their city can be seen to be locked. Xenakis' project, and Utopian discourse in general, will not exactly be understood to be a coming to consciousness of such antinomies and contradictions; it cannot yet be thought to be *critical* in the sense in which the Frankfurt School so described the distantiation and heightened awareness of contradictions afforded by the *negative*. Still, at some lower, still preconceptual level, the "neutralization" of such a contradiction by Utopian discourse may nonetheless be supposed to bring the mind up short before its own ideological limits, in a stunned and puzzled arrest of thought before the double-bind in which it suddenly finds itself paralyzed.

The principal anxiety we have about the city today can probably be best expressed in terms of sheer urban concentration. Here the stereotypes of science fiction usefully document the unconscious agoraphobia of contemporary bourgeois consciousness, with its monitory images of overpopulation and its clogged dystopias of all kinds. From a diachronic perspective, this fear or urban concentration is clearly a twentieth-century variant, a coded or "sedimented" persistence, of that older, ideologically far more transparent, nineteenth-century terror of the mob itself, the revolutionary crowd, which such anxieties thematize in terms of looting and arson, of damage to property (Scott, Manzoni, and Dickens offer rich dramatizations), but whose real credentials for menace are to be sought in the great revolutionary "days" of 1789-94. What interests us in the present context is that this anxiety-fantasy about urban concentration represents a profound structural reversal of the older bourgeois concept of the "freedom of the city" which developed during the revitalization of the city life in the high and late Middle Ages; from this ideological perspective, the city was the place where you went to shake off the constraints of village life, or, even more fundamentally, those of serfdom and the feudal order. Such an ideal of the "free" city is thus at one with the initial strategies of legitimation of capitalism and of the market itself, and the individualism it promises was closely related to the civilizing, beneficent effects of that *douceur du commerce* celebrated by the earlier ideologies of free enterprise.

This earlier ideal of the city as a place of individual freedom is therefore at one with the emergence of "individualism" as such and of the bourgeois subject. Its negation by the nightmarish visions of concentration in the mid- and late twentieth century—as in those thronged bodies passing the night indoors on the staircases of the apartment buildings of a privileged elite in the twenty-first-century Manhattan of *Soylent Green*—may be expected to be less a reversal of the ideology of individualism than a confused and figural coming-to-the-surface of the latter's internal contradictions.

For meanwhile, in some other register of our minds and at some other level of collective representation, the city has a quite different ideological function to play and serves as the support for an ideal antithetical to that of bourgeois individualism, lending its content to visions of perfected community or collective existence from the image of the heavenly city of Christian eschatology all the way down to the conception of the commune itself. These two quite different ideologies—that of individualism and that of collectivity—are no doubt in the normal run of things able to coexist without any great discordance in that vast lumber-room of stereotypes and fantasies which Althusser calls the *idéologique,* since ordinarily they serve different functions and are wheeled out for different purposes and on different occasions. But in a crisis their structural incompatibility becomes clear, and the fundamental contradiction about capitalism that they express (the paradox of a collective social form organized on the basis of individual profit) makes its presence felt as a conceptual antinomy. We may dramatize it most simply by observing that the solution most appropriate to assuage the individualistic terror about urban concentration—it is, obviously enough, the idea of *decentralization*—turns out at one and the same time to cancel out that other fundamental vocation of the city to stand as the locus and the figure of collective life.

It should be added that the distinction we have made here between a contradiction in the social infrastructure and the form it takes when it becomes registered in the realm of thought and ideology, or in the superstructure—namely the antinomy—is an essential one, which is crucial if we want on the one hand to refute the reproach of a Hegelian idealism sometimes extended to Marxism itself, and on the other to propose a more adequate solution to the problem raised by the insistence of contemporary historians like Michel Foucault on the fundamental discontinuity of epistemes as they succeed themselves in "history" (*Les Mots et les choses* offered a catalog of such epistemic discontinuities, whereas *The Archeology of Knowledge* proposed their theory). This insistence—and the attack on linear and continuous, "idealistic" historiography that accompanied it—sprang from the conviction that ideology is a closed system, that a given epistémé is not something that can be modified or developed or "resolved" or *aufgehoben* according to the conventional sterotype of the Hegelian dialectic; but rather that ideology generates all the logical possibilities and permutations implicit in its structure and is then abandoned, a new epistémé gradually taking its place. It is for this reason that we have couched our own description of ideology in terms of antinomies rather than of contradiction, for the latter, subcellared in the deeper structures of mental life, must be understood as betraying its operations through those surface clicks and malfunctionings in which the former consist, and which serve to signal an approach to the conceptual limits or closure of a given ideological system. Such antinomies cannot be solved or resolved in their own terms; rather, they are violently restructured by an infrastructural praxis, which, rendering the older oppositions meaningless, now lays the preconditions for some new conceptual system or ideology which has no *immediate* link with the preceding one. In this sense, even a social contradiction itself cannot be resolved; it can only be disarticulated and destroyed in its turn and its elements fundamentally reorganized; and this is no doubt the Marxian equivalent for that figure of "death" by which, in the *Phenomenology*, Hegel signals that discontinuous jolt from "moment" to "moment" so often wrongly construed as a kind of "synthesis" of the preceding contradiction.

If we now stress its closure as a system, we will find Greimas' semiotic rectangle a useful instrument for mapping both the content and the logical limits of a given ideology. In particular, it allows us to rearticulate the ideology of the contemporary city in the following manner:

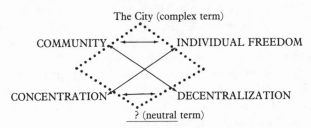

The City (complex term)

COMMUNITY ←——→ INDIVIDUAL FREEDOM

CONCENTRATION ←——→ DECENTRALIZATION

? (neutral term)

Greimas' scheme makes it plain that the negation of any single term of this antinomic system locks us only more deeply into the double-bind of the closed system itself. It also suggests the vocation of the as yet vacant neutral term to permit a desperate (and impossible) final attempt to eradicate the contradictions of the system by some extreme gesture. Unexpectedly, this gesture is none other than Xenakis' mile-high-city, which now falls into place as the inconceivable union of the two negative terms of concentration and decentralization. Xenakis' verticality is thus a tangible squaring of the circle, whose existence as a discourse and a text (but not as an image or a social reality, even a future one) dramatically repudiates the older conceptual dilemma as a flat and two-dimensional effort to think the city on a plane surface, an ideological contradiction locked into the impossible alternatives of point and dispersal. For in some paradoxical, unthinkable fashion, rising out of "centrality" into some other dimension, Xenakis' cosmic city is *both* decentralized and concentrated all at once, and designates, as a figure, that place in which some future urban conceptuality, the categories of some concrete collective and city life as yet inconceivable to use, remain to be invented.

We cannot leave the example of Xenakis' Utopia without a final qualification, which deals precisely with this "absence of the concept" in Utopian textualization. Although Marin does not say so (but for an example of his own form of ideological analysis see what has become the best-known chapter of his book, "Disneyland as a Degenerate Utopia"), it is implicit in his historical scheme that in our own time, the critical value of Xenakis' Utopia—its function as a machine for neutralizing ideological contradictions—does not at all guarantee its immunity from a more properly ideological use as well. Quite the contrary; and Xenakis' transcendence of an older ideological system proves perfectly consistent with his elaboration of a new one, in the event that we may call the contemporary ideology of communication: "The problems of urban concentration are not going to be solved, writes Xenakis, by the vigorous pencil-slashes of decentralization on a map, nor by advocating the dispersal of the living complexity of Paris into smaller centers which will simply reduplicate its inconveniences, but rather *by energetic attention to the general problem of communication, of exchange and of information in urban agglomerations"* (Marin, p. 328/p. 261; italics mine). (It is not without interest that the same motif returns in LeGuin's "solution" to the problem—not merely of urban concentration—but also of the necessary centralization of industrial society as a whole, on Anarres the new decentralized organizational principle being ensured, as in Xenakis' cosmic city, by computers [LeGuin, pp. 84-85].) So the Utopian neutralization of the old ideology ends up making a contribution to the production of that new communicational one whose variants may be found in McLuhanism, systems theory, Habermas' "communications theory of society," and structuralism, to the degree to which each of these, above and beyond its value as an instrument of analysis, projects a more properly ideological anthropology or theory of "human nature" according to which it is proposed that society be organized.

We may now at last return to the full-dress analysis of More's *Utopia* itself, where Marin's initial model is enriched with the content of history and complicated by all the discontinuities of a form in the process of emergence. Book One, with its lengthy debate between Hythloday and the courtiers about conditions in England, supplies the raw material and sketches the fundamental social contradictions on which Book Two must perform its work of transformation and neutralization and Utopian production.

The contradiction is already implicit, as Marin notes, in that remarkable and prophetic diagnosis of English social turmoil with which Hythloday justifies his attack on capital punishment, the point being that the diagnosis is itself heterogeneous and envelops two relatively distinct explanatory systems. On the one hand, Hythloday suggests that the immense increase in the number of beggars—what would today be called a rural lumpenproletariat—is the result of the breakdown of the older feudal manor, that extended social unit which includes, besides the lord and his family, and the peasants and artisans who support them, the feudal retinue which ensures his power. In More's day, indeed, under the twofold pressure of worldwide inflation and royal centralization, the feudal lords find it increasingly expedient to divest themselves of this expensive multitude of soldiers and petty nobility; the latter, suddenly without employment, are thus thrown in the way of highway robbery and brigandage, if not of revolution itself (as in the German peasant wars during the same period). The explicit link More establishes between the social disorder of the countryside and the inner collapse of feudalism as a system has long been appreciated as one of the most original insights of his book.

The trouble is that this initial diagnosis is then reduplicated by a second one of a rather different type: this is the historically and economically crucial indictment by Hythloday of the contemporary movement of enclosure, by which, as is well known, masses of peasants were evicted and transformed into a rural lumpenproletariat of a different type than that rabble of unemployed petty nobles referred to above. But unlike the previous critique, of the inner distintegration of feudalism, this one is a critique of nascent capitalism, and determines a perspective whose distance from the first can most dramatically be measured at the end of Book Two, when Hythloday identifies the vices or transgressions that threaten the Utopian system as such.

For it is too easy to say that the critique of feudal decadence and the denunciation of the various modes of corruption of the market system are both subsumed under a nostalgia for a healthier feudal order which is a coherent class position in its own right. This is not the place to ask whether a genuinely coherent critique of capitalism from a feudal perspective is structurally and ideologically possible. What is certain is that when Hythloday at the end of his description of the island comes to give an account of Utopian virtue, the two quite distinct opposites or vices projected by this ideal value— they are, on the one hand, *pride* and, on the other, *money*—betray their sociological origins in the quite distinct milieux of feudal ostentation and of commerce (thus, Bénichou has shown how later, in the seventeenth century, the humiliation of pride becomes a strategy, if not of the middle classes, then of the *noblesse de robe*, for undermining feudal pretensions.[15] The structural inconsistency between these two ultimate diagnoses may also be expressed as the widening distance between a proto-economic analysis of society and one that remains ethical in the immemorial religious framework of the hierarchy of virtues and vices. What may at least be allowed is that the distance between two ideologies—between two forms of class consciousness—opens up the empty place in which *Utopia* itself emerges.

For the oscillation between these two explanatory systems itself reflects the conceptual limits of this transitional period (for which no alternative to feudalism or capitalism is yet conceivable) and explains why, in the absence of any genuine historical and social self-consciousness, what has been conceptually unformulizable becomes the raw material and the occasion for a very different type of mental operation, namely what must be called the work of *figuration*.

We are, indeed, at the very heart of Marin's book when we begin to grasp the originality of its demonstration of a "work of figuration" of a different order than that already familiar to us in the analysis of myth or dream. Nor is it without interest to observe the deeper affinities between this aspect of his work and the direction in which some of Althusser's group have evolved, most notably Pierre Macherey, whose pioneering work, *Pour une théorie de la production littéraire,*[16] in particular the chapter on Jules Verne, describes the day in which a given ideology ends up betraying itself and providing its own self-critique through the very process by which it attempts (in vain) to endow itself with literary and narrative figuration.

But precisely because we are dealing with figuration, in other words, with preconceptual thinking or discourse, the ideological "contradiction" just outlined cannot be the starting point for our analysis of the text but must rather come as the latter's confirmation and interpretation. Marin's own starting point, indeed, has a unique methodological specific which it owes, less to the more traditional models of figurative analysis already enumerated (Freud, Lévi-Strauss, etc.), than to his work in the field of the semiotics of painting (see in particular his *Etudes sémiologiques,*[17] where his privileged objects of study have been those images already in some way structurally associated with a verbal text, a text either visible within the image itself as motto, script, or emblem, or else implied by it as its historical or mythological source and the classical allusion therewith illustrated. The peculiar duality of registers observable in such visual objects guarantees them against any temptation to collapse one of them back into the other, to see the text as a mere pretext, or, on the other hand, to reduce the visual register to the merely fictional or illustrative. It is indeed Marin's constitution of his object of study as a relationship, or, more precisely, as a structural discontinuity *(écart),* which accounts for the evolution of his more recent work in the direction of those literary texts in which a similar duality of registers can be detected (as in fables or fairy tales which juxtapose the discursive structure of a concluding moral with the quite different narrative texture of the fable proper.)

This duality of the registers of image and text has its equivalent in the structure of More's *Utopia* (and indeed, to varying degrees, in that of all properly Utopian discourse): it is simply the relationship between, and the gap that separates, the *map* of the imaginary nonplace and the verbal *discourse* in which the place and its institutions are recounted. Unlike the painted objects of the *Etudes sémiologiques,* however, the two registers are here both immanent to the verbal text itself, in the sense that the map is not given as an accompanying plate or illustration bound within the volume, but must rather be reconstructed from the data furnished by Hythloday's account. (This immanence is then what accounts for the ingenious reversal of two of the later chapters of *Utopiques,* in which Marin reconstructs the latent verbal text implicit in a series of classical maps of historical places.)

There thus emerges a tension, profoundly characteristic of all Utopian discourse, between description and narrative, between the effort of the text to establish the coordinates of a stable geographical entity, and its other vocation as sheer movement and restless displacement, as itinerary and exploration and, ultimately, as event. This is no doubt a tension present in all travel narrative as such, with which Utopia has an obvious generic kinship. Yet classically the traveler's narrative, which bears within itself the resistant nucleus of some genuinely contingent and irreducible, historical and topographical reality, tends to become a process of transformation whereby the object given, the hitherto unexplored landscape—Nature—is worked over until it can be dissolved and assimilated by the older value systems of some more properly European superego—in other words, Culture.[18] In Utopian discourse, on the contrary, it is the narrative itself that tends to be effaced by and assimilated to sheer description, as anyone knows who has ever nodded over the more garrulous explanatory passages in the classical Utopias. Indeed, one of the basic constraints of the form would seem to be its incompatibility between action or events and that timeless maplike extension of the nonplace itself; in other words, if things can really happen in Utopia, if real disorder, change, transgression, novelty, in brief if history is possible at all, then we begin to doubt whether it can really be a Utopia after all, and its institutions—from a promise of the fulfillment of collective living—slowly begin to turn around into their opposite, a more properly dystopian repression of the unique existential experience of individual lives. (And the same inversion may be detected on the level of the characters, where, to the degree to which the Utopian citizens take on individual specificity, their exemplary value as abstract citizens is undermined and they come to stand as figures for discord, for what is unassimilable to a Utopian harmony that has itself correlatively undergone a dialectical reversal into tyrannical unanimity.)

Nonetheless, even in More the absorption of narrative by description is far from complete; and its is precisely the lack of coincidence between the two that yields the clues and provides the instrument of analysis for Marin's reading. The discrepancy, indeed, between the verbal account of the island given by Hythloday and its possibilities of geometrical realization leads us to the most important findings of *Utopiques*, which can only be briefly summarized here. These findings bear on the noncongruence of text and geography in the three fundamental areas of Utopian social structure, political organization, and economic activity respectively, the point being that in none of the three can Hythloday's account be perfectly matched, in a one-to-one correspondence, against the "ideal map" projected by the data he supplies. But this is something more than mere sloppiness or imaginative failure: rather, the inconsistencies thereby revealed are systematic, and the structural discrepancies are not random but determinate ones, their absences and lacunae now readable as symptoms of some deeper contradiction within the text.

Foremost among the problems raised by the description of the social structure of Utopia is the difficulty of reconciling the internal organization of its subgroups with the external network of relations they entertain among one another. The attempt to coordinate all of Hythloday's data in this respect results in a kind of imbalance between the division of the quarters into communal groups which share a garden around which they live, and the jurisdiction of their collective dining halls which, drawing their membership from opposite sides of the streets that separate the gardens, thus presumably, but inexplicably, mingle people from two different communities:

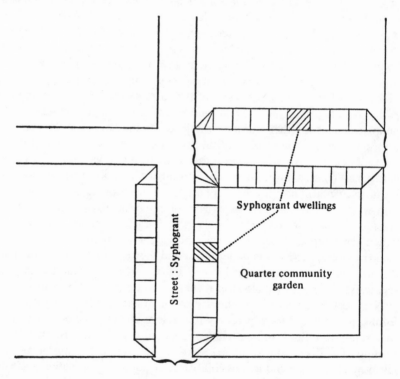

Map of a quarter and street (Marin, p. 166/p. 127)

This particular imbalance is then perpetuated in the impossibility of working out the seating plan of the dining halls themselves, where the elders are supposed to be placed at regular intervals between the other citizens in an attempt to combine a political or administrative structure harmoniously with the more fundamental social and economic structure of the family units. That this is no mere lapse on More's part, but rather to be interrogated as a meaningful symptom, may be demonstrated by the translation of this cartographic dilemma into the more properly conceptual form of an antinomy; for we can read this apparently insignificant failure in technical execution as the ideological difficulty of reconciling a hierarchical social order—based on the authority of the elders within the family group—with the ideal of absolute equality that is supposed to govern the organization of Utopia as a whole.

It will therefore not be surprising to find that this particular contradiction has its equivalent on the level of the overall political organization of the Utopian state itself. The island is a federation of fifty-four city-states, all equal; meanwhile Amaurotum, the capital, and therefore the home of the Prince and the seat of the representative assembly, stands at the exact geometrical center of the island. But how can a federation have a center, and what is still worse, how can a federation of city-states have a Prince? The historical source of this dilemma lies clearly in the centralizing absolutism characteristic of More's own time, in which the monarch increases his own power by proposing himself as an abriter, "above the parties," of the conflict between the feudal nobility and the city bourgeoisie. On the map, the result is that although the Prince's palace and the national senate are supposed to be located at the exact geographical center of the city of Amourotum, the city has no center, being divided equally into four identical districts.

These cartographic discrepancies reach their climax on the economic level of the text, which assigns the island's commercial activity to central market for which no place can be found in the strict letter of Hythloday/More's account. When we remember, however, that the lasting historical originality of More's conception of Utopia springs from the radical elimination from it of money as such, it becomes difficult to resist the feeling that this structural absence of the marketplace betrays some deeper contradiction than any of the foregoing and, through the very difficulty it suggests of thinking an exchange system that would somehow be separate from money itself as a medium, designates that fundamental blank or blind spot in the episteme of the time which is the notion of capitalism itself, and which will therefore only gradually be filled in by the developing political economy of the eighteenth and nineteenth centuries. This absence of a theoretical discourse yet to be developed, this figural anticipation, in the form of a blank or gap, of what could not in the very nature of things be conceptualized, is for Marin the very place of origin and inauguratory impulse of the genre itself: "Utopian discourse is the one form of ideological discourse that has anticipatory value of a theoretical kind: but it is a value which can only appear as such *after* theory itself has been elaborated, that is to say, subsequent to the emergence of the material conditions for the new productive forces" (p. 255/p. 199).

Such, broken, yet carrying within itself that absence of which it is itself but the fragmentary and uneven surcharge, is the Utopian figure. It now remains for us to rewrite the essentials of Marin's account in terms of the latter's production; and as we do so Book One (written later than the description of the island, but evidently generated by the latter as a precondition of its own production) will once more become of interest to us. For above and beyond the incommensurability between the historical reforms proposed by Book One and the Utopian "vision" of Book Two, the reader who has begun to grasp the spirit of Marin's method will find his or her attention jogged and arrested by the insertion, within the discursive texture of the former, of a puzzling and partial Utopian figure—the example of the Polylerites—which seems in some ways an anticipation of the latter on a small and anecdotal scale. Already, then, in the midst of a political debate on historical conditions by "real-life" historical figures, the emergence of a Utopian figure almost in spite of itself would seem a privileged occasion for understanding the process of Utopian production in general.

But to do this, we must go back to the terms of Hythloday's debate with the courtiers, in order to identify that radical insufficiency in it which seems to demand the generation of a Utopian anecdote for its own completion. We have already noted one of the fundamental contradictions of Hythloday's great speech to the Cardinal (the coexistence of the critique of feudalism with a critique of nascent capitalism); it is now worth underscoring a rather different one, which is simply that—already underscored by Marx and Engels in their critique of Utopian socialism—of an overemphasis on the power of rationality in general and a basic and constitutive overestimation of the functional role of rhetoric and persuasion in particular in the historical process whereby an imperfect world may be transformed into a more satisfactory one. Hythloday's appeal to the Cardinal may thus be said to block out the place, and the concrete social and historical situation, of the Renaissance humanists themselves, of whom Max Weber has said that their intellectual program amounted to nothing less than an abortive revolution and the attempt of a certain aristocratic caste to constitute itself as a bureaucratic ruling class on the order of the mandarins in classical China. (Their failure to do so then left the door ajar for the emergence of that more properly middle-class bureaucracy which was to form around the absolute monarchs of succeeding centuries.) In hindsight, therefore, we may associate the Archimedean space of Renaissance rhetoric and humanist persuasion, that imaginary fulcrum projected outside the two worlds of late feudal England and some Tudor and Stuart bureaucracy to come, as the more general position of the intellectuals as a group, whose tendency to overestimate their own structural role in the political and historical process is familiar to all of us. Yet this permits a somewhat different reading of the qualitative distinction we continue to sense between More's *Utopia* and those only characteristic expressions of the humanist discourse of the period *(The Praise of Folly, II Cortegiano*, indeed even *The Prince* itself) with which it otherwise seems to have so much in common: the Utopian figure would in this case be the sign of More's dawning awareness of the inefficacy of those fundamental humanist instruments and categories that are rhetoric and pursuasion. *Utopia* would then be generated, not so much by an overestimation of the powers of reason, as rather by an unformulated consciousness of its failure, and by Hythloday's experience (in Book One) of the impotence of discursive argument and disputation in the making or at least the transformation of history.

Such an interpretation finds confirmation in Marin's analysis of the "preliminary Utopia" of the Polylerites. The latter are introduced, it will be remembered, as an answer to the courtier's objections to Hythloday's views on capital punishment, as his "proof" that the replacement of the death sentence by forced labor which he proposes (as a punishment for theft) is in fact practically realizable; this is to say, in our present context, that it is narratable, in other words, capable of narrative figuration. Hence the shifting of gears from a rhetorical presentation to a narrative example.

Nonetheless, there turns out to be a structural inconsistency between the Utopian and anecdotal, narrative "proof" of the example of the Polylerites and that abstract policy whose wisdom and/or practicality it was supposed to document. The Utopian community of the Polylerites, "altogether satisfied with the products of their own land," living "a life more comfortable than splendid and more happy than renowned or famous" (More, p. 31), is in one sense of course little more than a pretext for illustrating the effects of the policy Hythloday proposes and for giving a picture of what the convicts themselves would look like," dressed in clothes of the same color, their hair. . . not shaved but cropped a little above the ears, from one of which the top is cut off (p. 32). The real problem is that by Hythloday's own account of the matter there ought not to have been any thieves in this happy land to begin with, so that the very possibility of a just (that is to say, a Utopian) punishment is necessarily at one with the disappearance of the crime it was designed for. We here glimpse a kind of totalizing logic in the imagination of Utopia, a logic which, gathering its own momentum, undermines and discredits all the partial and purely reformist "insights" it was supposed to generate on its passage through; thus even the use of Utopian materials as illustrations or examples for the reforming argumentation of humanist rhetoric involves a contradiction and drives the text inexorably on into its own paradoxical realization as a full-dress Utopia.

The process may be observed even more strikingly in another feature of the preliminary Utopia of the Polylerites, insofar as this narrative material, as anecdotal and illustrative as it may be, nonetheless presupposes a certain number of preconditions before it can achieve narrative representability or figuration. Chief among these, in the example of the kingdom of the Polylerites, is the textual obligation to reconcile their existence *within* the historical world contemporary with Tudor society (which can alone make them available as a pedagogical or political model for the latter) with that necessary disjunction from the imperfection of existing historical space and historical societies without which the Utopian purity of their customs must remain inconceivable. More squares this circle, as Marin points out, with a trick, which is, however, extremely suggestive in our present context: the Polylerite state is said to be a protectorate of the Persian Empire and thus doubly isolated from the historical world, first by the chain of mountains that surrounds it, but then also, and far more significant, by this permission to exist granted to it by a historical society that undertakes to leave it alone. Shades of Huxley's Pala, its hallucinogenic *bonheur* precariously sheltered from the imminent menace of the Sears-Roebuck catalog! But where Huxley's imagination, having produced his Utopia, must then resign itself to the implacable narrative and historical logic whereby the latter is then once more effaced and reabsorbed into the violence and stupidity of the outside real world itself, More's—generated by an inverse logic inherent even in this tiny Utopian fragment—evolves in the opposite direction of the production of a Utopian text ever less historically dependent, and guaranteed by a set of Utopian boundaries ever more absolute, by a disjunction ever more fundamental and preemptory.

This new boundary is, as is well known, the great trench that King Utopus causes to be dug to sunder from the mainland that promontory thereby transformed into the island of Utopia; and it is also the empty atmosphere through which a few ancient spaceships ferry the Odonian settlers to their barren planet, their Utopia of scarcity.[19] The operation is of course not only that of disjunction but one of exclusion as well: indeed, the other basic feature of Utopian economics (not touched on above) provides for the location of many of the unpleasant tasks associated with market and commercial activity—such as the slaughter of animals—outside the city's walls. To this still local mode of exclusion within Utopia corresponds a more global one that governs its relations with the outside world in general: not only is money itself excluded—and then used exclusively in foreign trade and for corrupting enemy governments and the like—but violence itself—embodied by mainland mercenaries hired to fight the Utopians' wars for them—is ejected and then reestablished outside the charmed circle that confirms the Utopian commonwealth. Violence and money—was this not the very alternation we found at work in More's diagnosis of Tudor England, as well as in his ultimate formulation of the twin vices rebuked by Utopian virtue?—the trampling arrogance of the feudal retinues and mercenaries, on the one hand, the silent and invisible solvent of the market system, on the other, as it corrodes the older social forms—twin evils now externally negated by geographical fiat, just as their inner principles have been structurally neutralized by the order of Utopian discourse itself.

This act of disjunction/exclusion that founds Utopia as a genre is also the source of everything problematical about it, and about the position of the "neuter" in general, both within and without the system, an observation post which is, however, unlike the ideologies of science itself and the *sujet supposé savior*, without any real term or position of its own (on the philosophical status of the neuter, see Marin's opening chapter, "Du neutre pluriel et de l'utopie"). In a reflection on Utopian reading that echoes some of the basic hypotheses of the Russian Formalists, Marin writes: "We first ask the question: 'What does this story narrate? What is the object described by this description?' But no sooner have we done so than this initial question is converted into a different one: 'How does the story narrate this object? How can its description go about describing it?' And we end up with the realization that the way in which the story is told is the story itself, that the narrative never in reality narrates anything other than its own narrative procedures [*la maniére dont elle s'y prend pour raconter*], these being indeed its truest subject matter" (p. 151/pp. 114-15). From this point of view, then, the Utopian narrative might be described as one that having come into being by a radical act of disjunction, must then summon up all its energies into a "motivation" of that initial disjunction into an elaborate, endless, impossible demonstration that such unimaginable separation from the inextricable totality of Being of that Real world in which history and indeed the reader exist was in fact "imaginable" in the first place. The ultimate subject matter of Utopian discourse would then turn out to be its own conditions of possibility as discourse. Yet such desperate formalism, and the spectacle of a genre lifting itself up into being by its own bootstraps, is perhaps only the obverse and the corollary of its most genuine chance for authenticity; for it would follow, in that case, that Utopia's deepest subject, and the source of all that is most vibrantly political about it, is precisely our inability to conceive it, our incapacity to produce it as a vision, our failure to project the Other of what is, a failure that, as with fireworks dissolving back into the night sky, must once again leave us alone with *this* history. This is surely the ultimate sense in which "Utopian discourse accompanies ideological discourse as its converse and designates the still empty place of a scientific theory of society" (p. 253/p. 198).

Summer 1977

Chapter 5
The Politics of Theory
Ideological Positions in the
Postmodernism Debate

The problem of postmodernism—how its fundamental characteristics are to be described, whether it even exists in the first place, whether the very *concept* is of any use or is, on the contrary, a mystification—this problem is at one and the same time an aesthetic and a political one. The various positions that can logically be taken on it, whatever terms they are couched in, can always be shown to articulate visions of history, in which the evaluation of the social moment in which we live today is the object of an essentially political affirmation or repudiation. Indeed, the very enabling premise of the debate turns on an initial, strategic, presupposition about our social system: to grant some historic originality to a postmodernist culture is also implicitly to affirm some radical structural difference between what is sometimes called consumer society and earlier moments of the capitalism from which it emerged.

The various logical possibilities, however, are necessarily linked with the taking of a position on that other issue inscribed in the very designation "postmodernism" itself, namely the evaluation of what must now be called high or classical modernism itself. Indeed, when we make some initial inventory of the varied cultural artifacts that might plausibly be characterized as postmodern, the temptation is strong to seek the "family resemblance" of such heterogeneous styles and products, not in themselves, but in some common high modernist impulse and aesthetic against which they all, in one way or another, stand in reaction.

The seemingly irreducible variety of the postmodern can be observed fully as problematically within the individual media (of arts) as between them: what affinities, besides some overall generational reaction, to establish between the

103

elaborate false sentences and syntactic mimesis of John Ashbery and the much simpler talk poetry that began to emerge in the early 1960s in protest against the new-critical aesthetic of complex, ironic style? Both register, no doubt, but in very different ways indeed, the institutionalization of high modernism in the same period, the shift from an oppositional to a hegemonic position of the classics of modernism, the latter's conquest of the university, the museum, the art gallery network and the foundations, the assimilation, in other words, of the various high modernisms, into the "canon" and the subsequent attenuation of everything in them felt by our grandparents to be shocking, scandalous, ugly, dissonant, immoral, and antisocial.

The same heterogeneity can be detected in the visual arts, between the inaugural reaction against the last high modernist school in painting—abstract expressionism—in the work of Andy Warhol and so-called pop art, and such quite distinct aesthetics as those of conceptual art, photorealism, and the current new figuration or neoexpressionism. It can be witnessed in film, not merely between experimental and commercial production, but also within the former itself, where Godard's "break" with the classical filmic modernism of the great "auteurs" (Hitchcock, Bergman, Fellini, Kurasawa) generates a series of stylistic reactions against itself in the 1970s, and is also accompanied by a rich new development of experimental video (a new medium inspired by, but significantly and structurally distinct from, experimental film). In music also, the inaugural moment of John Cage now seems far enough from such later syntheses of classical and popular styles in composers like Phil Glass and Terry Riley, as well as from punk and new-wave rock of the type of The Clash, The Talking Heads, and The Gang of Four, themselves significantly distinct from disco or glitter rock. (In film or in rock, however, a certain historical logic can be reintroduced by the hypothesis that such newer media recapitulate the evolutionary stages or breaks between realism, modernism, and postmodernism, in a compressed time span, such that the Beatles and the Stones occupy the high modernist moment embodied by the "auteurs" of 1950s' and 1960s' art films.)

In narrative proper, the dominant conception of a dissolution of linear narrative, a repudiation of representation, and a "revolutionary" break with the (repressive) ideology of storytelling generally, does not seem adequate to encapsulate such very different work as that of Burroughs, but also of Pynchon and Ishmael Reed; of Beckett, but also of the French *nouveau roman* and its own sequels, and of the "nonfictional novel" as well, and the New Narrative. Meanwhile, a significantly distinct aesthetic has seemed to emerge both in commercial film and in the novel with the production of what may be called nostalgia art (or *la mode rétro*).

But it is evidently architecture which is the privileged terrain of struggle of postmodernism and the most strategic field in which this concept has been debated and its consequences explored. Nowhere else has the "death of modernism" been felt so intensely, or pronounced more stridently; nowhere else have the theoretical and practical stakes in the debate been articulated more programmatically. Of a burgeoning literature on the subject, Robert Venturi's *Learning from Las Vegas* (1971), a series of discussions by Christopher Jencks, and Pier Paolo Portoghesi's Biennale presentation, *After Modern Architecture*, may be cited as usefully illuminating the central issues in the attack on the architectural high modernism of the international style (LeCorbusier, Wright, Mies): namely, the bankruptcy of the monumental (buildings which, as Venturi puts it, are really *sculptures*), the failure of its protopolitical or Utopian program (the transformation of all social life by way of the transformation of space), its elitism including the authoritarianism of the charismatic leader, and finally its virtual destruction of the older city fabric by a proliferation of glass boxes and of high rises that, disjoining themselves from their immediate contexts, turn these last into the degraded public space of an urban no-man's land.

Still, architectural postmodernism is itself no unified or monolithic period style, but spans a whole gamut of allusions to styles of the past, such that within it can be distinguished a baroque postmodernism (say, Michael Graves), a rococo postmodernism (Charles Moore or Venturi), a classical and a neoclassical postmodernism (Rossi and De Porzemparc respectively), and perhaps even a Mannerist and a Romantic variety, not to speak of a high modernist postmodernism itself. This complacent play of historical allusion and stylistic pastiche (termed "historicism" in the architecture literature) is a central feature of postmodernism more generally.

Yet the architectural debates have the merit of making the political resonance of these seemingly aesthetic issues inescapable, and allowing it to be detectable in the sometimes more coded or veiled discussions in the other arts. On the whole, four general positions on postmodernism may be disengaged from the variety of recent pronouncements on the subject; yet even this relatively neat scheme or *combinatoire* is further complicated by one's impression that each of these possibilities is susceptible of either a politically progressive or a politically reactionary expresssion (speaking now from a Marxist or more generally Left perspective).

One can, for example, salute the arrival of postmodernism from an essentially antimodernist standpoint.[1] A somewhat earlier generation of theorists (most notably Ihab Hassan) seems already to have done something like this when they dealt with the postmodernist aesthetic in terms of a more properly poststructuralist thematics (the *Tel quel* attack on the ideology of representation, the Heideggerian or Derridean "end of Western metaphysics"); here what is often not yet called postmodernism (see the Utopian prophecy at the end of Foucault's *The Order of Things*) is saluted as the coming of a whole new way of thinking and being in the world. But since Hassan's celebration also includes a number of the more extreme monuments of high modernism (Joyce, Mallarmé), this would be a relatively more ambiguous stance, were it not for the accompanying celebration of a new information high technology which marks the affinity between such evocations and the political thesis of a properly *postindustrial society.*

All of this is largely disambiguated in Tom Wolfe's *From Bauhaus to Our House* (1981), an otherwise undistinguished book report on the recent architectural debates by a writer whose own New Journalism itself constitutes one of the varieties of postmodernism. What is interesting and symptomatic about this book is, however, the absence of any Utopian celebration of the postmodern and—far more strikingly—the passionate hatred of the modern that breathes through the otherwise obligatory camp sarcasm of the rhetoric; and this is not a new passion, but a dated and archaic one. It is as though the original horror of the first middle-class spectators of the very emergence of the modern itself—the first Corbusiers, as white as the first freshly built cathedrals of the twelfth century, the first scandalous Picasso heads, with two eyes on one profile like a flounder, the stunning "obscurity" of the first editions of *Ulysses* or *The Waste Land*—as though this disgust of the original philistines, Spiessbürger, bourgeois, or Main Street Babbitry, had suddenly come back to life, infusing the newer critiques of modernism with an ideologically very different spirit, whose effect is on the whole to reaweaken in the reader an equally archaic sympathy with the protopolitical, Utopian, antimiddle-class impulses of a now extinct high modernism itself. Wolfe's diatribe thus offers a stunning example of the way in which a reasoned and contemporary, theoretical repudiation of the modern—much of whose progressive force springs from a new sense of the urban and a now considerable experience of the destruction of older forms of communal and urban life in the name of a high modernist orthodoxy—can be handily reappropriated and pressed into the service of an explicitly reactionary cultural politics.

These positions—antimodern, propostmodern—then find their opposite number and structural inversion in a group of counterstatements whose aim is to discredit the shoddiness and irresponsibility of the postmodern in general by way of a reaffirmation of the authentic impulse of a high modernist tradition still considered to be alive and vital. Hilton Kramer's twin manifestos in the inaugural issue of his new journal, *The New Criterion*, articulate these views with force, contrasting the moral responsibility of the "masterpieces" and monuments of classical modernism with the fundamental irresponsibility and superificiality of a postmodernism associated with camp and with the "facetiousness" of which the Wolfe style is a ripe and obvious example.

What is more paradoxical is that politically Wolfe and Kramer have much in common; and there would seem to be a certain inconsistency in the way in which Kramer must seek to eradicate from the "high seriousness" of the classics of the modern their fundamentally antimiddle-class stance and the protopolitical passion that informs the repudiation, by the great modernists, of Victorian taboos and family life, of commodification, and of the increasing asphyxiation of a desacralizing capitalism, from Ibsen to Lawrence, from Van Gogh to Jackson Pollock. Kramer's ingenious attempt to assimilate this ostensibly antibourgeois stance of the great modernists to a "loyal opposition" secretly nourished, by way of foundations and grants, by the bourgeoisie itself—while most unconvincing indeed—is surely itself enabled by the contradictions of the cultural politics of modernism proper, whose negations depend on the persistence of what they repudiate and entertain—when they do not, very rarely indeed (as in Brecht), attain some genuine political self-consciousness—asymbiotic relationship with capital.

It is, however, easier to understand Kramer's move here when the political project of *The New Criterion* is clarified: for the mission of the journal is clearly to eradicate the 1960s and what remains of that legacy, to consign that whole period to the kind of oblivion that the 1950s was able to devise for the 1930s, or the 1920s for the rich political culture of the pre-World-War-I era. *The New Criterion* therefore inscribes itself in the effort, ongoing and at work everywhere today, to construct some new conservative cultural counterrevoluton, whose terms range from the aesthetic to the ultimate defense of the family and or religion. It is therefore paradoxical that this essentially political project should explicitly deplore the omnipresence of politics in contemporary culture—an infection largely spread during the 1960s, but which Kramer holds responsible for the moral imbecility of the postmodernism of our own period.

The problem with the operation—an obviously indispensable one from the conservative viewpoint—is that for whatever reason its paper-money rhetoric does not seem to have been backed by the solid gold of state power, as was the case with McCarthyism or in the period of the Palmer raids. The failure of the Vietnam War seems, at least for the moment, to have made the naked exercise of repressive power impossible,[2] and endowed the 1960s with a persistence in collective memory and experience which it was not given to the traditions of the 1930s or the pre-World-War-I period to know. Kramer's "cultural revolution" therefore tends most often to lapse into a feebler and sentimental nostalgia for the 1950s and the Eisenhower era.

It will not be surprising, in the light of what has been shown for an earlier set of positions on modernism and postmodernism, that in spite of the openly conservative ideology of this second evaluation of the contemporary cultural scene, the latter can also be appropriated for what is surely a far more progressive line on the subject. We are indebted to Jürgen Habermas[3] for this dramatic reversal and rearticulation of what remains the affirmation of the supreme value of the modern and repudiation of the theory, as well as the practice, of postmodernism. For Habermas, however, the vice of postmodernism consists very centrally in its politically reactionary function, as the attempt everywhere to discredit a modernist impulse Habermas himself associates with the bourgeois Enlightenment and with the latter's still universalizing and Utopian spirit. With Adorno himself, Habermas seeks to rescue and to recommemorate what both see as the essentially negative, critical, and Utopian power of the great high modernisms. On the other hand, his attempt to associate these last with the spirit of the eighteenth-century Enlightenment marks a decisive break indeed with Adorno and Horkheimer's somber *Dialectic of Enlightenment,* in which the scientific ethos of the *philosophies* is dramatized as a misguided will to power and domination over nature, and their own desacralizing program as the first stage in the development of a sheerly instrumentalizing worldview which will lead straight to Auschwitz. This very striking divergence can be accounted for by Habermas' own vision of history, which seeks to maintain the promise of "liberalism" and the essentially Utopian content of the first, universalizing bourgeois ideology (equality, civil rights, humanitarianism, free speech, and open media) over against the failure of those ideals to be realized in the development of capital itself.

As for the aesthetic terms of the debate, however, it will not be adequate to respond to Habermas' resuscitation of the modern by some mere emperical certification of the latter's extinction. We need to take into account the possibility that the national situation in which Habermas thinks and writes is rather different from our own: McCarthyism and repression are, for one thing, realities in the Federal Republic today, and the intellectual intimidation of the Left and the silencing of a Left culture (largely associated, by the West German Right, with "terrorism") has been on the whole a far more successful operation than elsewhere in the West.[4] The triumph of a new McCarthyism and of the culture of the Speissburger and the philistine suggests the possibility that in this particular national situation Habermas may well be right, and the older forms of high modernism may still retain something of the subversive power that they have lost elsewhere. In that case, a postmodernism that seeks to enfeeble and to undermine that power may well also merit his ideological diagnosis in a local way, even though the assessment remains ungeneralizable.

Both of the previous positions—antimodern/propostmodern, and promodern/antipostmodern—are characterized by an acceptance of the new term, which is tantamount to an agreement on the fundamental nature of some decisive "break" between the modern and the postmodern moments, however these last are evaluated. There remain, however, two final logical possibilities, both of which depend on the repudiation of any conception of such a historical break and which therefore, implicitly or explicitly, call into question the usefulness of the very category of postmodernism. As for the works associated with the latter, they will then be assimilated back into classical modernism proper, so that the "postmodern" becomes little more

than the form taken by the authentically modern in our own period, and a
mere dialectical intensification of the old modernist impulse toward innovation. (I must here omit yet another series of debates, largely academic, in
which the very continuity of modernism as it is here reaffirmed is itself called
into question by some vaster sense of the profound continuity of romanticism
itself, from the late eighteenth-century on, of which both the modern and the
postmodern will be seen as mere organic stages.)

The two final positions on the subject thus logically prove to be a positive
and negative assessment respectively of a postmodernism now assimilated back
into the high modernist tradition. Jean-François Lyotard[5] thus proposes that
his own vital commitment to the new and the emergent, to a contemporary or
postcontemporary cultural production now widely characterized as
"postmodern," be grasped as part and parcel of a reaffirmation of the
authentic older high modernisms very much in Adorno's spirit. The ingenious twist or swerve in his own proposal involves the proposition that
something called "postmodernism" does not *follow* high modernism proper,
as the latter's waste product, but rather very precisely *precedes* and prepares
it, so that the contemporary postmodernisms all around us may be seen as the
promise of the return and the reinvention, the triumphant reappearance, of
some new high modernism endowed with all its older power and with fresh
life. This is a prophetic stance, whose analyses turn on the antirepresenta-
tional thrust of modernism and postmodernism; Lyotard's aesthetic positions, however, cannot be adequately evaluated in aesthetic terms, since what
informs them is an essentially social and political conception of a new social
system beyond classical capitalism (our old friend, "postindustrial society");
the vision of a regenerated modernism is in that sense inseparable from a certain prophetic faith in the possibilities and the promise of the new society
itself in full emergence.

The negative inversion of this position will then clearly involve an
ideological repudiation of modernism of a type that might conceivably range
from Lukács' older analysis of modernist forms as the replication of the
reification of capitalist social life all the way to some of the more articulated
critiques of high modernism of the present day. What distinguishes this final
position from the antimodernisms already outlined above is, however, that it
does not speak from the security of an affirmation of some new postmodernist
culture, but rather sees even the latter itself as a mere degeneration of the
already stigmatized impulses of high modernism proper. This particular position, perhaps the bleakest of all and the most implacably negative, can be
vividly confronted in the works of the Venetian architecture historian Manfredo Tafuri, whose extensive analyses[6] constitute a powerful indictment of
what we have termed the "protopolitical" impulses in high modernism (the
"Utopian" substitution of cultural politics for politics proper, the vocation to
transform the world by transforming its forms, space, or language). Tafuri is,

however, no less harsh in his anatomy of the negative, demystifying, "critical" vocation of the various modernisms, whose function he reads as a kind of Hegelian "ruse of History," whereby the instrumentalizing and desacralizing tendencies of capital itself are ultimately realized through just such demolition work by the thinkers and artists of the modern movement. Their "anticapitalism" therefore ends up laying the basis for the "total" bureaucratic organization and control of late capitalism, and it is only logical that Tafuri should conclude by positing the impossibility of any radical transformation of culture before a radical transformation of social relations themselves.

The political ambivalence demonstrated in the earlier two positions seems to me to be maintained here, but *within* the positions of both of these very complex thinkers. Unlike many of the previously mentioned theorists, Tafuri and Lyotard are both explicitly political figures, with an overt commitment to the values of an older revolutionary tradition. It is clear, for example, that Lyotard's embattled endorsement of the supreme value of aesthetic innovation is to be understood as the figure for a certain kind of revolutionary stance; whereas Tafuri's whole conceptual framework is largely consistent with the classical Marxist tradition. Yet both are also, implicitly, and more openly at certain strategic moments, rewritable in terms of a post-Marxism that at length becomes indistinguishable from anti-Marxism proper. Lyotard has, for example, very frequently sought to distinguish his "revolutionary" aesthetic from the older ideals of political revolution, which he sees either as Stalinist, or as archaic and incompatible with the conditions of the new postindustrial social order; while Tafuri's apocalyptic notion of the total social revolution implies a conception of the "total system" of capitalism that, in a period of depolitization and reaction, is only too fatally destined for the kind of discouragement that has so often led Marxists to a renunciation of the political altogether (Adorno and Merleau-Ponty come to mind, along with

	ANTIMODERNIST	PROMODERNIST
PROPOSTMODERNIST	Wolfe- Jencks+	Lyotard $\left\{ {+ \atop -} \right.$
ANTIPOSTMODERNIST	Tafuri $\left\{ {- \atop +} \right.$	Kramer – Habermas +

many of the ex-Trotskyists of the 1930s and 1940s and the ex-Maoists of the 1960s and 1970s).

The combination scheme outlined above can now be schematically represented as in the accompanying diagram, the plus and minus signs designating the politically progressive or reactionary functions of the positions in questions.

With these remarks we come full circle and may now return to the more positive potential political content of the first position in question, and in particular to the question of a certain *populist* impulse in postmodernism that it has been the merit of Charles Jencks (but also of Venturi and others) to have underscored—a question which will also allow us to deal a little more adequately with the absolute pessimism of Tafuri's Marxism itself. What must first be observed, however, is that most of the political positions that we have found to inform what is most often conducted as an aesthetic debate are in reality moralizing ones, which seek to develop final judgments on the phenomenon of postmodernism, whether the latter is stigmatized as corrupt or, on the other hand, saluted as a culturally and aesthetically healthy and positive form of innovation. But a genuinely historical and dialectical analysis of such phenomena—particularly when it is a matter of a present of time and of history in which we ourselves exist and struggle—cannot afford the impoverished luxury of such absolute moralizing judgments; the dialectic is "beyond good and evil" in the sense of some easy taking of sides, whence the glacial and inhuman spirit of its historical vision (something that already disturbed contemporaries about Hegel's original system). The point is that we are *within* the culture of postmodernism to the point where its facile repudiation is as impossible as any equally facile celebration of it is complacent and corrupt. Ideological judgment on postmodernism today necessarily implies, one would think, a judgment on ourselves as well as on the artifacts in question; nor can an entire historical period, such as our own, be grasped in any adequate way by means of global moral judgments or their somewhat degraded equivalent, pop-psychological diagnosis (such as those of Lasch's *Culture of Narcissism*). On the classical Marxian view, the seeds of the future already exist within the present and must be conceptually disengaged from it, both through analysis and through political praxis (the workers of the Paris Commune, Marx once remarked in a striking phrase, *"have no ideals to realize"*; they merely sought to disengage emergent forms of new social relations from the older capitalist social relations in which the former had already begun to stir). In place of the temptation either to denounce the complacencies of postmodernism as some final symptom of decadence, or to salute the new forms as the harbingers of a new technological and technocratic Utopia, it seems more appropriate to assess the new cultural production within the working hypothesis of a general modification of culture itself within the social restructuration of late capitalism as a system.[7]

As for emergence, however, Jencks' assertion that postmodern architecture distinguishes itself from that of high modernism through its populist priorities,[8] may serve as the starting point for some more general discussion. What is meant, in the specifically architectural context, is that where the now more classical high modernist space of a Corbusier or a Wright sought to differentiate itself radically from the fallen city fabric in which it appears—its forms thus dependent on an act of radical disjunction from its spatial context (the great *pilotis* dramatizing separation from the ground and safeguarding the *Novum* of the new space)—postmodernist buildings, on the contrary, celebrate their insertion into the heterogeneous fabric of the commercial strip and the motel and fast-food landscape of the postsuperhighway American city. Meanwhile a play of allusion and formal echoes ("historicism") secures the kinship of these new art buildings with the surrounding commercial icons and spaces, thereby renouncing the high modernist claim to radical difference and innovation.

Whether this undoubtedly significant feature of the newer architecture is to be characterized as *populist* must remain an open question, since it would seem essential to distinguish the emergent forms of a new commercial culture—beginning with advertisements and spreading to formal *packaging* of all kinds, from products to buildings and not excluding artistic commodities such as television shows (the "logo") and bestsellers and films—from the older kinds of folk and genuinely "popular" culture which flourished when the older social classes of a peasantry and an urban *artisanat* still existed and which, from the mid-nineteenth century on, have gradually been colonized and extinguished by commodification and the market system.

What can at least be admitted is the more universal presence of this particular feature, which appears more unambiguously in the other arts as an effacement of the older distinction between high and so-called mass culture, a distinction on which modernism depended for its specificity, its Utopian function consisting at least in part in the securing of a realm of authentic experience over against the surrounding environment of philistinism, of schlock and kitsch, of commodification and of Reader's Digest culture. Indeed, it can be argued that the emergence of high modernism is itself contemporaneous with the first great expansion of a recognizable mass culture (Zola may be taken as the marker for the last coexistence of the art novel and the bestseller wthin a single text).

It is now this constitutive differentiation which seems on the point of disappearing; we have already mentioned the way in which, in music, after Schönberg and even after Cage, the two antithetical traditions of the "classical" and the "popular" once again begin to merge. In a more general way, it seems clear that the artists of the "postmodern" period have been fascinated precisely by the whole new object world, not merely of the Las Vegas strip, but also of the late show and the grade-B Hollywood film, of so-called paraliterature with its airport paperback categories of the gothic and romance, the popular biography, the murder mystery and the science-fiction or fantasy novel (in such a way that the older generic categories discredited by modernism seem on the point of living an unexpected reappearance). In the visual arts, the renewal of photography as a significant medium in its own right and also as the "plane of substance" in pop art or photorealism is a crucial symptom of the same process. At any rate, it becomes minimally obvious that the newer artists no longer "quote" the materials, the fragments and motifs, of a mass or popular culture, as Joyce (and Flaubert) began to do, or Mahler; they somehow incorporate them to the point where many of our older critical and evaluative categories (founded precisely on the radical differentiation of modernist and mass culture) no longer seem functional.

But if this is so, it seems at least possible that what wears the mask and makes the gestures of "populism" in the various postmodernist apologias and manifestos is in reality a mere reflex and symptom of a (to be sure momentous) cultural mutation, in which what used to be stigmatized as mass or commercial culture is now received into the precincts of a new and enlarged cultural realm. In any case, one would expect a term drawn from the typology of political ideologies to undergo basic semantic readjustments when its initial referent (that Popular-front class coalition of workers, peasants, and petty bourgeois generally called "the people") has disappeared.

Perhaps, however, this is not so new a story after all. One remembers, indeed, Freud's delight at discovering an obscure tribal culture, which alone among the multitudinous traditions of dream-analysis on the earth had managed to hit on the notion that all dreams had hidden sexual meanings— except for sexual dreams, which meant something else! So also it would seem in the postmodernist debate, and the depoliticized bureaucratic society to which it corresponds, where all seemingly cultural positions turn out to be symbolic forms of political moralizing, except for the single overtly political note, which suggests a slippage from politics back into culture again. I have the feeling that the only adequate way out of this vicious circle, besides praxis itself, is a dialectical view that seeks to grasp the present as history.

Fall 1964

Chapter 6
Beyond the Cave
Demystifying the Ideology of Modernism

There is a novel by Iris Murdoch in which one of the characters—an elderly philosophy professor—reminds us of Plato's conclusions, in the *Phaedrus*, on the use and misuse of language. "Words," Socrates is there supposed in essence to have said, "words can't be moved from place to place and retain their meaning. Truth is communicated from a particular speaker to a particular listener."[1]

Is is an odd remark for a novelist to have one of her characters make. For, of course, if it is true, there could never be such a thing as a novel in the first place. Literature is presumably the preeminent example of words that *can* be moved from place to place without losing their meaning. What else can possibly be meant by the idea of the autonomy of the work of art—one of the great terroristic fetishes of present-day American literary criticism—if it be not this essential *portability* of all literary language? So what we want to ask ourselves first and foremost is not whether the work of art is or is not autonomous, but rather, how it *gets to be* autonomous; how language—in context, in situation—worldly language—gradually manages to separate itself out, to organize itself into relatively self-sufficient bodies of words which can then be grasped by groups and individuals widely divided from one another in space and in time, and by social class or by culture.

Now, although I do not intend here to attempt an answer to the aesthetic and philosophical problem I have just raised—that of the autonomy of the work of art—I think it may be instructive, as a way of leading into my own subject, to tick off a few of the possible solutions to this problem, by way of seeing whether they do not all lead back—however deviously and indirectly—

115

to the social and historical situations that form the absolute horizon of our individual existences.

For it is clear that if you begin by interrogating the origins of a given form, if you take as your object of study, in other words, not the present-day autonomy of a given form or genre, but rather its *autonomization*, you will always end up observing the emergence of such forms from social life in general and everyday language in particular; and this is so whether, with Fischer and Lukács,[2] on the one hand, or with the Cambridge school, on the other, you seek the moment when artistic activity differentiates itself from the unspecialized ritualistic world of primitive social life; or whether, with a writer like André-Jolles, in his *Simple Forms,* you seek the key to some specific genre in a determinate speech act within a determinate social situation—thus, for instance, you might seek to understand how the maxim or epigram separated itself out of the conversational life of a certain type of salon society. In both of these ways of studying autonomization, the worldliness of form is of necessity reaffirmed.

But it may be objected that the forms or genres are only initially a part of the practical world of everyday social life: once differentiated from it, they lose all traces of their origins and become in fact quite independent and autonomous linguistic products in their own right. Yet this is to forget, it seems to me, that genre is itself a social institution, something like a social contract in which we agree to respect certain rules about the appropriate use of the piece of language in question. Far from proving the autonomy of the work of art, therefore, the very existence of the generic convention explains how an illusion of autonomy could come into being, for the generic situation formalizes and thus absorbs into the formal structure worldly elements that would otherwise be passed on in the work of art itself, as content.

Even here, however, I imagine that a final position is possible, one which, while admitting the social nature of the generic situations, declares that the old-fashioned genres have ceased in our time to exist and that we no longer consume a tragedy, a comedy, a satire, but rather literature in general in the form of each work, the Book of the world, the text as an impersonal process. The answer here would be, I think, that at that point all the generic situations have been telescoped into one, that of the consumption of Literature itself, which then becomes the hobby of a small group—I won't really call us an elite—centered in the universities and in a few major cultural centers.

What I really want to stress, however, is the way in which our initial question seems to have come full circle. The idea of the autonomy of the work of art—which at first seemed a proud boast and a value to be defended—now begins to look a little shameful, like a symptom into whose pathology one would want to inquire more closely. At this point, then, we are tempted to ask, not whether literary works are autonomous, nor even how art manages to lift itself above its immediate social situation and to free itself from its social context, but rather what kind of society it can be in which works of art have become autonomous to this degree, in which the older social and cultic functions of literature have become so unfamiliar as to have made us forgetful (and this in the strong, Heideggerian sense of the term) of the power and influence that a socially living art can exercise.

A question like this evidently demands that we are able, in some way, to get outside of ourselves and of our own local tastes and literary values, and to see all that with something like a Brechtian estrangement-effect, as though they were the values and the institutions of an utterly alien culture. Were we able to do so, I suggest that we would suddenly become aware of the degree to which a coherent and quite systematic ideology—I will call it the ideology of modernism—imposes its conceptual limitations on our aesthetic thinking and our taste and judgments, and in its own way projects an utterly distorted model of literary history—which is evidently one of the privileged experiences through which we as scholars at least have access to History itself.

When one is the prisoner of such an ideology—or *Weltanschauung,* if you prefer—or paradigm or epistémé—how could one ever become aware of it in the first place, let alone patiently undo—or deconstruct—its complicated machinery, through which hitherto we have alone learned to see reality?

I suppose that the first step in doing so is to take an inventory of the things excluded from this ideology, and to make ourselves more acutely aware of the kinds of literary works explicitly rejected from the machine (and which may in many cases not even be classified as Literature at all) such as mass or media culture, lower-class or working-class culture, but also those few surviving remnants of genuine popular or peasant culture from the precapitalist period, and in particular of course the oral storytelling of tribal or primitive societies. Yet to say so is not necessarily to endorse the new-worlds-to-conquer imperialism that has been the spirit of so much of recent Western thought in the cultural realm, for it is not so much a question now of feeling satisfaction at the infinite elasticity and receptivity of our own cultural outlook, but rather of locating the ultimate structural limits of that outlook and coming to terms with its negation, with what it cannot absorb without losing its own identity and wholly transforming itself. For we all know that capitalism is the first genuinely global culture and has never renounced its mission to assimilate everything alien into itself—whether that be the African masks of the time of Picasso, or the little red books of Mao Zedong on sale in your corner drugstore.

No, what I have in mind is a more difficult process than that, one that can be completed successfully only by a painful realization of the ethnocentrism in which we are all, in one way or another, caught. And to put it in its most exaggerated and outrageous form, I will suggest that our first task is not to persuade ourselves of the validity for us of these alien or primitive art forms, but rather to attempt to measure the whole extent of our boredom with them and our almost visceral refusal of what can only be (to our own jaded tastes) the uninventive simplicity and repetition, the liturgical slowness and predictability, or else the senseless and equally monotonous episodic meandering, of an oral tradition that has neither verbal density and opacity, nor psychological subleties and violence to offer us. Not interest or fascination, therefore, but rather that sense of dreariness with which we come to the end of our own world and observe with a certain self-protective lassitude that there is nothing for us on the other side of the boundary—this is the unpleasant condition in which, I suggest, we come to the realization of the Other which is at the same time a dawning knowledge of ourselves as well.

Now I want to borrow a concept from another discipline in order to explain why this should be so, and, perhaps, indeed, to suggest what might be done about it. This is the concept of repression, which, like so much else in Freud's language, is drawn from the political realm, to which, in the medieval languages, its original purely descriptive sense had already been applied. Yet the notion of repression is by no means so dramatic as it might at first appear, for in psychoanalytic theory, whatever its origins, and whatever the final effect of repression on the personality, its symptoms and its mechanisms are quite the opposite of violence, and are nothing quite so much as looking away, forgetting, ignoring, losing interest. Repression is reflexive, that is, it aims not only at removing a particular object from consciousness, but also and above all, at doing away with the traces of that removal as well, at repressing the very memory of the intent to repress. This is the sense in which the boredom I evoked a moment ago may serve as a powerful hermeneutic instrument: it marks the spot where something painful is buried, it invites us to reawaken all the anguished hesitation, the struggle of the subject to avert his or her eyes from the thought with which brutal arms insist on confronting him.

Now, of course, I will make only metaphoric use of this concept, for it cannot be any part of my intention here to assess the possibility of some consequent Freudo-Marxism or to come to terms with the relationship of Freud's own object of study, namely sexuality, to the cultural phenomena that concern us. I would only observe that Georg Lukács' classic analysis of ideology in *History and Class Consciousness* (1923) is very consistent with the description of repression we have just given. Lukács there draws the consequences from his idea that the fundamental category of Marxism is that of Totality, or, in other words, that the fundamental strength of Marxist thinking is its ability—indeed its determination—to make all the connections and to put back together all those separate fields—economics, say, and literature—that middle-class thought had been so intent on keeping apart. It follows, then, that bourgeois ideology, or, in our present terms, the middle-class method of repressing reality, is not so much an affair of distortion and of false consciousness in the sense of outright cynicism or lies (although, obviously there is also enough of that in our discipline to satisfy the most demanding observer), but rather, primarily and constitutively, of leaving out, of strategic omissions, lapses, a kind of careful preliminary preparation of the raw material such that certain questions will never arise in the first place.

This, then, is the sense in which an exploration of repression or of ideological bias in literary criticism demands an attention to the outer and constitutive limits of the discipline just as much as to the positive acts committed on a daily basis in its name and within its confines. I cannot, however, resist an appeal to a very different kind of authority than that of Lukács, and since I have already pronounced the word, I will agree that this problem is on the whole coterminous with what relatively right-wing and theological current in both France and Germany today have decided once again to call hermeneutics, that is, the whole science of interpretation, the problematics of the encounter with the alien text—whether from the distant past or from other cultures. I will only point out that my own appeal to boredom is not essentially different from that of Hans-Georg Gadamer, Heidegger's principal disciple and the central figure in German hermeneutics, to what he quite deliberately and provocatively calls prejudice, *Vorurteile*,[3] and what we might very quickly describe as the class habits and ideological thought-modes inherent in our own concrete social and historical situation. To say that we understand what is other than ourselves through such *Vorurteile*, or situational prejudice, is therefore to reaffirm the dual character of all understanding and to remind ourselves that it can never take place in the void, "objectively" or out of situation, that all contact with otherness is also at one and the same time of necessity a return upon ourselves and our own particular culture and class affiliation that cannot but implicitly or explicitly call the latter into question.

Now let us try to see what this would mean in a practical sense, as a way of assessing the organization of literature as a field of study. I have suggested elsewhere that our habit of studying individual writers one by one, in a kind of respectful stylistic isolation, was a very useful strategy in preventing genuinely social and historical problems from intruding into literary study.[4] The position I want to defend here is not unlike this one, but for whole periods rather than individual writers. I suggest that the ghettoization of primitive storytelling is an excellent example of this, but the ambiguity of the word "myth," as loosely brandished in our discipline today, makes primitive storytelling a fairly complicated example to use. Our own myth school—or rather, what it might be clearer to call archetypal criticism—obviously has in mind a very different object of study, and a very different kind of textual satisfaction, than that afforded by the primitive storytellers of, say, the Bororo Encyclopedia. Indeed, whatever the ultimate usefulness of the intellectual brilliance invested in Claude Lévi-Strauss' *Mythologiques*, those four volumes will at least have had the effect of giving us a feeling for those genuinely episodic, molecular strings of events in which the Jungian hero, wearing all his archetypal masks, must inevitably find himself structurally ill at ease.

So we set aside the problem of myth for one much closer to home, which indeed involves that literature most explicitly repudiated by the practice and the values of the ideology of modernism: I refer to realism itself. And perhaps my point about boredom may now make a little more sense to you, when you think, on the one hand, of the inevitable tediousness for us today, programmed by the rapid gearshifts of television, of the old endless three-decker novels; and when, on the other hand, you heave a sigh at the thought of yet another rehearsal of the tiresome polemics waged in the name of realism, to accept the terms of which is perhaps already to find yourself compromised in advance.

Now obviously I share that feeling too to some degree, and am not interested here in making some puritanical attack on modernism in the name of the older realistic values; I simply want to underscore the limits of the ideology of modernism in accounting for the great realistic works, and to suggest that to prove Dickens was really a symbolist, Flaubert the first modernist, Balzac a myth-maker, and George Eliot some Victorian version of Henry James if not even of Dostoevsky, is an intellectually dishonest operation that skirts all the real issues.

Modern literary theory has in fact given us what are essentially two irreconcilable accounts of realism. On the one hand, there are the classical apologias for this narrative mode, most dramatically associated with the position of Georg Lukács, but of which Erich Auerbach provides a less controversial and perhaps more patient documentation. For this position, the realistic mode—like the sonata form in music, or the conquest of perspective in painting—is one of the most complex and vital realizations of Western culture, to which it is indeed, like those other two artistic phenomena I mentioned, well-nigh unique. Any reader of Auerbach's *Mimesis* will have retained a vivid picture of the way in which realism slowly takes shape over many centuries by a progressive enlargement and refinement of literary techniques—from the unlimbering of epic sentence structure and the development of narrative perspective to the great plots of the nineteenth-century novels—an expansion of the literary and linguistic recording apparatus in such a way as to make ever larger areas of social and individual reality accessible to us. Here realism is shown to have epistemological truth, as a privileged mode of knowing the world we live in and the lives we lead in it; and for a position of this kind, of course, the modern dissatisfaction or boredom with realism cannot be expected to be taken very seriously.

Yet when we turn to that dissatisfaction itself and to the repudiation of realism in the name of modernism and in the interests of the latter's own developing apologia, we may well find that this other position is by no means dismissed as easily as all that. For the ideologues of modernism[5] do not indeed seek to refute the Lukács-Auerbach defense of the realistic mode in its own terms, which are primarily aesthetic and cognitive; rather they sense its weak link to be preaesthetic, part and parcel of its basic philosophical presuppositions. Thus, the target of their attack becomes the very concept of reality itself which is implied by the realistic aesthetic as Lukács or Auerbach outline it, the new position suggesting that what is intolerable for us today, aesthetically, about the so-called old-fashioned realism is to be accounted for by the inadmissible philosophical and metaphysical view of the world which underlies it and which it in its turn reinforces. The objection is thus, clearly, a critique of something like an *ideology of realism*, and charges that realism, by suggesting that representation is possible, and by encouraging an aesthetic of mimesis or imitation, tends to perpetuate a preconceived notion of some external reality to be imitated, and indeed, to foster a belief in the existence of some such common-sense everyday ordinary shared secular reality in the first place. Yet the great discoveries of modern science—relativity and the uncertainty principle—the movement in modern philosophy toward theories of models and various linguistic dimensions of reality, present-day French investigations of the category of representation itself—above all, however, the sheer accumulated weight and habit of the great modern works of art from the cubists and Joyce all the way to Beckett and Andy Warhol—all these things tend to confirm the idea that there is something quite naive, in a sense quite profoundly *un*realistic, and in the full sense of the word ideological, about the notion that reality is out there simply, quite objective and independent of us, and that knowing it involves the relatively unproblematical process of getting an adequate picture of it into our own heads.

Now I have to confess that I find both these positions—the defense of realism just as much as the denunciation of it—equally convincing, equally persuasive, equally true; so that, even though they would appear to be logically incompatible, I cannot persuade myself that they are as final as they look. But before I suggest a resolution that has seemed satisfactory to me, I want to remind you again of the reason we brought the subject up in the first place. The quarrel we have evoked is more fundamental, it seems to me, than a mere difference in aesthetic theories and positions (or else, if you prefer, such mere differences are perhaps themselves more fundamental than we have been accustomed to think): to be sure, in one sense, they simply correspond to differences in taste—it is clear that Lukács and Auerbach, for whatever reasons of background and upbringing and the like, deep down really don't like modern art. But again: perhaps what we call taste is not so simple either. I want to suggest that these two conflicting aesthetic positions correspond in the long run to two quite different cultures: there was a culture of realism, that of the nineteenth century—and a few of its inhabitants still survive here and there, native informants who provide us with very useful reports and testimony about its nature and values—and there is today a different culture altogether, that of modernism. Alongside these two, as we suggested earlier, there is yet a third kind, namely what we called in the most general way primitive or at least precapitalist, and whose products—incomprehensible to both modernist and realist aesthetics alike—we call myths or oral tales. So the limits of our own personal tastes have brought us to the point where we can see our need, not to pick and choose and assimilate selected objects from the older aesthetics or cultures into our own, but rather to step outside our own culture—outside the culture of modernism—entirely and to grasp its relationship to the others and its difference from them by means of some vaster historical and supracultural model.

Before I suggest one, however, I have an obligation, even in the most sketchy way, to complete my account of the quarrel between the realists and the modernists: what both leave out, you will already have guessed, is simply history itself. Both positions are completely ahistorical, and this in spite of the fact that *Mimesis* is a history, one of the few great contemporary literary histories we possess, and in spite of the fact, also, that Lukács is a Marxist (that the modernists are ahistorical will probably be less surprising, since after all by and large that is exactly what they set out to be). Briefly, I would suggest that realism—but also that desacralized, postmagical, common-sense, everyday, secular reality which is its object—is inseparable from the development of capitalism, the quantification by the market system of the older hierarchical or feudal or magical environment, and thus that both are intimately linked to the bourgeoisie as its product and its commodity (and this is, it seems to me, where Lukács himself is ahistorical, in not positing an exclusive link between realism and the life of commerce, in suggesting that a wholly different social order like that of socialism or communism will still want to maintain this particular—historically dated—mode of reality-construction). And when in our own time the bourgeoisie begins to decay as a class, in a world of social anomie and fragmentation, then that active and conquering mode of the representation of reality which is realism is no longer appropriate; indeed, in this new social world which is ours today, we can go so far as to say that the very object of realism itself—secular reality, objective reality—no longer exists either. Far from being the world's final and definitive face, it proves to have been simply one historical and cultural form among many others, such that one might argue a kind of ultimate paradox of reality itself: there once was such a thing as objective truth, objective reality, but now that "real world" is itself a thing of the past. Objective reality—or the various possible objective realities—are in other words, the function of genuine group existence or collective vitality; and when the dominant group disintegrates, so also does the certainty of some common truth or being. Thus the problem about realism articulates in the cultural realm that profound ambivalence that Marx and Engels have about the bourgeoisie in history in general: the secularization and systematization that capitalism brought about is both more brutal and alienating, *and* more humane and liberating, than the effects of any previous social system. Capitalism destroys genuine human relationships, but also for the first time liberates humankind from village idiocy and the tyranny and intolerance of tribal life. This simultaneous positive and negative coding of capitalism appears everywhere in the works of Marx, but most strikingly and programmatically perhaps in the *Communist Manifesto;* and it is this very complex and ambivalent, profoundly dialectical assessment of capitalism that is reflected in the notion of the historical necessity of capitalism as a stage; whereas in the literary realm it takes the form of the hesitations just expressed about the realistic mode that corresponds to classic nineteenth-century capitalism, hesitations which can be measured in all their ambiguity by the simultaneous assertion that realism is the most complex epistemological instrument yet devised for recording the truth of social reality, and also, at one and the same time, that it is a lie in the very form itself, the prototype of aesthetic false consciousness, the appearance that bourgeois ideology takes on in the realm of narrative literature.

The model I now want to submit to you derives no doubt ultimately from Engels also, who had it himself from Morgan's *Ancient Society,* who in turn drew it from a still older anthropological tradition. But the form in which I am going to use this model—which in essence is nothing more than the old classification of cultures and social forms into the triad of savage, barbarian, and civilized types—comes more directly from a recent French work that gives us the means of transforming his otherwise purely historical typology into a rather sensitive instrument of practical literary analysis.

Now I should preface all this by saying that I don't intend here to give anything like a complete account, let alone a critique, of this more recent work—the *Anti-Oedipus* of Gilles Deleuze and Félix Guattari[6]—around which there has been a great deal of controversy, and whose usefulness for us lies in its reintroduction of genuinely historical preoccupations into the hitherto resolutely a- or antihistorical problematics of structuralism. Deleuze and Guattari, indeed, give us a vision of history based once more firmly on the transformation of fundamental social forms, and on the correlation between shifts in meaning and conceptual categories, and the various types of socioeconomic infrastructures.

But I must at least explain that, as the book's title, the *Anti-Oedipus,* suggests, its official theme is the now familiar one of the reactionary character of Freud's doctrine of the Oedipus complex—a position for which Karl Kraus' famous aphorism might serve as a motto: "Psychoanalysis is that illness of which it believes itself to be the cure." I will content myself with observing that the violence with which this rather hysterical assertion is argued goes a long way toward making me suspect that Freud must have been right about the Oedipus complex in the first place. The real interest of the book, I would think, lies elsewhere, in its energetic attempt to synthesize a great number of contemporary intellectual trends and currents which have not all been confronted with one another before in quite so systematic a way. Here the alternate title, *Capitalism and Schizophrenia,* may suggest the approach, and indeed, within these pages, we find, alongside Freud and Marx, in both original and dubbed versions, phenomenological reflections on the body, Mumford on the city, linguistics and anthropological materials, studies of the commodity society, but also of kinship systems, theories of genetic codes, references to modern painting, and all this bathed in the familiarity of the great contemporary literary works like those of Beckett and Artaud, of which, of course, the term "schizophrenic" is meant to furnish both a description and a relatively new literary classification which is of no little practical interest.

Schizophrenia, however, has a more fundamental strategic value for Deleuze and Guattari, one which is very directly related to the historical typology with which we are ourselves concerned. For schizophrenia provides something like a zero degree against which we can assess the various—shall I call them more complex?—forms of human life, and by comparison serves as a kind of base line against which we can then measure and deconstruct the various determinate structures of individual and social reality which in their unending succession make up what we call history. Schizophrenia is, then, for Deleuze and Guattari something like the primordial flux that underlies existence itself; and clinically, to be sure, what characterizes the schizophrenic is this almost druglike dissolution of the bonds of time and of logic, the succession of one experiential moment after another without the organization and perspective imposed by the various kinds of abstract orders of meaning—whether individual or social—which we associate with ordinary daily life. So—to begin to construct our model—we can say that schizophrenia is something like a flux which is then, in the various social forms, ordered into some more elaborate, but also clearly, in one way or another, more repressive structure; to put it in the terminology of Deleuze, we will say that organized social life in one way or another then *codes* this initial flux, organizes it into ordered hierarchical meanings of one kind or another, makes the hallucinatory landscape suddenly fall into meaningful perspectives and become the place of work but also of the kinds of determinate values that characterize a given social order.

Now at this point we come upon our now-familiar triad of savage, barbarian, and civilized societies, and here also the approach of Deleuze and Guattari—this terminology of flux and codes—adds a handle that suddenly makes this rather antiquated piece of historical typology into a relatively sophisticated item of technical equipment. Let us remember what we needed to have our model do: we needed something like a unified field theory of the various hitherto wholly unrelated bodies of literature, something that would give us a terminology sufficiently responsive to deal in the same breath with primitive storytelling, precapitalist literatures, bourgeois realism, and the various modernisms of the present postindustrial world of late monopoly capital and of the superstate; such a common terminology or unified field theory ought then to allow us to see all these social and literary forms somehow as permutations of a common structure, or at least rearrangements of terms they hold in common.

Now it is clear that Deleuze and Guattari understood Engels' and Morgan's old historical triad in a fairly free and loose way: for Morgan, savagery was the first stage of human social life, which ran from the invention of language to that of the bow-and-arrow; barbarism is the next, more complex stage, in which agriculture and pottery are developed, and which is characterized above all by the use of metals; civilization, finally, begins with the invention of writing. Yet it seems to me that within the purely archaeological confines of the paradigm, there lies a deeper imaginative truth, and this poetic or Viconian vision of human societies is what is used and exploited by Deleuze and Guattari, and what presently interests us. On this view, peoples living in the state of savagery are those we generally call primitive cultures, neolithic tribes, village societies of all kinds, of which, in the golden age of American anthropology in the nineteenth century, the supreme example was the American Indian, and for which, particularly since Lévi-Strauss and *Tristes tropiques*, we have developed a nostalgia that does not shrink from an explicit invocation of Rousseau himself. Now barbarian society is somehow thought to be more complex than that of savagery, but also more dynamic, and, if I may put it that way, more fearsome and dangerous; it is not an accident that with barbarism we instinctively associate cruelty, whether it be on the level of the raids of nomadic predators or of the great and inhuman Asiatic city-states and oriental despotisms; and here cruelty—whether it be that of Attila or of Babylon—is a code-word for a war machine, that is to say, essentially for the poetic truth of metals and metalurgy. When we arrive at length at what is called civilization, it is clear that for Deleuze and Guattari, that is to be measured, not so much by inscriptions, as rather simply by the primacy of commerce, by the progress of a money economy and a market system, of organized production and exchange, in short, of what must sooner or later answer to the name of capitalism.

Let me quickly resume their hypothesis: the savage state is the moment of the coding of the original or primordial schizophrenic flux; in barbarism we have, then, to do with a more complex construction on this basis, which will be called an overcoding of it; under capitalism, reality undergoes a new type of operation or manipulation, and the desacralization and laicization, the quantification and rationalization of capitalism will be characterized by Deleuxe and Guattari precisely as a decoding of these earlier types of realities or code-constructions; and finally, our own time—whatever it may be thought to be as a separate social form in its own right, and it is obviously to this question on that we will want to return shortly—our own time is marked by nothing quite so much as a recoding of this henceforth decoded flux—by *attempts* to recode, to reinvent the sacred, to go back to myth (now understood in Frye's archetypal sense)—in brief, that whole host of recoding strategies which characterize the various modernisms, and of which the most revealing and authentic, as far as Deleuze and Guattari are concerned, is surely the emergence of schizophrenic literature, or the attempt to come to terms with the pure primordial flux itself.

Now I will try, not so much to explain these various moments, as to show why this way of thinking and talking about them may be of use to us (and if it is not, of course we have been mistaken in our choice of a model, and there remains nothing but to jettison this one and to find some paradigm better able to do the work we require from it).

The application of the terminology of flux and codes to primitive life and storytelling may be overhastily described in terms of symbolism or of Lévi-Strauss' conception of the "primitive mind," of that *pensée sauvage* or primitive thought which has not yet invented abstraction, for which the things of the outside world are, in themselves, meanings, or are indistinguishable from meanings. The medieval conception of the world as God's book, in which, for example, the beasts are so many sentences in a bestiary, is still close enough to this naive coding to convey its atmosphere to us. Yet in the primitive world, the world of the endless oral stories and of the simple and naively or, if you prefer, "naturally" coded flux, none of those things are really organized systematically; it is only when this omnipresent and decentered primitive coding is somehow ordered and the body of the world *territorialized*, as Deleuze and Guattari put it, that we find ourselves in the next stage of the social (but also the literary) order, namely that of barbarism, or of the despotic machine. Here the world-book is reorganized into what Lewis Mumford calls a megamachine, and the coded flux, now overcoded, acquires a center; certain signifiers become privileged over others in the same way that the despot himself gradually emerges from tribal indistinction to become the very center of the world and the meeting place of the four points of the compass; so a kind of awesome Forbidden City of language comes into being, which is not yet abstraction in our sense either, but far more aptly characterized, in my opinion, by that peculiar phenomenon we call allegory, and in which a single coded object or item of the outside world is suddenly overloaded with meaning, lifted up into a crucial element of a new and complicated object-language or overcoding erected on the basis of the older, simpler, "natural" sign-system. So in the passage from savagery to barbarism, it may be said that we pass from the *production* of coded elements to the *representation* of them, a representation that indicates itself and affirms its own splendor as privilege and as sacred meaning.

Civilization, capitalism, then come as an attempt to annul this barbaric overcoding, this despotic and luxurious sign-system erected parasitically upon the basis of the older "natural" codes; and the new social form, the capitalist one, thus aims at working its way back to some even more fundamental and uncoded reality—scientific or objective—behind the older signs. This changeover is, of course, a familiar historical story, of which we possess a number of different versions, and I have the obligation clearly enough to explain what advantages there are to us—in our practical work as teachers and students of literature—in the one I am proposing here. For we know that the ideologues of the rising bourgeoisie—in that movement called the Enlightenment—set themselves the explicit task of destroying religion and superstition, of extirpating the sacred in all of its forms; they were then quite intensely aware of the struggle to *decode*, even if they did not call it that and even if subsequent generations of a bourgeoisie complacently installed in power preferred to forget the now rather frightening corrosive power of that ambitious effort of negativity and destructive criticism.

So gradually the bourgeoise invents a more reassuring, more positive account of the transformation: in this view, the older superstitious remnants simply give way to the new positivities of modern *science;* or, if you prefer—now that a model-building science in our own time has seemed a less reliable ally—to the positive achievements of modern technology and invention. But both these accounts—that of the Enlightenment itself and that of positivism—are concerned more with abstract knowledge and control than with the facts of individual existence. From the point of view of our particular discipline, in other words, this positive science- or technology-oriented account of the secularization of the world seems more appropriate to the history of ideas than to narrative analysis. The dialectical version of the story—that of Hegel as well as of Marx and Engels—still seems to provide the most adequate synthesis of these older purely negative or purely positive accounts. Here the changeover is seen in terms of a passage from quality to quantity: in other words, the gradual substitution of a market economy for the older forms of barter or payment in kind amounts to the increasing primacy of the principle of generalized equivalence, as it is embodied in the money system. This means that where before there was a qualitative difference between the objects of production, between, say, shoes and beef, or oil paintings and leather belts or sacks of grain—all of them, in the older systems, coded in unique and qualitative ways, as objects of quite different and incommensurable desires, invested each with a unique libidinal content of its own—now suddenly they all find themselves absolutely interchangeable, and through equivalence and the common measure of a money system reduced to the gray tastelessness of abstraction.

The advantage now of the addition to this view of Deleuze and Guattari's concept of the decoded flux is that we will come to understand quantification, the pure equivalence of the exchange world, henceforth no longer as a reality in its own right, but rather as a process, an outer limit, a secular ideal, a kind of absence of quality that can never really be reached once and for all in any definitive form, but only approached in that infinite and teasing approximation of the asymptote to a curve with which it will never completely coincide. This is why the periodization of the ideologues of modernism, when they talk about the break with the classical novel, or the realistic novel or the traditional nineteenth-century novel, always proves so embarrassing, because, of course, as a positive phenomenon the classical novel is not there at all when you look for it, realism proving to be, as Darko Suvin put it, simply the zero degree of allegory itself.

Now I can give only two brief illustrations of the usefulness of the view for practical criticism of these so-called realistic novels. In the first place, it seems to me that the idea of a decoded flux for the first time gives content to the very formalistic suggestions—in the Jakobson-Tynianov theses on realism, for instance—that each realism constitutes a demystification of some preceding ideal or illusion. Obviously, the prototype for such a paradigm is the *Quijote* of Cervantes, but it would seem to me that the idea of realism as a decoding tends to direct our attention far more insistently to the very nature of the codes thus canceled, the older barbaric or savage signifiers thus dismantled; this view, in other words, forces us to attend far more closely to the page-by-page and incident-by-incident operations, whereby the novel effectuates this desacralization, thus effectively preserving us, at the same time, from any illusion that secular reality could be anything but provisional terminus of the narrative process.

The other point I want to make is the close identity between realism and historical thinking, an identity revealed by the model of decoded flux. It has been claimed—by the tenets of the rise-of-science explanation I mentioned a moment ago—that the new scientific values, particularly those of causality and causal explanation, are responsible for the new perspectivism shown by critics like Auerbach to constitute the very web of the new realistic narrative texture. Let me suggest, on the contrary, that causality is not a positive but rather a negative or privative concept: causality is simply the form taken by chronology itself when it falls into the world of quantification, of the indifferently equivalent and the decoded flux. Angus Fletcher's book *Allegory*, (1964) gives us an excellent picture of the literary phenomena that played the role in the older high allegory or barbaric overcoding of what will later become causality in realism: action by contiguity, emanation, magical contamination, the hypnotic and in-gathering spell of a kosmos or spatial form— all of these must then disappear from the decoded narrative, and the continuity of time must be dealt with in some more secular way, if it is not to decay and disintegrate back into the random sequence of unrelated instants which is the very nature of the primordial schizophrenic flux itself. Historical thinking, causality, is now a way of making things yield up their own meanings immanently, without any appeal to transcendental or magical outside forces; the process by which a single item deteriorates in time is now seen to be meaningful in itself, and when you have shown it, you have no further need of any external or transcendental hypotheses. Thus realism is par excellence the moment of the discovery of changing time, of the generation-by-generation and year-by-year dynamics of a new kind of social history. Realism is at one, I am tempted to say, with a world of *worn things*, things among which, of course, one must number people as well, and those discarded objects that are used-up human lives.

At length, as the nineteenth century itself wears on, we begin to detect signs of a kind of fatigue with the whole process of decoding; indeed, as the very memory of feudalism and the ancien régime grows dim, there appear perhaps to be fewer and fewer codes in the older sacred sense to serve as the object of such semiotic purification. This is, of course, the moment of the emergence of modernism, or rather, of the various modernisms, for the subsequent attempts to *recode* the henceforth decoded flux of the realistic, middle-class, secular era are many and varied, and we cannot hope even to give a sense of their variety here. So I will simply attempt to make one point, which seems to me absolutely fundamental for the analysis of modern literature, and which, to my mind, constitutes the most useful contribution to our future work of the model here under consideration. It is simply this: that it follows, from what we have said, and from the very notion of a recoding of secular reality or of the decoded flux, that all modernistic works are essentially simply canceled realistic ones, that they are, in other words, not apprehended directly, in terms of their own symbolic meanings, in terms of their own mythic or sacred immediacy, the way an older primitive or over-coded work would be, but rather indirectly only, by way of the relay of an imaginary realistic narrative of which the symbolic and modernistic one is then seen as a kind of stylization; and this is a type of reading, and a literary structure, utterly unlike anything hitherto known in the history of literature, and one to which we have been insufficienty attentive until now. Let me suggest, in other words, to put it very crudely, that when you make sense of something like Kafka's *Castle*, your process of doing so involves the substitution for that recoded flux of a realistic narrative of your own devising—one which may be framed in terms of Kafka's supposed personal experience—psychoanalytic, religious, or social—or in terms of your own, or in terms of some hypothetical destiny of "modern man" in general. Whatever the terms of the realistic narrative appealed to, however, I think it's axiomatic that the reading of such a work is always a two-stage affair, first, substituting a realistic hypothesis—in narrative form—then interpreting that secondary and invented or projected core narrative according to the procedures we reserved for the older realistic novel in general. And I suggest that this elaborate process is at work everywhere in our reception of contemporary works of art, all the way from those of Kafka down to, say, *The Exorcist*.

And since I mentioned chronology a moment ago, let me briefly use the fate of chronology in the new artistic milieu of the recoded flux to give you a clearer sense of what is meant by the process. It has been said, for instance, that in Robbe-Grillet's novel *La Jalousie*, chronology is abolished: there are two separate sets of events that ought to permit us to reestablish the basic facts of the story in their proper order, only they do not: "the crushing of the centipede which, in a novel telling a story, would provide a good point of reference around which to situate the other events in time, is [in fact] made to occur *before* the trip taken by Franck and A., *during* their trip, and *after* it."[7] Yet it would be wrong to conclude that Robbe-Grillet had really succeeded thereby in shaking our belief in chronology, and along with it, in that myth of a secular, objective, "realistic" reality of which it is a sign and a feature. On the contrary, as every reader of Robbe-Grillet knows, this kind of narrative exasperates our obsession with chronology to a veritable fever pitch, and the absence of any realistic "solution," far from being a return to the older non-causal narrative consciousness of primitive peoples, as in allegory for instance, in fact drives us only deeper into the contradictions of our own scientific and causal thought-modes. So it is quite wrong to say that Robbe-Grillet has abolished the story; on the contrary, we read *La Jalousie* by substituting for it a realistic version of one of the oldest stories in the world, and its force and value come from the paradoxical fact that by canceling it, the new novel tells this realistic story more forcefully than any genuinely realistic, old-fashioned, decoded narrative could.

Now from a sociological point of view it is clear why this had to happen with the breakdown of a homogeneous public, with the social fragmentation and anomie of the bourgeoisie itself, and also its refraction among the various national situations of Western or Nato capitalism, each of which then speaks its own private language and demands its own particular frame of reference. So the modern work comes gradually to be constructed as a kind of multipurpose object, Umberto Eco's so-called opera aperta or open form,[8] designed to be used by each subgroup after its own fashion and needs, so that its realistic core, that "concrete" emotion, but also situation, which we call, simply, *jealousy*, seems the most abstract and empty starting point of all, inasmuch as every private audience is obliged to recode it afresh in terms of its own sign-system.

The first conclusion one would draw from this peculiar historical and aesthetic situation is that Lukács (whose limits I hope I have already admitted) turns out in the long run to have been right after all about the nature of modernism: very far from a break with that older overstuffed Victorian bourgeois reality, it simply reinforces all the latter's basic presuppositions, only in a world so thoroughly subjectivized that they have been driven underground, beneath the surface of the work, forcing us to reconfirm the concept of a secular reality at the very moment when we imagine ourselves to be demolishing it.

This is a social and historical contradiction, but for the writer it is an agonizing dilemma, and perhaps that would be the most dramatic way of expressing what we have been trying to say. No one here, after all, seriously wants to return to the narrative mode of nineteenth-century realism; the latter's rightful inheritors are the writers of bestsellers, who—unlike Kafka or Robbe-Grillet—really do concern themselves with the basic secular problems of our existence, namely, money, power, position, sex, and all those humdrum daily preoccupations that continue to form the substance of our daily lives all the while that art literature considers them unworthy of its notice. I am not suggesting that we go back and read or write in the older way, only that in their heart of hearts—as the Goldwater people used to say—everyone knows that John O'Hara's novels still give a truer picture of the facts of life in the United States than anything of Hemingway or Faulkner, with all their tourist or magnolia exoticism. Yet—yet—the latter are palpably the greater writers. So we slowly begin to grasp the enormity of a historical situation in which the truth of our social life as a whole—Lukács would have said, as a totality—is increasingly irreconcilable with the aesthetic quality of language or of individual expression; of a situation about which it can be asserted that if we can make a work of art from our experience, if we can tell it in the form of a story, it is no longer true; and if we can grasp the truth about our world as totality, as something transcending mere individual experience, we can no longer make it accessible in narrative or literary form. So a strange malediction hangs over art in our time, and for the writer this dilemma is felt as an increasing (structural) incapacity to generalize or universalize private or lived experience. The dictates, not only of realism, but of narrative in general, tend gradually to restrict writing to sheer autobiography, at the same time that they transform even autobiographical discourse itself into one more private language among others: reduced to the telling of the truth of a private situation alone, that no longer engages the fate of a nation, but merely a single locality; and no longer even for that, but a particular neighborhood—and even that only as long as it still remains a neighborhood in the traditional, ethnic or ghetto, sense; even therein, speaking henceforth only for a specific family, and then not even for its older generations; at length reduced to a single household, and finally, within it, to a single gender. So little by little the writer is reduced to so private a speech that it is henceforth bereft of any public consequences or resonances, so that only symbolic recoding holds out the hope of saying something meaningful to a wider and more heterogeneous public. Yet, as we have seen, that new kind of meaning is quite different from the old one. But in this wholly subjectivized untruth, the modern writer nonetheless in another sense remains profoundly true and profoundly representative: for everyone else is equally locked into his or her private language, imprisoned in those serried ranks of monads that are the ultimate result of the social fragmentation inherent in our system.

Many are the images of this profound subjectivization and fragmentation of our social life, and of our very existences, in the world of late monopoly capitalism. Some strike terror and inspire us with a kind of metaphysical pathos at our condition, like that persona of Lautréamont sealed since birth in an airtight, soundproof membrane, dreaming of the shriek destined to rupture his isolation and to admit for the first time the cries of pain of the world outside.

All are, of course, figures, and it is a measure of our dilemma that we cannot convey the situation in other than a figurative way; yet some figures seem more liberating than others, and since we began with a reference to Plato, let us conclude with a Platonic vision, which was once itself the foundation of a metaphysic, but which now, today, and owing to historical developments quite unforeseeable in Plato's time, seems—like the gravest of all figures and metaphors—henceforth to have been intended in the most *literal* sense.

> Imagine [says Socrates], an underground chamber, like a cave
> with an entrance open to the daylight and running a long way
> underground. In this chamber are men who have been prisoners
> there since they were children, their legs and necks being so fastened
> that they can only look straight ahead of them and cannot turn their
> heads. Behind them and above them a fire is burning, and between
> the fire and the prisoners runs a road, in front of which a curtain-
> wall has been built, like the screen at puppet-shows....Imagine fur-
> ther that there are men carrying all sorts of artefacts along behind
> the curtain-wall, including figures of men and animals made of wood
> and stone and other materials...
>
> An odd picture [responds Socrates' listener] and an odd sort of
> prisoner.
>
> They are drawn from life, I replied. For tell me, do you think our
> prisoners could see anything of themselves or their fellows save the
> shadows thrown by the fire upon the wall of the cave opposite?[9]

There are, of course, ways of breaking out of this isolation, but they are not literary ways and require complete and thoroughgoing transformation of our economic and social system, and the invention of new forms of collective living. Our task—specialists that we are in the reflections of things—is a more patient and modest, more diagnostic one. Yet even such a task as the analysis of literature and culture will come to nothing unless we keep the knowledge of our own historical situation vividly present to us: for we are least of all, in our position, entitled to the claim that we did not understand, that we thought all those things were real, that we had no way of knowing we were living in a cave.

Chapter 7
Reflections on the Brecht-Lukács Debate

It is not only political history that those who ignore are condemned to repeat. A host of recent "post-Marxisms" document the truth of the assertion that attempts to "go beyond" Marxism typically end by reinventing older pre-Marxist positions (from the recurrent neo-Kantian revivals, to the most recent "Nietzschean" returns through Hume and Hobbes all the way back to the Pre-Socratics). Even within Marxism itself, the terms of the problems, if not their solutions, are numbered in advance, and the older controversies— Marx versus Bakunin, Lenin versus Luxemburg, the national questions, the agrarian question, the dictatorship of the proletariat—rise up to haunt those who thought we could now go on to something else and leave the past behind us.

Nowhere has this "return of the repressed" been more dramatic than in the aesthetic conflict between realism and modernism, whose navigation and renegotiation is still unavoidable for us today, even though we may feel that each position is in some sense right and yet that neither is any longer wholly acceptable. The dispute is itself older than Marxism, and in a longer perspective may be said to be a contemporary political replay of the seventeenth century *Querelle des anciens et des modernes*, in which, for the first time, aesthetics came face to face with the dilemmas of historicity.

Within the Marxism of this century, the precipitant of the controversy over realism and modernism was the living fact and persisting influence of expressionism among the writers of the German Left in the 1920s and 30s. An implacable ideological denunciation by Lukács in 1934 set the stage for the series of interconnected debates and exchanges between Bloch, Lukács,

Brecht, Benjamin, and Adorno generally referred to as the "realism debate." Much of the fascination of these jousts, indeed, comes from the internal dynamism by which all the logical possibilities are rapidly generated in turn, so that it quickly extends beyond the local phenomenon of expressionism, and even beyond the ideal type of realism itself, to draw within its scope the problems of popular art, naturalism, socialist realism, avant-gardism, media, and finally modernism—political and nonpolitical—in general. Today, many of its fundamental themes and concerns have been transmitted by the Frankfurt School, and in particular by Marcuse, to the student and antiwar movements of the 1960s, while the revival of Brecht has ensured their propagation among political modernisms of the kind exemplified by the *Tel Quel* group.

The legacy of German expressionism provided a more propitious framework for the development of a major debate within Marxism than its contemporary French counterpart, surrealism, was to do. For in the writings of the surrealists, and in particular of Breton, the problem of realism largely fails to arise—in the first instance owing to their initial repudiation of the novel as a form. For their principal adversary, Jean-Paul Sartre—the only important writer of his generation not to have passed through surrealism's tutelage, and whose notion of "commitment" *(engagement)* Adorno was later to take as the very prototype of a political aesthetic—the realism/modernism dilemma did not arise either, but for the opposite reason: because of Sartre's preliminary exclusion of poetry and the lyric from his account of the nature and function of literature in general (in *What Is Literature?* [1948]). Thus in France, until that second wave of modernism (or postmodernism) represented by the *nouveau roman* and the *nouvelle vague, Tel Quel* and "structuralism," the terrain for which realism and modernism were elsewhere so bitterly to contend—that of *narrative*—was effectively divided up between them in advance, as though in amicable separation. If the problem of narrative does not loom large in the earlier debate, that is in part because Lukács' principal exhibits were novels, while Brecht's main field of activity was the theater. The increasing importance, in turn, of film in artistic production since the time of these debates (witness the frequent juxtapositions of Brecht and Godard) likewise suggests that structural differences in medium and in genre may play a larger part in compounding the dilemmas of the realism/modernism controversy than its earliest participants were willing to admit.

More than this, the history of aesthetics itself suggests that some of the more paradoxical turns in the Marxist debate within German culture spring from contradictions within the very concept of realism, an uneasily different quantity from such traditional aesthetic categories as comedy and tragedy, or lyric, epic, and dramatic. The latter—whatever social functionality may be invoked for them in this or that philosophical system—are purely aesthetic concepts, which may be analyzed and evaluated without any reference outside the phenomenon of beauty or the activity of artistic play (traditionally the terms in which the "asethetic" has been isolated and constituted as a separate realm or function in its own right). The originality of the concept of realism, however, lies in its claim to cognitive as well as aesthetic status. A new value, contemporaneous with the secularization of the world under capitalism, the ideal of realism presupposes a form of aesthetic experience that yet lays claim to a binding relationship to the real itself, that is to say, to those realms of knowledge and praxis that had traditionally been differentiated from the realm of the aesthetic, with its disinterested judgments and its constitution as sheer appearance. But it is extremely difficult to do justice to both these properties of realism simultaneously. In practice, an overemphasis on its cognitive function often leads to a naïve denial of the necessarily fictive character of artistic discourse or even to iconoclastic calls for the "end of art" in the name of political militancy. At the other pole of this conceptual tension, the emphasis of theorists like Gombrich or Barthes on the "techniques" whereby an "illusion" of reality or *effet de réel* is achieved, tends surreptitiously to transform the "reality" of realism into appearance and to undermine that affirmation of its own truth—or referential—value, by which it differentiates itself from other types of literature. (Among the many secret dramas of Lukács' later work is surely to be counted the adeptness with which he walks this particular tightrope, from which, even at his most ideological or "formalistic," he never quite falls.)

This is not to say that the concept of modernism, realism's historical counterpart and its dialectical mirror image, is not equally contradictory.[1] and in ways that it will be instructive to juxtapose to the contradictions of realism itself. For the moment, suffice it to observe that neither of these sets of contradictions can be fully understood, unless they are replaced within the broader context of the crisis of historicity itself, and numbered among the dilemmas a dialectical criticism faces when it tries to make ordinary language function simultaneously on two mutually exclusive registers: the absolute (in which case realism and modernism veer toward timeless abstractions like the lyric or the comic), and the relative (in which case they inexorably revert to the narrow confines of an antiquarian nomenclature, whose use is restricted to specific literary movements in the past). Language, however, does not submit peacefully to the attempt to use its terms dialectically—that is, as relative and sometimes even extinct concepts from an archaeological past, which nonetheless continue to transmit faint but absolute claims upon us.

Meanwhile, poststructuralism has added yet a different kind of parameter to the realism/modernism controversy, one which—like the question of narrative and the problems of historicity—was implicit in the original exchange but scarcely articulated or thematized as such. The assimilation of realism as a value to the old philosophilcal concept of mimesis by such writers as Foucault, Derrida, Lyotard, and Deleuze has reformulated the realism/modernism debate in terms of a Platonic attack on the ideological effects of representation. In this new (and old) philosophical polemic, the stakes of the original discussion find themselves unexpectedly elevated, and their issues—once largely political in focus—begin to take on metaphysical (or antimetaphysical) implications. Such philosophical artillery is, of course, intended to increase the defensiveness of the defenders or realism; yet believe we will not fully be able to assess the consequences of the attack on representation, and of poststructuralism generally, until we are able to situate its own work within the field of the theory of ideology itself.

It is at any rate clear that the realism/modernism controversy loses its interest if one side is programmed to win in advance. The Brecht-Lukács debate alone is one of those rare confrontations in which both adversaries are of equal stature, both of incomparable significance for the development of contemporary Marxism, the one a major artist and probably the greatest literary figure to have been produced by the Communist movement, the other a central philosopher of the age and heir to the whole German philosophical tradition, with its unique emphasis on aesthetics as a discipline. It is true that in recent accounts of their opposition,[2] Brecht has tended to get the better of Lukács, the former's "plebeian" style and Schweikian identifications proving currently more attractive than the "mandarin" culture to which the latter appealed.[3] In these versions, Lukács is typically treated as a professor, a revisionist, a Stalinist—in general "in the same way as the brave Moses Mendelssohn in Lessing's time treated Spinoza as a 'dead dog,'" as Marx described the standard view of Hegel current among his radical contemporaries.

To the degree to which Lukács single-handedly turned the expressionism debate around into a discussion of realism, and forced the defenders of the former to fight on his own ground and in his own terms, their annoyance with him was understandable (Brecht's own animosity toward him comes through particularly vividly in these pages). On the other hand, such meddling interference was at one with everything that made Lukács a major figure in twentieth-century Marxism—in particular his lifelong insistence on the crucial significance of literature and culture in any revolutionary politics. His fundamental contribution here was the development of a theory of mediations that could reveal the political and ideological content of what had hitherto seemed purely formal aesthetic phenomena. One of the most famous instances was his "decoding" of the static descriptions of naturalism in terms of reification.[4] Yet at the same time, it was precisely this line of research—itself an implicit critique and repudiation of traditional content analysis—that was responsible for Brecht's characterization of Lukács' method as *formalistic:* by which he meant the latter's unwarranted confidence in the possibility of deducing political and ideological positions from a protocol of purely formal properties of a work of art. The reproach sprang from Brecht's experience as a man of the theater, in which he constructed an aesthetic of performance and a view of the work of art in situation that was in diametric contrast to the solitary reading and individualized bourgeois public of Lukács' privileged object of study, the novel. Can Brecht then be enlisted in current campaigns against the very notion of mediation? It is probably best to take Brecht's attack on Lukács' formalism (along with the Brechtian watchword of *plumpes Denken)* at a somewhat less philosophical and more practical level, as a therapeutic warning against the permanent temptation of idealism present in any ideological analysis as such, the professional proclivity of intellectuals for methods that need no external verification. There would then be *two* idealisms: one, the common-or-garden variety to be found in religion, metaphysics, and literalism; the other a repressed and unconscious danger of idealism within Marxism itself, inherent in the very ideal of science itself in a world so deeply marked by the division of mental and manual labor. To that danger the intellectual and the scientist can never sufficiently be alerted. At the same time, Lukács' work on mediation, rudimentary as at times it may have been, can on another reading be enlisted as a precursor of the most interesting work in the field of ideological analysis today—that which, assimilating the findings of psychoanalysis and of semiotics, seeks to construct a model of the text as a complex and symbolic ideological act. The reproach of "formalism," whose relevance to Lukács' own practice is only too evident, may consequently have a wider extension to present-day research and speculation.

The charge of "formalism" was only one item of Brecht's attack on Lukács' position; its corollary and obverse was indignation at the ideological judgments which the latter used his method to substantiate. The primary exhibit at the time was Lukács' denunciation of alleged links between expressionism and trends within Social-Democracy (in particular the USPD), not to speak of fascism, which launched the realism debate in the German emigration and which Ernst Bloch's essay was designed to refute in some detail. Nothing has, of course, more effectively discredited Marxism than the practice of affixing instant class labels (generally "petty bourgeois") to textual or intellectual objects; nor will the most hardened apologist for Lukács want to deny that of the many Lukácses conceivable, this particular one—epitomized in the shrill and outrageous postscript to *Die Zersörung der Vernunft*—is the least worthy of rehabilitation. But abuse of class ascription should not lead to overreaction and mere abandonment of it. In fact, ideological analysis is inconceivable without a conception of the "ultimately determining instance" of social class. What is really wrong with Lukács' analyses is not too frequent and facile a reference to social class, but rather to incomplete and intermittent a sense of the relationship of class ideology. A case in point is one of the more notorious of Lukács' basic concepts, that of "decadence"—which he often associates with fascism, but even more persistently with modern art and literature in general. The concept of decadence is the equivalent in the aesthetic realm of that of "false consciousness" in the domain of traditional ideological analysis. Both suffer from the same defect: the common presupposition that in the world of culture and society such a thing as pure error is possible. They imply, in other words, that works of art or systems of philosophy are conceivable which have no content, and are therefore to be denounced for failing to grapple with the "serious" issues of the day, indeed distracting from them. In the iconography of the political art of the 1920s and 30s, the "index" of such culpable and vacuous decadence was the champagne glass and top hat of the idle rich, making the rounds of an eternal night-club circuit. Yet even Scott Fitzgerald and Drieu la Rochelle are more complicated than that, and from our present-day vantage point, disposing of the more complex instruments of psychoanalysis (in particular the concepts of repression and denial, or *Verneinung)*, even those who might wish to sustain Lukács' hostile verdict on modernism would necessarily insist on the existence of a repressed social content even in those modern works that seem most innocent of it. Modernism would then not so much be a way of avoiding social content—in any case an impossibility for beings like ourselves who are "condemned" to history and to the implacable sociability of even the most apparently private of our experiences—but rather of managing and containing it, secluding it out of sight in the very form itself, by means of specific techniques of framing and displacement which can be identified with some precision. If so, Lukács' summary dismissal of "decadent" works of art should yield to an interrogation of their buried social and political content.

The fundamental weakness in Lukács' view of the relationship of art and ideology surely finds its ultimate explanation in his politics. What is usually called his "Stalinism" can, on closer examination, be separated into two quite distinct problems. The charge that he was complicit with a bureaucratic apparatus and exercised a kind of literary terrorism (particularly against political modernists, for example, of the Proletkult variety) is belied by his resistance in the Moscow of the 30s and 40s to what was later to be known as Zhdanovism—that form of socialist realism which he disliked as much as Western modernism but was obviously less free to attack openly. "Naturalism" was his pejorative code word for it at the time. Indeed, the structural and historical identification for which he argued between the symbolic techniques of modernism and the "bad immediacy" of a photographic naturalism was one of his most profound dialectical insights. As for his continuing party membership, which he called his "entry ticket to history," the tragic fate and wasted talents of so many oppositional Marxists of his generation, like Korsch and Reich, are powerful arguments for the relative rationality of Lukács' choice—one, of course, that he shared with Brecht. A more serious problem is posed by the "popular frontism" of his aesthetic theory. That betokened a formal mean between a modernistic subjectivism and an overly objectivistic naturalism, a mean which, like most Aristotelian strategies of moderation, has never aroused much intellectual excitement. Even Lukács' most devoted supporters failed to evince much enthusiasm for it. So far as the political alliance between revolutionary forces and the progressive sections of the bourgeoisie went, it was rather Stalin who belatedly authorized a version of the policy that Lukács had advocated in the "Blum Theses" of 1928-29, which foresaw a first-stage, democratic revolution against the fascist dictatorship in Hungary, prior to any socialist revolution. Yet it is precisely that distinction, between an antifascist and an anticapitalist strategy, that seems less easy to maintain today and less immediately attractive a political program over wide areas of a "free world" in which military dictatorships and "emergency regimes" are the order of the day—indeed multiplying precisely to the degree that genuine social revolution becomes a real possibility. From our present perspective, nazism itself, with its charismatic leader and unique exploitation of a nascent communications technology in the widest sense of the term (including transportation and autobahns as well as radio and television), now seems to represent a transitional and special combination of historical circumstances not likely to recur as such; whereas routine torture and the institutionalization of counterinsurgency techniques have proved perfectly consistent with the kind of parliamentary democracy that used to be distinguished from fascism. Under the hegemony of the multinational corporations and their "world system," the very possibility of a progressive bourgeois culture is problematic—a doubt that obviously strikes at the very foundation of Lukács' aesthetic.

Finally, the preoccupations of our own period have seemed to reveal in Lukács' work the shadow of a literary dictatorship somewhat different in kind from the attempts to prescribe a certain type of production which were denounced by Brecht. It is Lucács as a partisan, less of a specific artistic style than of a particular critical method, who is the focus of new polemics today—an atmosphere in which his work has found itself regarded by admirers and opponents alike as a monument to old-fashioned content-analysis. There is some irony in this transformation of the name of the author of *History and Class Consciousness* into a signal not unlike that emitted by the names of Belinsky and Chernyshevsky in an earlier period of Marxist aesthetics. Lukács' own critical practice is in fact very much genre-oriented, and committed to the mediation of the various forms of literary discourse, so that it is a mistake to enlist him in the cause of a naïve mimetic position that encourages us to discuss the events or characters of a novel in the same way we would look at "real" ones. On the other hand, insofar as his critical practice implies the ultimate possibility of some full and nonproblematical "representation of reality," Lukácsian realism can be said to give aid and comfort to a documentary and sociological approach to literature which is correctly enough thought to be antagonistic to more recent methods of construing the narrative text as a free play of signifiers. Yet these apparently irreconcilable positions may prove to be two distinct and equally indispensable moments of the hermeneutic process itself—a first naïve "belief" in the density or presence of novelistic representation, and later "bracketing" of that experience in which the necessary distance of all language from what it claims to represent—its substitutions and displacements—is explored. At any rate, it is clear that as long as Lukács is used as a rallying cry (or bogeyman) in this particular methodological conflict, there is not much likelihood of any measured assessment of his work as a whole.

Brecht, meanwhile, is certainly much more easily rewritten in terms of the concerns of the present, in which he seems to address us directly in an unmediated voice. His attack on Lukács' formalism is only one aspect of a much more complex and interesting stand on realism in general, to which it is surely no disservice to observe a few of the features that must seem dated to us today. In particular, Brecht's aesthetic, and his way of framing the problems of realism, are intimately bound up with a conception of science that it would be wrong to identify with the more scientistic currents in contemporary Marxism (for example, the work of Althusser and Colletti). For Colletti, science is an epistemological concept and a form of abstract knowledge, and the pursuit of a Marxian "science" is closely linked to recent developments in the historiography of science—the findings of scholars like Koyré, Bachelard, and Kuhn. For Brecht, however, "science" is far less a matter of knowledge and epistemology than it is a sheer experiment and of practical, well-nigh manual activity. His is more an ideal of popular mechanics, technology, the home chemical set, and the tinkering of a Galileo, rather than one of "epistēmēs" or "paradigms" in scientific discourse. Brecht's particular vision of science was for him the means of annulling the separation between physical and mental activity and the fundamental division of labor (not least that between worker and intellectual) that resulted from it: it puts knowing the world back together with changing the world, and at the same time unites an ideal of praxis with a conception of production. The reunion of "science" and practical, change-oriented activity—not without its influence on the Brecht-Benjamin analysis of the media, as we will see in a moment— thus transforms the process of "knowing" the world into a source of delight or pleasure in its own right; and this is the fundamental step in the construction of a properly Brechtian aesthetics. For it restores to "realistic" art that principle of play and genuine aesthetic gratification which the relatively more passive and cognitive aesthetic of Lukács had seemed to replace with the grim duty of a proper reflection of the world. The age-old dilemmas of a didactic theory of art (to teach or to please?) are thereby also overcome, and in a world where science is experiment and play, where knowing and doing alike are forms of production, stimulating in their own right, a didactic art may now be imagined in which learning and pleasure are no longer separate from each other. In the Brechtian aesthetic, indeed, the idea of realism is not a purely artistic and formal category, but rather governs the relationship of the work of art to reality itself, characterizing a particular stance toward it. The spirit of realism designates an active, curious, experimental, subversive—in word, *scientific*—attitude toward social institutions and the material world; and the "realistic" work of art is therefore one that encourages and disseminates this attitude, yet not merely in a flat or mimetic way or along the lines of imitation alone. Indeed, the "realistic" work of art is one in which "realistic" and experimental attitudes are tried out, not only between its characters and their fictive realities, but also between the audience and the work itself, and—not least significant—between the writer and his or her own materials and techniques. The threefold dimensions of such a practice of "realism" clearly explode the purely representational categories of the traditional mimetic work.

What Brecht called science is thus in a larger sense a figure for non-alienated production in general. It is what Bloch would call a Utopian emblem of the reunified and satisfying praxis of a world that has left alienation and the division of labor behind it. The originality of the Brechtian vision may be judged by juxtaposing his figure of science with the more conventional image of art and the artist which, particularly in bourgeois literature, has traditionally had this Utopian function. At the same time, it must also be asked whether Brecht's vision of science is still available to us as a figure today, or whether it does not itself reflect a relatively primitive stage in what has now come to be known as the second industrial revolution. Seen in this perspective, the Brechtian delight in "science" is rather of a piece with Lenin's definition of communism as "the Soviets plus electrification," or Diego Rivera's grandiose Rockefeller Center mural (repainted for Bellas Artes) in which, at the intersection of microcosm and macrocosm, the massive hands of Soviet New Man grasp and move the very levers of creation.

Together with his condemnation of Lukács' formalism and his conception of a union of science and aesthetics in the didactic work of art, there is yet a third strain in Brecht's thinking—in many ways the most influential—which deserves attention. This is, of course, his fundamental notion of *Verfremdung*. It is the so-called estrangement effect which is most often invoked to sanction theories of political modernism today, such as that of the *Tel Quel* group.[5] The practice of estrangement—staging phenomena in such a way that what had seemed natural and immutable in them is now tangibly revealed to be historical, and thus the object of revolutionary change—has long seemed to provide an outlet from the dead end of agitational didacticism in which so much of the political art of the past remains confined. At the same time it allows a triumphant reappropriation and a materialist regrounding of the dominant ideology of modernism (the Russian Formalist "making strange,"

Pound's "make it new," the emphasis of all the historical varieties of modernism on the vocation of art to alter and renew perception as such) from the ends of a revolutionary politics. Today, traditional realism—the canon defended by Lukács, but also old-fashioned political art of the socialist realist type—is often assimilated to classical ideologies of representation and to the practice of "closed form," whereas even bourgeois modernism (Kristeva's models are Lautréamont and Mallarmé) is said to be revolutionary precisely to the degree to which it calls the older formal values and practices into question and produces itself as an open "text." Whatever objections may be made to this aesthetic of political modernism—and we will reserve a fundamental one for our discussion of similar views of Adorno—it would seem most difficult to associate Brecht with it. Not only was the author of "On Abstract Painting"[6] as hostile to purely formal experimentation as was Lukács himself; that might be held to be a historical or generational accident, and simply to spell out the limits of Brecht's personal tastes. What is more serious is that his attack on the formalism of Lukács' literary analyses remains binding on the quite different attempts of the political modernists to make ideological judgments (revolutionary/bourgeois) on the basis of the purely formal characteristics of closed or open forms, "naturality," effacement of the traces of production in the work, and so forth. For example, it is certainly the case that a belief in the natural is ideological and that much of bourgeois art has worked to perpetuate such a belief, not only in its content but through the experience of its forms as well. Yet in different historical circumstances the idea of nature was once a subversive concept with a genuinely revolutionary function, and only the analysis of the concrete historical and cultural conjuncture can tell us whether, in the postnatural world of late capitalism, the categories of nature may not have acquired such a critical charge again.

It is time, indeed, to make an assessment of those fundamental changes that have taken place in capitalism and its culture since the period when Brecht and Lukács spelled out their options for a Marxist aesthetics and a Marxian conception of realism. What has already been said about the transitional character of nazism—a development which has done much to date many of Lukács' basic positions—is not without its effect on those of Brecht as well. Here it is necessary to emphasize the inextricable relationship between Brecht's aesthetic and the analysis of the media and its revolutionary possibilities worked out jointly by him and Walter Benjamin, and most widely accessible in the latter's well-known essay "The Work of Art in the Age of Mechanical Reproduction."[7] For Brecht and Benjamin had not yet begun to feel the full force and constriction of that stark alternative between a mass audience or media culture, and a minority "elite" modernism, in which our thinking about aesthetics today is inevitably locked. Rather, they foresaw a revolutionary utilization of communications technology such that the most striking advances in artistic technique—effects such as those of "montage," for instance, which today we tend to associate almost exclusively with modernism as such—could at once be harnessed to politicizing and didactic purposes. Brecht's conception of "realism" is thus not complete without this perspective in which the artist is able to use the most complex, modern technology in addressing the widest popular public. Yet if nazism itself corresponds to an early and still relatively primitive stage in the emergence of the media, so does Benjamin's cultural strategy for attacking it, and in particular his conception of an art that would be revolutionary precisely to the degree to which it was technically (technologically) "advanced." In the increasingly "total system" of the media societies today, we can unfortunately no longer share this optimism. Without it, however, the project of a specifically political modernism becomes indistinguishable from all the other kinds—modernism, among other things, being characterized by its consciousness of an absent public.

In other words, the fundamental difference between our own situation and that of the 1930s is the emergence in full-blown and definitive form of that ultimate transformation of late monopoly capitalism variously known as the *sociéte de consommation* or as postindustrial society. This is the historical stage reflected by Adorno's two postwar essays, so different in emphasis from the prewar materials. It may appear easy enough in retrospect to identify his repudiation of *both* Lukács *and* Brecht, on the grounds of their political praxis, as a characteristic example of an anticommunism now outmoded with the Cold War itself. More relevant in the present context, however, is the Frankfurt School's premise of a "total system," which expressed Adorno's and Horkheimer's sense of the increasingly closed organization of the world into a seamless web of media technology, multinational corporations, and international bureaucratic control.[8] Whatever the theoretical merits of the idea of the "total system"—and it would seem to me that where it does not lead out of politics altogether, it encourages the revival of an anarchist opposition to Marxism itself and can also be used as a justification for terrorism—we may at least agree with Adorno that in the cultural realm, the all-pervasiveness of the system, with its "culture-industry" or (Enzensberger's variant) its "consciousness-industry," makes for an unpropitious climate for any of the older, simpler forms of oppositional art, whether it be that proposed by Lukács, that produced by Brecht, or indeed those celebrated in their different ways by Benjamin and by Bloch. The system has a power to co-opt and to defuse even the most potentially dangerous forms of political art by transforming them into cultural commodities (witness, if further proof be needed, the grisly example of the burgeoning Brecht-Industrie itself!). On the other hand, it cannot be said that Adorno's rather astonishing "resolution" of the problem is any more satisfactory: he proposes the classical stage of high modernism itself as the very prototype of the most "genuinely" political art ("this is not a time for political art, but politics has migrated into autonomous art, and nowhere more so than where it seems to be politically dead"[9]) and suggests that it is therefore Beckett who is the most truly revolutionary artist of our time. To be sure, some of Adorno's most remarkable analyses—for instance, his discussion of Schoenberg and the twelve-tone system in the *Philosophy of Modern Music*—document his assertion that the greatest modern art, even the most apparently un- or antipolitical, in reality holds up a mirror to the "total system" of late capitalism. Yet in retrospect, this now seems a most unexpected revival of a Lukács-type "reflection theory" of aesthetics, under the spell of a political and historical despair that plagues both houses and finds praxis henceforth unimaginable. What is ultimately fatal to this new and finally itself once more antipolitical revival of the ideology of modernism is less the equivocal rhetoric of Adorno's attack on Lukács or the partiality of his reading of Brecht,[10] than very precisely the fate of modernism in consumer society itself. For what was once an oppositional and antisocial phenomenon in the early years of the century, has today become the dominant style of commodity production and an indispensable component in the machinery of the latter's ever more rapid and demanding reproduction of itself. That Schoenberg's Hollywood pupils used their advanced techniques to write movie music, that the masterpieces of the most recent schools of American painting are now sought to embellish the splendid new structures of the great insurance companies and multinational banks (themselves the work of the most talented and "advanced" modern architects), are but the external symptoms of a situation in which a once scandalous "perceptual art" has found a social and economic function in supplying the styling changes necessary to the *société de consommation* of the present.

The final aspect of the contemporary situation relevant to our subject concerns the changes that have taken place within socialism itself since the publication of the expressionism debate in *Das Wort* some forty years ago. If the central problem of a political art under capitalism is that of co-optation, one of the crucial issues of culture in a socialist framework must surely remain that of what Ernst Bloch calls the *Erbe:* the question of the uses of the world's cultural past in what will increasingly be a single international culture of the future, and of the place and effects of diverse heritages in a society intent on building socialism. Bloch's formulation of the problem is obviously a strategic means of transforming Lukács' narrow polemics—which were limited to the realistic novelists of the European bourgeois tradition—and of enlarging the framework of the debate to include the immense variety of popular or peasant, precapitalist or "primitive" arts. It should be understood in the context of his monumental attempt to reinvent the concept of Utopia for Marxism and to free it from the objections correction made by Marx and Engels themselves to the "Utopian socialism" of Saint-Simon, Owen, and Fourier. Bloch's Utopian principle aims at jarring socialist thought loose from its narrow self-definition in terms that essentially prolong the categories of capitalism itself, whether by negation or adoption (terms like industrialization, centralization, progress, technology, and even production itself, which tend to impose their own social limitations and options on those who work with them). Where Lukács' cultural thinking emphasizes the continuities between the bourgeois order and that which is to develop out of it, Bloch's priorities suggest the need to think of the "transition to socialism" in terms of radical difference, of a more absolute break with that particular past, perhaps of a renewal or recovery of the truth of more ancient social forms. The newer Marxist anthropology, indeed, reminds us—from within our "total system"—of the absolute difference of older precapitalist and tribal societies; and at a historical moment when such an interest in a much more remote past seems less likely to give rise to the sentimentalizing and populistic myths that Marxism had to combat in the late nineteenth and early twentieth centuries, the memory of precapitalist societies may now become a vital element of Bloch's Utopian principle and of the invention of the future. Politically, the classical Marxian notion of the necessity, during the transition to socialism, of a "dictatorship of the proletariat"—that is, a withdrawal of effective power from those with a vested interest in the reestablishment of the old order—has surely not become outmoded. Yet it may emerge conceptually transformed as soon as we think of it together with the necessity for a cultural revolution that involves collective reeducation of all the classes. This is the perspective in which Lukács' emphasis on the great bourgeois novelists seems most adequate to the task, but it is one in which the antibourgeois thrust of the great modernisms also appears inappropriate. It is then that Bloch's mediation on the *Erbe*, on the repressed cultural difference of the past and the Utopian principle of the invention of a radically different future, will for the first time come into its own, at a point when the conflict between realism and modernism recedes behind us.

But surely in the West, and perhaps elsewhere as well, that point is still beyond us. In our present cultural situation, if anything, both alternatives of realism and of modernism seem intolerable to us: realism because its forms revive older experiences of a kind of social life (the classical inner city, the traditional opposition city/country) that is no longer with us in the already decaying future of consumer society; modernism because its contradictions have proved in practice even more acute than those of realism. An aesthetic of novelty today—already enthroned as the dominant critical and formal ideology—must seek desperately to renew itself by ever more rapid rotations of its own axis, modernism seeking to become postmodernism without ceasing to be modern. Thus today we witness the spectacle of a predictable return, after abstraction has itself become a tired convention, to figurative art, but this time to a figurative art—so-called hyperrealism or photorealism—that turns out to be the representation, not of things themselves, but of the latter's photographs: a representational art that is really "about" art itself! In literature, meanwhile, amid a weariness with plotless or poetic fiction, a return to intrigue is achieved, not by the latter's rediscovery, but rather by the pastiche of older narratives and depersonalized imitation of traditional voices, similar to Stravinsky's pastiche of the classics criticized by Adorno's *Philosophy of Music.*

In these circumstances, indeed, there is some question whether the ultimate renewal of modernism, the final dialectical subversion of the now automatized conventions of an aesthetics of perceptual revolution, might not simply be... realism itself! For when modernism and its accompanying techniques of "estrangement" have become the dominant style whereby the consumer is reconciled with capitalism, the habit of fragmentation itself needs to be "estranged" and corrected by a more totalizing way of viewing phenomena.[11] In an unexpected dénouement, it may be Lukács—wrong as he might have been in the 1930s—who has some provisional last word for us today. Yet this particular Lukács, if he be imaginable, would be one for whom the concept of realism has been rewritten in terms of the categories of *History and Class Consciousness*, in particular those of reification and totality. Unlike the more familiar concept of alienation, a process that pertains to activity and in particular to work (dissociating workers from their labor, their product, their fellow workers, and ultimately from their very "species being" itself), reification is a process that affects our cognitive relationship with the social totality. It is a disease of that mapping function whereby the individual subject projects and models his or her insertion into the collectivity. The reification of late capitalism—the transformation of human relations into an appearance of relationships between things—renders society opaque: it is the lived source of the mystifications on which ideology is based and by which domination and exploitation are legitimized. Since the fundamental structure of the social "totality" is a set of class relationships—an antagonistic structure such that the various social classes define themselves in terms of that antagonism and by opposition with one another—reification necessarily obscures the class character of that structure, and is accompanied, not only by anomie, but also by that increasing confusion as to the nature and even the existence of social classes which can be abundantly observed in all the "advanced" capitalist countries today. If the diagnosis is correct, the intensification of class consciousness will be less a matter of a populist or ouvrierist exaltation of a single class by itself, than of the forcible reopening of access to a sense of society as a totality, and of the reinvention of possibilities of cognition and perception that allow social phenomena once again to become transparent, as moments of the struggle *between* classes.

Under these circumstances, the function of a new realism would be clear: to resist the power of reification in consumer society and to reinvent that category of totality which, systematically undermined by existential fragmentation on all levels of life and social organization today, can alone project structural relations between classes as well as class struggles in other countries, in what has increasingly become a world system. Such a conception of realism would incorporate what was always most concrete in the dialectical counterconcept of modernism—its emphasis on violent renewal of perception in a world in which experience has solidified into a mass of habits and automatisms. Yet the habituation that it would be the function of the new aesthetic to disrupt would no longer be thematized in the conventional modernistic terms of desacralized or dehumanizing reason, of mass society and the industrial city or technology in general, but rather as a function of the commodity system and the reifying structure of late capitalism.

Other conceptions of realism, other kinds of political aesthetics, obviously remain conceivable. The realism/modernism debate teaches us the need to judge them in terms of the historical and social conjuncture in which they are called to function. To take an attitude of partisanship toward key struggles of the past does not mean either choosing sides or seeking to harmonize irreconcilable differences. In such extinct yet still virulent intellectual conflicts, the fundamental contradiction is between history itself and the conceptual apparatus, which, seeking to grasp its realities, succeeds only in reproducing their discord within itself in the form of an enigma for thought, an aporia. It is to this aporia that we must hold, which contains within its structure the crux of a history beyond which we have not yet passed. It cannot of course tell us what our conception of realism ought to be; yet its study makes it impossible to us not to feel the obligation to reinvent one.

1977

Chapter 8
Marxism and Historicism

The relationship of Marxism to historicism is part of a larger problem—that of a properly Marxist *hermeneutic*—which cannot fully be dealt with here. Let us merely observe that the two thematic paths along which this problem is generally approached—that of historicism and that of an interpretive master code—form, along with the third and more distantly related theme of *representation*, the three major polemic and ideological targets of most forms of poststructuralism today, even though full-dress philosophical onslaughts on these three concepts have rarely been mounted. Still, the work of the *Tel Quel* group, Barthes, Derrida, Baudrillard, Lyotard, and others, presupposes this polemic at the same time that it contributes locally to this or that aspect of it; whereas the most systematic statement of the repudiation of historicism has been made by Foucault (in *The Order of Things* [1966] and *The Archaeology of Knowledge* [1969]), and the most systematic statement of the repudiation of interpretation is expressed in the *Anti-Oedipus* (1972) of Deleuze and Guattari. All these statements, however, presuppose a more basic master text, namely, Althusser's *Reading Capital* (1968), which, owing to its explicitly Marxist framework, is probably less familiar to American readers than other texts in French theory today. Althusser's attacks on Marxist historicism and on classical hermeneutics (which he calls *expressive causality*) are therefore basic reference points in what follows, even if we cannot here engage Althusser's fundamental work directly.[1]

As for interpretation, I can only assert here what I will argue more systematically in another place,[2] namely the semantic priority of Marxist interpretation over the other interpretive codes that are its rivals in the theoretical marketplace today. If indeed one construes interpretation as a rewriting operation, all the various critical methods or positions may be grasped as positing, either explicitly or implicitly, some ultimate privileged interpretive *code* in terms of which the cultural object is allegorically rewritten: such codes have taken the various forms of language or communication (in structuralism), desire (as for some Freúdianisms but also some post-Marxisms), anxiety and freedom (in classical existentialism), temporality (for phenomenology), collective archetypes (in Jungianism or myth criticism), various forms of ethics or psychological "humanism" (in criticism whose dominant themes are the integration of the personality, the quest for identity, alienation and nonalienation, the reunification of the psyche, and so forth). Marxism also proposes a master code, but it is not, as is sometimes commonly thought, either that of economics or production in the narrow sense, or that of class struggle as a local conjuncture or event, but rather that very different category which is the "mode of production" itself, which we may therefore expect to make its appearance at the conclusion of the present argument. For the moment, suffice it to say that the concept of a mode of production projects a total synchronic structure in terms of which the themes and the concrete phenomena valorized by the other methods listed above necessarily find the appropriately subordinate structural position. This is to say that no intelligent contemporary Marxism will wish to exclude or repudiate any of the themes listed above, which all in their various ways designate objective zones in the fragmentation of contemporary life. Marxism's "transcendence" of these other methods therefore does not spell the abolition or dissolution of their privileged objects of study, but rather the demystification of the various frameworks or strategies of containment by means of which each could lay claim to being a total and self-sufficient interpretive system. To affirm the priority of Marxist analysis as that of some ultimate and untranscendable semantic horizon—namely the horizon of the *social*—thus implies that all other interpretive systems conceal a *seam* which strategically seals them off from the social totality of which they are a part and constitutes their object of study as an apparently closed phenomenon. Thus, for instance, the powerful closed hermeneutic of the Freudian psychic models is unexpectedly and dialectically reopened and transcended when it is understood that such models ultimately depend on the concrete social reality of the family as an institution. As to the final state—in all the poststructuralist critiques of interpretation—in which allegorical rewriting always presupposes some ultimately privileged form of *representation*—in the present instance, presumably, the representation of something called History itself—we can merely assert here that it is percisely in this respect that a Marxist hermeneutic can be radically distinguished from all the other types enumerated above, since its "master code,'' or transcendental signified, is precisely not given as a representation but rather as an *absent cause,* as that which can never know full representation. I must here limit myself to a formula I have proposed elsewhere, namely that History is not in any sense itself a text or master text or master narrative, but that it is inaccessible to us except in textual or narrative form, or, in other words, that we approach it only by way of some prior textualization or narrative (re)construction.

These preliminary remarks about the problem of interpretation would therefore seem to have restructured in advance the other related problem that is our official subject here, namely that of historicism, to which we now turn. I will speak in a moment about the curious destiny of this term, which cannot today be pronounced without furtively turning up one's lapels and glancing over one's shoulder. Let us for the moment construe this problem in a more empirical or commonsense fashion as being simply that of our relationship to the past, and of our possibility of understanding the latter's monuments, artifacts, and traces.

The dilemma of any "historicism" can then be dramatized by the peculiar, unavoidable, yet seemingly unresolvable alternation between Identity and Difference. This is indeed the first arbitrary decision we are called on to make with respect to any form or object from out of the past, and it is a decision which founds that contact; so that on the one hand, as with Sartrean freedom, we cannot *not* opt for one or the other of these possibilities (even when for the most part we remain oblivious of a choice made in an unthematized and unreflexive way), while on the other, the decision itself, since it inaugurates the experience, is something like an absolute presupposition that is itself beyond any further philosophical argument (thus, we cannot appeal to any empirical findings about the past, since they are themselves grounded on this initial presupposition). That this is meanwhile an intolerable option may quickly be conveyed by an oversimplified demonstration: if we choose to affirm the Identity of the alien object with ourselves—if, in other words, we decide that Chaucer, say, or a steatopygous Venus, or the narratives of nineteenth-century Russian gentry, are more or less directly or intuitively accessible to us with our own cultural *moyens du bord*—then we have presupposed what was to have been demonstrated, and our apparent "comprehension" of these alien texts must be haunted by the nagging suspicion that we have all the while remained locked in our own present—the present of the *société de consommation* with its television sets and superhighways, its Cold War, and its postmodernisms and poststructuralisms—and that we have never really left home at all, that our feeling of *Verstehen* is little better than mere psychological projection, that we have somehow failed to touch the strangeness and the resistance of a reality genuinely different from our own. Yet if, as a result of such hyperbolic doubt, we decide to reverse this initial stance, and to affirm, instead and from the outset, the radical Difference of the alien object from ourselves, then at once the doors of comprehension begin to swing closed and we find ourselves separated by the whole density of our own culture from objects or cultures thus initially defined as Other from ourselves and thus as irremediably inaccessible.

The status of the classical world has long been paradigmatic of this dilemma. When Greek forms and Latin texts were considered classical for us, what was affirmed was not merely the Identity of these formal languages and sign systems with our own aesthetic values and ideals, but rather also, and through the symbolic medium of the aesthetic experience, a whole political analogy between two forms of social life. We are in a position to grasp this better today, when Greek forms—and the ideal of classical beauty that derives from them and of which the art of Raphael has generally been taken as the supreme embodiment—to come to be viewed as insipid and when the temptation arises to rewrite them more "strongly" in terms of Difference. Then the Nietzschean reassertion of the Dionysian and of the orgiastic counterreligion of the mysteries, the ritual studies of the Cambridge school, Freud himself (and *Lévi-Strauss'* rewriting of the Oedipus legend in terms of primitive myth), decisive reversals in classical scholarship (such as the work of George Thompson, Dodds' *The Greeks and the Irrational,* and the newer French classical scholarship), and above all, perhaps, contemporary aesthetic reinterpretations of the Greek fact (such as Karl Orff's opera *Antigone)*—all converge to produce an alternative Greece, not that of Pericles or the Parthenon, but something savage or barbaric, tribal or African, or Mediterranean-sexist—a culture of masks and death, ritual ecstasies, slavery, scapegoating, phallocratic homosexuality, an utterly non- or anticlassical culture to which something of the electrifying otherness and fascination, say, of the Aztec world, has been restored. That this powerful counterimage is no less conditioned by our own collective fantasies than the *edle Einfalt und stille Grösse* of the Apollonian classicism which it replaced may be deduced from its kinship with other persistent historical motifs, such as the constellation of "totalitarian" fantasies expressed in *1984,* images of Wittvogel's *Oriental Despotism,* popular representations of Stalinist "bureaucracy" and of the cyclical return (particularly in science fiction) of various images of imperial domination and of archaic power systems. Nonetheless, the content of these new motifs allows us to reevaluate the older vision of the classical world, which now proves to be less a matter of individual taste than a whole social and collective mirror image, in which the production of a new artistic style—neoclassicism—comes to serve as the vehicle for political legitimation; now it is a whole dominant social class, the English aristocratic oligarchy as it persists as a privileged enclave within the hostile environment of industrialization and commerce and the alien element of a brutalized and mentally and corporeally alienated proletariat, which contemplates its own ideal image in and is validated by the culture of a slaveholding aristocratic polis from which only the cultural forms themselves triumphantly survive.

It is clear that these two images of the classical world—that of Identity and that of Difference, that of the harmonious polis and that of the "Orientalism" of a radically alien form of social life—float side by side as alternative worlds that can never intersect. That both are profoundly ideological visions should not encourage us too rapidly to conclude that a "value-free" and henceforth "scientific" historiography is capable of freeing us from the binary opposition of Identity and Difference, and of piercing such ideological representations in order to replace them with an "objective" account of the realities of the ancient world. Perhaps, on the contrary, we need to take into account the possibility that our contact with the past will always pass through the imaginary and through its ideologies, will always in one way or another be mediated by the codes and motifs of some deeper historical classification system or *pensée sauvage* of the historical imagination, some properly political unconscious. This is at any rate the hypothesis we now want to explore.

II

I begin by suggesting that the traditional "solutions" to the dilemma of historicism are fourfold, and indeed organize themselves into something like a *combinatoire* or structural permutation scheme. It is, however, sufficient to enumerate these possibilities—which I call antiquarianism, existential historicism, structural typology, and Nietzschean antihistoricism—to note that two of these positions amount essentially to refusals or repudiations of the problem itself.

This refusal may be observed most immediately in simple antiquarianism, for which the past does not have to justify its claim of interest on us, nor do its monuments have to present their credentials as proper "research subjects" or furnish appropriate reasons for a passionate commitment to *The Fairie Queene* or to nineteenth-century industrial novels, which now—validated as sheer historical facts with the irrevocable claim on us of all historical fact—lead a ghostly second existence as mere private hobbies. One is tempted to say that this position "solves" the problem of the relationship between present and past by the simple gesture of abolishing the present as such, and that its emblem might well be found in Melville's "late consumptive usher to a grammer school [who] loved to dust his old grammars; it somehow mildly reminded him of his mortality." The graduate school anxieties of the first scene of Goethe's *Faust* sufficiently express the asphyxiating distress of this position, to which Nietzsche's "Use and Abuse of History" then comes as a fairly predictable dialectical reaction and counterblast.

Yet it should not be thought that the antiquarian position is utterly without theoretical justification may take the form of the repudiation of theory as such. It is in fact the cultural equivalent and afterimage of a far more powerful ideology in the realm of historiography itself, namely of empiricism proper. It should not be necessary today to rehearse the many powerful indictments that have been made by empirical and empiracist historiography, which can be resumed by the twin diagnosis that the repudiation of theory is itself a theory, and that the concept of the objective "fact" is itself a theoretical construct. I will therefore limit myself to observing that the empiricist position is essentially a second-degree, reactive, critical, or demystifying one, a form of what Deleuze and Guattari conveniently term the "decoding" of preexistent, conventionally received interpretive codes, whether they be those of folk and popular legend (as in ancient historiography), or essentially theological visions of history (as in Enlightenment historiography), of the naive chronicle narratives of the deeds and destines of the great (as in the nascent social history of the nineteenth century), or of a hegemonic Marxian vision of history in the present day.[3] If this is so, however, then empirical historiography or antiquarianism is never a first-degree position in its ownright, but rather presupposes for its own vitality as a stance the existence of those other visions of history which its mission lies in subverting.

III

The first theoretical stance toward the past that has genuine content will therefore be what we here call "existential historicism," a term which, now designating an ideological position in its own right and a whole theoretical program, rather than a conceptual dilemma, demands, owing to the well-nigh universal stigmatization of these words, some preliminary comment.[4] The postcontemporary reader can still sense something of the irony of this reversal by juxtaposing Auerbach's celebration of German historism with Althusser's canonical onslaught on what he understands this term to imply. It will then be seen that something quite different is meant by these two authors, but that the term has, for better or for worse, become an ideological and polemic battleground whose framework must, at least for the moment, be respected.

The poststructural attack on "historicism," which emerges from a no less problematic affirmation of the priority of "synchronic" thought, can best be resumed in my opinion as a repudiation of two related and essentially *narrative* forms of analysis which can be termed the *genetic* and the *teleological*, respectively. This second term may be resumed most rapidly, for it amounts to little more than the reappearance, within a Marxian (and also, today a post-Marxist framework, of that critique and repudiation of the idea of "progress" which for rather different reasons characterizes bourgeois thought as well from Henry Adams and H. G. Wells down to the anti-Utopian "end of ideology" thinkers of our own Cold War Period. Teleology here designates the belief in any "positive" future or "end of history" in whose name you might be expected to be willing to sacrifice your own present. Salvational, "humanist," or Stalinist, such spurious images of the future are then denounced as symptoms of an essentially theological (and totalitarian) mode of thought. As desirable as it may be to rid Marxism of any vestiges of a properly bourgeois notion of "progress," it would seem a good deal less desirable nervously to abandon any Marxian vision of the future altogether (an operation in which Marxism itself is generally abandoned in the process). Meanwhile, if this is what "teleology" means, it will be possible to show that what we here call "existential historicism" does not presuppose it in the least.

As for "genetic" historicism, while it may well be ideologically linked to teleological thought, which can then be seen as the former's projection and its metaphysic, in its strict form this kind of analysis—which we will examine as a specific trope of a certain nineteenth-century thought—is not necessarily wedded to the idea of the future and of progress either, although there are narrative similarities between the two forms. What teleological thought reads as a narrative progression from a fallen present to a fully constituted future, genetic thought now displaces onto the past, constructing an imaginary past term as the evolutionary precursor of a fuller term that has historical existence. Because the example of nineteenth-century historical linguistics (and Saussure's revolutionary "synchronic" reaction against it) is well known, I will give the rather different illustration of Bachofen's reconstruction of some "original" matriarchy, which precedes the patriarchal classical culture evident to us in classical texts and artifacts, and which is, in Bachofen's hypothesis, affirmed as a genuine historical event or stage: "In all the myths relating to our object of study, we find inscribed the memory of real events which happened to the human race. These are not fictions but historical destinies which people really experienced."[5] Bachofen's theoretical defense of this hypothesis is the exemplary expression of the genetic or "evolutionary" method: "A genuinely scientific epistemology consists not merely in answering the question about the nature of the object. It finds its completion in discovering the source of the object's emergence and connecting the latter to its subsequent development. Knowledge is only then transformed into Understanding when it has been able to encompass origin, development and ultimate fate."[6]

The genetic trope should, however, not be consigned to the ash can of history without a few preliminary qualifications. For one thing, in spite of the unself-conscious use of the term "origin," this trope is quite distinct from the characteristically eighteenth-century fascination with absolute origins (as in the debates about the contractual origin of society, the origin of language, the creation of the universe, or pre-Darwinian evolutionism)—a kind of speculation to which Kant may be said to have put an end once and for all. Nineteenth-century "historicism," even of the genetic kind, is, in the sense of Edward Said's convenient distinction, less concerned with absolute origins than with beginnings, and its historical narratives—whatever their ideological inspirations—organize a world of facts from which the problem of origins has been excluded from the outset and in which we must deal instead with more properly Althusserian *toujours-déjà-données*.

On the other hand, it must also be observed that the genetic approach is quite different from the seemingly analogous dilemmas of a more properly structural historiography: the former works with a single term in order artificially to construct a merely hypothetical preliminary opposite term, as in Bachofen's notion of "matriarchy," Morgan's notion of "savagery" and promiscuous group marriage, and the linguistic hypothesis of proto-Indo-European. Structural historiography, on the other hand, works with two already fully constituted terms, such as "feudalism" and "capitalism"; it does not seek to reconstruct the former as an Ur-stage of the latter, but rather to build a model of the *transition* from one form to the other, and this is no longer then a genetic hypothesis but rather an investigation of structural transformations.

Finally, in order to forestall still further confusions, it seems important to affirm, with Althusser, that Marx's *Capital* is not a genetic construction of this kind but rather a synchronic model. Indeed, even though the reproach of evolutionism generally accompanies that of geneticism, it seems appropriate to observe that Darwin is also—in contrast to earlier evolutionisms or later Darwinianisms—synchronic in this sense, and that the whole scandalous force of the synchronic mechanism of natural selection, as a rigorously "meaningless" and nonteleological process, is lost when it is appropriated for the cornerstone of some vast divine master plan. What must be added to both these affirmations is that such synchronic models do not discredit History in any absolute sense as an object of study and representation, but rather determine a new and original form of historiography, a structural permutation in the latter's narrative form or trope. It is this new antigenetic form which Nietzsche will then theorize as the *genealogy* (and Foucault as the *archaeology)*, namely the narrative reconstruction of the conditions of possibility of any full synchronic form. Thus, to return to *Capital*, Marx's discussions of commerce and merchant capital, and his analysis of the "stage" of primitive accumulation, are reconstructions of what, once capital is fully emergent as such, can now be rewritten as the latter's preparatory requirements, it being understood that *within feudalism* these phenomena were not anticipatory of anything, since in that synchronic system capital as such did not yet exist.

With these qualifications, we are now perhaps in a better position to raise the more interesting problems posed by the genetic trope, which do not involve its "truth" or "falsity" but rather arise only after we have decided that this form of thinking is ideological or inadequate. Saussure's own expression of impatience—"much against my own inclination all this will end up with a book in which I will explain without any passion or enthusiasm how there is not a single term used in linguistics today which has any meaning for me whatsoever"[7]—suggests a more satisfactory way of historicizing the genetic trope, namely to ask ourselves what this particular "meaning-effect" or "understanding-effect" must have been in the first place, and how it was that intelligent people felt satisfied with the kind of historical narrative it provided them. At that point, it might well prove possible to grasp the genetic trope as the conceptual hypostasis and phenomenological projection of a life experience unique to the industrializing nations of nineteenth-century capitalism, of the gradual dissolution of the older precapitalist *Gemeinschaften* of traditional village life and their replacement, within the unity of a single lifetime and a single biographical experience, by the nascent industrial city. For subjects whose life experience thus includes both these terms and spans two distinct social formations—unlike the inhabitants of relatively static precapitalist societies, and unlike those of the postnatural *société de consommation* of the present day—it would not seem farfetched to suppose that the empty form of the genetic trope might have provided a satisfying way of thinking the two terms together and thereby of resolving, by way of something like a conceptual narrative mechanism, the lived contradiction of "modernization" itself, as the bourgeois cultural revolution is often euphemistically termed today. However this may be, such regrounding of the "false consciousness" of the genetic trope in a concrete historical situation has the additional merit for us, in the present context, of suggesting a historicizing operation and a model of a different possible "historicism" which has nothing in common with the genetic approach itself.

IV

With such a model we may now leave genetic or teleological "historicism" behind and examine that quite different theoretical stance which is existential historicism proper. Its theoretical origins may no doubt be fixed in the work of Dilthey, and beyond it, perhaps, in Ranke's great dictum that "every age is immediate to God" (or, in other words, that every culture is immanently comprehensible in its own terms). The fundamental practitioners of existential historicism are then surely the cultural historians, linguists, and iconologists of the great and now virtually extinct tradition of German philology, of which Auerbach and Spitzer, and in the history of art, Panofsky and the work of the Warburg Institute, remain the most vital presences in English-language cultural study. But we must not forget to mention the original forms taken by this historicism in other national traditions, most notably in the work of Croce, Collingwood, and the important Spanish variant expressed in that of Ortega and Americo Castro. Yet from an institutional point of view, the most powerful and authoritative monument to existential historicism is not to be found in the official "humanities," but rather in American anthropology, in the school of Franz Boas, explicitly antigenetic and antievolutionist, in which the range of historical experience open to existential historicism is broadened to include the whole range of "primitive" cultures as such.[8] This is perhaps also the place to observe that, however "teleological" the form in which Hegel's histories proper are narrated (as the realization in matter of World Spirit), the much maligned concept of Absolute Spirit cannot accurately be assimilated to some final stage of History, but rather is meant to describe the historian's mind as it contemplates the variety of human histories and cultural forms.

Such names—in particular that of Boas—should warn us then that existential historicism does not involve the construction of this or that linear or evolutionary or genetic history, but rather designates something like a transhistorical event: the experience, rather, by which *historicity* as such is manifested, by means of the contact between the historian's mind in the present and a given synchronic cultural complex from the past. This is to say that the methodological spirit of existential historicism may be described as a historical and cultural aestheticism. On the one hand, as in classical German aesthetics itself, all praxis is in this experience suspended (whence the well-known Hegelian formulas of the "Sunday of life," and the dusk in which Minerva's owl takes flight). Meanwhile, the quality of rapt attention that existential historicism brings to the objects of its study—texts as expressions of moments of the historical past, or of unique and distant cultures—is essentially that of aesthetic appreciation and recreation, and the diversity of cultures and historical moments becomes thereby for it a source of immense aesthetic excitement and gratification. These twin constitutive strengths of existential historicism are also, as we will see in a moment, the places of its theoretical and ideological flaws. Already, in the face of the well-nigh infinite variety of cultures, it is clear that existential historicism requires some principle of unity in order to prevent its vision from collapsing into the sheer mechanical and meaningless succession of facts of empiricist historiography (where History, as one expert remarked, is just "one damned thing after another"). This principle of unity, or, in other words, the ideological underpinning of existential historicism, is then derived from German *Lebensphilosophie*, in which the infinite multiplicity of human symbolic acts is the expression of the infinite potentialities of a nonalienated human nature. The experience of historicity then restores something of this richness to a present in which few enough of those potentialities are practically available to any of us.

For existential historicism, then, the past has vital urgency for us, and this urgency, which distinguishes such a stance from that of simple antiquarianism, surely needs to be retained in any more adequate "solution" to the dilemma of historicism proper. In this sense, whatever its theoretical contradictions, existential historicism must be honored as an experience, indeed, as the fundamental inaugural experience of history itself, without which all work in culture must remain a dead letter. There can indeed be no cultural investigation worthy of the name, let alone any history proper, that does not breathe something of the spiritual enthusiasm of this tradition for the traces that life has left behind it, something of its visionary instinct for all the forms of living praxis preserved and still instinct within the monuments of the past.

Nor does the past itself remain unmodified by this experience. Rather, the historicist act revives the dead and reenacts the essential mystery of the cultural past, which, like Tiresias drinking the blood, is momentarily returned to life and warmth and allowed once more to speak its mortal speech and to deliver its long-forgotten message in surroundings unfamiliar to it. As I have mentioned the Germans and the Spaniards, the Italians and the English, it may be appropriate to dramatize this astonishing moment of the exchange of forces between present and past through the voice of its supreme French embodiment, and to reread the lines in which Michelet—arriving at the night of 4 August 1789, in his great narrative, at the sudden and irrevocable dissolution of the *ancien régime* and the feudal world, and the unexpected emergence of "modern times"—salutes a past become present once again:

> Que vous avez tardé, grand jour! combien de temps nos péres vous ont attendu et révé!...L'espoir que leurs fils vous verraient enfin a pu seul les soutenir; autrement ils n'auraient pas voulu vivre, ils seraient morts à a peine....Moi-même, leur compagnon, labourant à côté d'eux dans le sillon de l'histoire, buvant à leur coupe amère, qui m'a permis de revivre le douloureax moyen áge, et pourtant de n'en pas mourir, n'est-ce pas vous, ô beau jour, premier jour de la délivrance?...J'ai vécu pour vous raconter!"[9]

> How late you are in coming, great day! How long our forefathers had to wait for you and dream about you!...Only the hope their sons would see you sustained them; otherwise they would have cursed life and died at hard labor....And I myself, their comrade, toiling beside them in the furrow of history and drinking from their bitter cup—what was it that allowed me to relive the agonizing Middle Ages and to emerge live, if not you, oh glorious day, first day of our freedom?...I lived but to tell your story!

Yet if the past is thus construed as a *Kerygma*,[10] as a voice and a message and an annunciation which it is the historian's vocation to sense and to preserve, there must also come a falling cadence as this supreme event begins to fade and normal time returns; so Michelet, evoking that other supreme moment of his history which is the Fête de la Fédération of July 1790—and finding its documents "burning, after sixty years, as though written yesterday...love letters"—now expresses the pathos of the downward slope and the withdrawal from his vision:

> "Ainsi finit le meilleur jour de notre vie." Ce mot que les fédérés d'un village écrivent le soir de la fête à la fin de leur récit, j'ai été tout prés de l'écrire moi-même en terminant ce chapitre. Il est fini et rien de semblable ne reviendra pour moi. J'y laisse un irréparable moment de ma vie, une partie de moi-même, je le sens bien, qui restera là et ne me suivra plus; il me semble que je m'en vias appauvri et diminué.[11]

> "So ended the best day of our life." This sentence, inscribed at nightfall by the fédérés of a village at the close of their narrative—I almost wrote it again myself at the end of the present chapter. It is over, and nothing of the sort will ever happen to me again. I leave here an irreparable moment of my life, a part of myself, which must, I sense, remain behind and follow me no further; it seems to me that I am thereby impoverished and diminished.

Such dramatic outbursts, comparable only to the great trumpet call of *Fidelio* which signals the deliverance from the crypt of the *ancien régime* and the resurrection of the dead, ratify the vocation of the historian as custodian of the past and of the nameless generations of human life that have vanished without a trace. At the same time, there is already in Michelet something that inflects the stance of existential historicism in an unexpected direction, and which may allow us to sense a way out of its contradictions, which can now thereby be more accurately formulated.

For existential historicism, as we have suggested, the experience of history is a contact between an individual subject in the present and a cultural object in the past. Each pole of this experience is thereby at once open to complete relativization: to take up for the moment only the subjectivity of the historian, it is clear that given the tastes and receptivities of the individual subject, an infinity of possible histories is conceivable. It is this threat of infinite relativization which the more properly ideological presuppositions of existential historicism are then called upon to limit and to conjure. These consist, as we have said, in a certain psychology of human nature, or, better still, in a certain anthropology—the notion of some full development of human potentialities, as it is expressed diversely in Schiller, Humboldt, or the early Marx—which, as an ontological presupposition, cannot be satisfactory to us today, no matter how much sympathy we may have for its vision. Here the Althusserian critique of "humanism," and Althusser's systematic dissociation of the early—anthropological or "existential"—Marx from the later structural and synchronic model of *Capital*, is powerful and timely; we may in our present context rewrite Althusser's thematics of "humanism" as a warning that any "anthropology," any statement about "human nature," is necessarily and irredeemably ideological. This position can perhaps be grasped most immediately and practically on the polemic level, where it is clear that to any given anthropology or presupposition about human nature, any other may with equally peremptory force be opposed (as, for instance, the Hobbesian view, revived by Robert Ardrey and others, of the innate aggressivity of the human animal).

It should not be thought, however, that this dilemma can be adequately solved by way of the poststructuralist critique of the center subject: that existential historicism in its canonical form posits the historian as a centered subject of this type is evident (and were it not, the critiques of Hegelian Absolute Spirit from the most varied philosophical standpoints would be enough to demonstrate it). Yet as we have suggested, what is essential in this experience is less the construction of the subject itself than its enthusiasm, the spark of recognition, what would today be called its reception of unique intensities. Quite unexpectedly, therefore, we find, in the midst of the most powerful contemporary celebration of the decentered subject, a call for what can only be called a decentered, "schizophrenic" equivalent to existential historicism.

> Klossowski has admirably demonstrated in his commentary on Nietzsche: the presence of the *Stimmung* as a material emotion, constitutive of the most lofty thought and the most acute perception. "The centrifugal forces do not flee the center forever, but approach it once again, only to retreat from it yet again: such is the nature of the violent oscillations that overwhelm an individual so long as he seeks only his own center and is incapable of seeing the circle of which he himself is a part; for if these oscillations overwhelm him, it is because each one of them corresponds to an individual other than the one he believes himself to be, from the point of view of the unlocatable center. As a result, an identity is essentially fortuitous, and a series of individualities must be undergone by each of these oscillations, so that as a consequence the fortuitousness of this or that particular individuality will render all of them necessary." The forces of attraction and repulsion, of soaring ascents and plunging falls, produce a series of intensive states based on the intensity = 0 that designates the body without organs ("but what is most unusual is that here again a new afflux is necessary, merely to signify this absence"). There is no Nietzsche-the-self, professor of philology, who suddenly loses his mind and supposedly identifies with all sorts of strange people; rather, there is the Nietzschean subject who passes through a series of states, and who identifies these states with history's various names: "I am all the names of History!" The subject spreads itself out along the entire circumference of the circle, the

center of which has been abandoned by the ego. At the center is the desiring-machine, the celibate machine of the Eternal Return. A residual subject of the machine, Nietzsche-as-subject garners a euphoric reward (Voluptas) from everything that this machine turns out, a product that the reader had thought to be no more than the fragmented *oeuvre* by Nietzsche. "Nietzsche believes that he is now pursuing, not the realization of a system, but the application of a program...in the form of residues of the Nietzschean discourse, which have now become the repertory, so to speak, of his histrionics." It is not a matter of identifying with various historical personages, but rather identifying the names of history with zones of intensity on the body without organs; and each time Nietzsche-as-subject exclaims: "They're *me!* So it's me!" No one has ever been as deeply involved in history as the schizo, or dealt with it in this way. He consumes all of universal history in one fell swoop. We began by defining him as *Homo natura*, and lo and behold, he has turned out to be *Homo historia*. This long road that leads from the one to the other stretches from Hölderlin to Nietzsche, and the pace becomes faster and faster. "The euphoria could not be prolonged in Nietzsche for as long a time as the contemplative alienation of Hölderlin. . . . The vision of the world granted to Nietzsche does not inaugurate a more or less regular succession of landscapes or still lifes, extending over a period of forty years or so: it is, rather, a parody of the process of recollection of an event: a single actor will play the whole of it in pantomime in the course of a single solemn day—because the whole if it reaches expression and then disappears once again in the space of just one day—even though it may appear to have taken place between December 31 and January 6—in a realm above and beyond the usual rational calendar.[12]

Schizophrenic historicism does not change the basic terms of the historicist situation, for it still opposes an individual subject (here to be sure an individual "effect of subjectivity" rather than a fully constituted "bourgeois" centered subject) to an essentially collective object. Yet it now allows us to widen the range of effects or intensities that are thereby implied: now not merely enthusiasm of an aestheticizing type, or Nietzschean euphoria and exaltation, but also the whole gamut of quite different *Stimmungen*—dizziness, loathing, depression, nausea, and Freudian decathexis—are to be numbered among the possible modes of some "authentic" contact with the cultural past. In this sense, indeed, our contemporary distance from aesthetic historicism itself may be unexpectedly reevaluated; and the Althusserian exasperation with Michelet's rhetoric of the resurrection of the dead, the passionate repudiation of the *vecú* and of existential phenomenology as well as of Hegelian "expressive causality," indeed, the more general malaise and revulsion we may sometimes feel for the supreme and placeless sovereignty with which a (most often Germanic) bourgeois World Spirit dips into the cultures of the past and organizes them into "imaginary museums" for its own delectation—all these feelings signal some electrifying and authentically historical—indeed properly *historicist*—contact with that present of existential historicism itself which has now become but another moment of our own past and which we live, in the no less vital mode of the negative, or of repulsion.

From this vaster perspective, then, it would seem that only indifference suspends a lived relationship to the past that can be registered in intensities of any conceivable quality; for even boredom, in its strong Baudelairean form, is a way of sensing and living the specificity of certain moments of the cultural past. If this is the case with boredom, however, as a resistance of the organism to culturally alien and asphyxiating forms, we may want to take into consideration the possibility that indifference is itself ultimately also a mode of relationship, something like a defense mechanism, a repression, a neurotic denial, a preventive shutting off of affect, which itself finally reconfirms the vital threat of its object. In that case, the "nightmare of history" becomes inescapable: we are everywhere in relation to it, even in its apparent absences, and the therapeutic Nietzschean "forgetfulness" of history is fully as reactive to the fact of history as is Michelet's "resurrection." How are we to understand this "absent cause" (Althusser), to which we cannot *not* react with the whole range of our affective intensities, and which at the same time would seem to be so charged with dread as to make the occasional prospect of its occultation—its repression or its amnesia—come before us like a momentary relief? It does not seem to me that the immemorial record of violence and the most brutal as well as the most intangible forms of domination are sufficient to motivate this mental flight, these ingenious subterfuges. Violence is a sheerly ideological category, as the popularity of this "concept" in American social criticism today testifies; and as for domination, social Darwinism and neofascism make it plain that under certain circumstances this phenomenon can also be contemplated with complacency or even a somber exhilaration. For Marxism, indeed, the categories of power are not the ultimate ones, and the trajectory of contemporary social theory (from Weber to Foucault) suggests that the appeal to it is often strategic and involves a systematic displacement of the Marxian problematic. No, the ultimate form of the "nightmare of history" is rather the fact of labor itself, and the intolerable spectacle of the backbreaking millennial toil of millions of people from the earliest moments of human history. The more existential versions of this dizzying and properly unthinkable, unimaginable spectacle—as in horror at the endless succession of "dying generations," at the ceaseless wheel of life, or at the irrevocable passage of Time itself—are themselves only disguises for this ultimately scandalous fact of mindless alienated work and of the irremediable loss and waste of human energies, a scandal to which no metaphysical categories can give a meaning. This scandal is everywhere known, everywhere repressed—*un secret de tous connu.* It is, for example, instructive that the text of Tolstoy upon which the Russian Formalists founded their canonical theory of artistic defamiliarization should be a text about work—indeed, contemporary feminism makes the recognition of this labor as *housework*, women's work, the oldest form of the division of labor, quite unavoidable:

> I was cleaning a room and, meandering about, approached the sofa and couldn't remember whether or not I had dusted it. Since these movements are habitual and unconscious, I could not remember and felt that it was impossible to remember—so that if I had dusted it and forgot—that is, had acted unconsciously—then it was the same as if I had not. If some conscious person had been watching, then the fact could be established. If, however, no one was looking, or was looking on unconsciously, if the whole complex lives of many people go on unconsciously, then such lives are as if they had never been.[13]

This waste of human life—what Tillie Olsen has called the *silences* into which such large parts of so many people's lives, and not merely women's lives, disappear—is evidently not rectified by the self-consciousness by which the Formalists (and perhaps Tolstoy himself) proposed to recuperate it. The whole classical doctrine of aesthetics as play and a nonfinalizable finality, and the persistent ideological valorization of handicraft production, are also desperate attempts to think away the unthinkable reality of alienated labor. The latter finally grounds the phenomenon of reification itself, described, for instance, by the *Tel Quel* group as the "effacement of the traces of production on the object": yet even here the category of "production" remains a still too tolerable and recuperable one, which in a pinch any modernist would be willing to salute. The deeper hold of reification lies in its promise to obliterate from the object world that surrounds us the dizzying and culpabilizing presence of the stored alien labor of other people.

Neither the complacent aestheticizing contemplation of existential historicism proper, nor the more manic and Nietzschean exaltation of schizophrenic historicism, resolves the fundamental imbalance of such views of historical experience, which oppose the response of an individual subject to the collective realities of any moment of the past. It is precisely at this point that Michelet's inflection of such historicism suggests a rather different solution: in Michelet, indeed, the present of the observer-historian, far from being placeless, is doubly inscribed in the text as a concrete situation. It is above all the present of 4 August 1789, the present of the Revolution, which resurrects the lost "silences" of medieval labor, not through any "objective" historiographic reconstruction, but by the vital *Novum* of praxis; meanwhile the politically committed stance of the historian Michelet during the legitimation crisis of the final years of the July Monarchy, the politically symbolic value of his own historiography which will earn him suspension from the Collége de France on the very eve of the Revolution of 1848, reduplicates this reinvention of the past by an active present and allows Michelet himself to resurrect that very present—the night of August fourth—which has become his own past. What needs to be stressed here is that we no longer have to do with the contemplative relationship of an individual subject to the past, but rather with the quite different relationship of an objective *situation* in the present with an objective *situation* in the past. Indeed, insofar as Marxism is itself a historicism—not, to be sure, a geneticism or a teleology in Althusser's sense of this word, but rather, as I have termed it elsewhere, an "absolute historicism"—its historical grounding is analogous, and Marx takes pains at various places in *Capital* to underscore the objective and historical preconditions of his discovery of the labor theory of value in a social situation in which for the first time labor and land are fully commodified: "The capitalist epoch is therefore characterized by the fact that labor-power, in the eyes of the worker himself, takes on the form of a commodity which is his property; his labor consequently takes on the form of wage-labor. On the other hand, it is only from this moment that the commodity-form of the products of labor becomes universal."[14] Marx's "personal" discovery of this "scientific truth" is therefore itself grounded within his system and is a function of the originality of a historical situation in which for the first time the development of capital itself permits the production of a concept—the labor theory of value—which can retroactively "recover" the truth of even the millennia of precapitalist human history. "What Marx's analytical method reveals and concretely demonstrates is the historical character both of the *realities* that thought analyzes and of the *concepts* such thinking constructs to explain them. Marx's method thus excludes from the outset any possibility for theory to *alienate itself speculatively* in its own ideational products by presenting them either as ideal realities without a history of their own or as idealities that refer to a reality that would itself be nonhistorical."[15]

Still, in our present context, there must remain something scandalous about this conjunction between an absolute scientific truth and its enabling situation in contingent, empirical history: the Althusserian resistance to such an absolute Marxist historicism evidently springs from the fear that, as an existential historicism generally, "science" must necessarily thereby find itself relativized. This scandal is perhaps usefully intensified by that contemporary Marxist thinker who has reflected the most consequently on the experience of the past expressed in our quotes from Michelet: "History is the subject of a structure whose site is not homogeneous, empty time, but time filled by the presence of the now [*Jetztzeit*, or Ernst Bloch's *Novum*]. . . . Thus, to Robespierre ancient Rome was a past charged with the time of the Now which he blasted out of the continuum of history."[16] Benjamin's own version of the resurrection of the past—"Only that historian will have the gift of fanning the spark of hope in the past who is firmly convinced that *even the dead* will not be safe from the enemy if he wins"—and his vision of the present—"every second of historical time is the strait gate through which Messiah may enter"[17]—clearly lead us out of existential historicism (and of its well-known "dilemmas") into a different space in which for the first time the missing term—the Utopian future—is pronounced.

V

Before we explore this new historical space even in a tentative way, we must return to the enumeration of the more conventional theoretical options on the relationship to the past with which we began. The emphasis of existential historicism on the subject of the historical experience seemed to precipitate the latter's object into an optional heterogeneity and multiplicity of possible pasts and cultures which were distinguished from the random additive multiplicity of empiricist history only by libidinal investment. It is then predictable enough to find a dialectical counterposition emerge in which it is the logic of the historical object, rather than the intensity and authentic experiencing of the historian subject, that organizes our relationship to the past. This hypothetical logic of the historical object then generally organizes itself into a typology whose semic content and mechanism varies with the level of abstraction in which cultures or moments of the past are therein described. Such a typology can take the quite different forms of Dilthey's psychological types (or Mannheim's), of the stylistic oppositions of the great late nineteenth-century art historians, such as Wölfflin, one of the operative mechanisms of the Weberian "ideal types," of Spengler's stylistic classification of cultures, or, in our own time, of Lotman's tropological typology of cultures, which will serve us as our principal exhibit here.[18]

It should not be assumed, however, that these classification schemes or *combinatoires*—here all loosely designated as forms of "structural typology"— necessarily express a radically different or incommensurable impulse from those at work in existential historicism. On the contrary, semiotic analysis of such texts generally discloses the operation of "deep" semic oppositions—a kind of historical *pensée sauvage*—which can usually be found to project a whole structural typology of cultures imperceptible at the surface of the text and disguised or displaced by the emphasis on the sensitivity of the individual historian-subject. The importance of Dilthey was his sensing of the necessary interrelationship between synchronic *Verstehen* and a more general typology of historical moments or cultures (even though he formulated this in the psychological terms of various worldviews). Meanwhile, it is clear in the work of a historicist like Auerbach that his series of "synchronic" moments is intersected, albeit very imperfectly, by the structural opposition between paratactic and syntactic styles which inaugurates his work and whose historical status is never fully articulated. In much the same way, the "masterpieces" of Boasian anthropology—such as Ruth Benedict's well-known *Patterns of Culture*—in spite of their ideological stress on the infinite diversity of human cultures, can be shown to be articulated by a cultural classification system that is far from innocent.

Lotman's work is exemplary for us in the present context because it would seem to have drawn the methodological consequences of this apparently unavoidable, yet generally unformulated, tendency toward typology in existential historicism, and to have projected the most self-conscious and ambitious program for cultural classification that we yet have. (In anthropology proper, such programs are generally hampered by the institutional restriction of ethnological materials to so-called cold or primitive societies; that is, they operate within an unreflected previous and far too global typology which is simply the division between "primitive" and "historical" social forms.) The work of Lotman and his group would appear to take its point of departure in the Marxian problematic of social reproduction; indeed, the initial definition of culture as the "nonhereditary memory of the collectivity"[19] suggests a perspective in which the various possible mechanisms of cultural "storage" will be analyzed in terms of their function to reproduce a mode of production of a determinate type. This is not the direction taken by Lotman's work, however, nor does the preliminary restriction of his studies to the field of Slavic or Russian cultural history compel this perspective, insofar as such materials thereby find themselves reduced to documents from only two modes of production: feudalism and capitalism (I do not know of any cultural-typological work of this school on artifacts from the socialist period proper). Thus, Lotman's initial definition of culture operates at once to bracket the whole question of the infrastructural function of culture and to determine a framework in which the various cultural mechanisms can be studied in isolation.

These prove essentially to be twofold and to generate a kind of dualistic vision of history. "It is possible to distinguish between cultures directed mainly towards expression and those directed chiefly towards content."[20] Both types of culture—they are explicitly correlated with the medieval-ritualistic and the modern-rationalistic or scientific, respectively—are organized around textual constructions, or better still, around processes of textualization. But the first type of culture—that organized around the plane of expression—posits a master text (scripture) to which the other texts of culture and social life are assimilated. The basic evaluative mechanism of such a cultural mechanism will be the distinction between "correct" and "incorrect," and the world will be articulated according to this binary opposition, in which the "true" text or true culture—the culture of belief—is opposed to the false texts and cultures of heresies, superstitions, and the like.

Meanwhile, a certain conception of textuality organizes modern or rationalistic culture as well; but in this case, the opposite of the equivalent "master text" (scientific rationality) is not another heretical text, but merely the nontextualized, entropy, or disorder. Here the reproductive mechanism of culture is not directed toward the replication of the sacred text, but rather toward the imperializing transformation of everything that is as yet a nontext into the new master text of scientific rationality; and the evaluative system of such a mechanism is based on conceptions of rules and method, rather than conceptions of "correctness" or "incorrectness" (an opposition that might be reformulated in terms of the ethical binary of "good" and "evil").

It is apparent that this global opposition is a more complex expression of the classical linguistic or tropological distinction between metaphor and metonymy associated with the name of Roman Jakobson; the cultural production of a culture organized around a master text or scripture will then be a process of metaphorical ordering, whereas that of a culture of textualizing rules will reveal the mechanism of a kind of metonymic reclamation, in which ever greater quantities of content are drawn into the system. The obvious danger of such a stark opposition lies in its recuperation by this or that "natural" or "metaphysical" dualism; thus, in Jakobson himself, in the inaugural work on aphasia, the temptation is ever present to fold the opposition of these master tropes back into some more "fundamental" division of mental processes, into the analogical and the associative, and beyond that, into specific zones of the brain itself.

Yet tropological classification need not be a dualism, as the variety and multiplicity of tropes and figures in any manual of rhetoric might suggest. In the case of Lotman's own work, indeed, it will be observed that other types of cultural mechanism, touched on in passing, suggest that this particular tropological opposition need not constrict Lotman's fundamental project of a "description of cultural universals and the elaboration of a grammar of the 'languages' of culture [which] will furnish, it is to be hoped, the bases of that structural history which is one of our future tasks."[21] On the other hand, a closer inspection of the "exception" noted above—Lotman's account of neoclassicism—shows that this promise of variety may well be illusory.

Neoclassicism occupies something like an intermediary position between a culture based on a master text and one based on "scientific" rules. Ostensibly a culture of rules and canons, it nonetheless posits an ensemble of classical texts that have the authority of the older sacred master text: "The theoretical models were thought of as eternal and as preceding the actual act of creation. In art, only those texts considered 'correct,' that is, corresponding to the rules, were recognized as texts, i.e., having significance.... The bad in art is whatever breaks the rules. But even the violation of the rules can be described, in Boileau's opinion, as following certain 'incorrect' rules. Therefore, 'bad' texts can be classified; any unsatisfactory work of art serves as an example of some typical violation."[22] Thus, in Lotman's view, neoclassicism does not present us with some new and original form of cultural mechanism (or some new trope that would break us out of the dualism of metaphor and metonymy); it is merely a structural permutation of the two older types in which the rationalistic mechanism of cultural and scientific production by rules finds itself organized around the true/false, correct/incorrect, good/bad system of evaluation of an older sacred culture. Nor is there anything particularly surprising in this. Greimas' semantic rectangle shows us that any initial binary opposition can, by the operation of negations and the appropriate syntheses, generate a much larger field of terms which, however, all necessarily remain locked in the closure of the initial system. The stark and mythical Jakobsonian dualism—as soon as it is articulated into semic variables of the type of Lotman's "truth" versus "rules"—becomes similarly capable of generating a more complex *combinatoire* or permutation scheme.

At this point, however, it becomes interesting to ask ourselves what further permutations the Lotmanian typology can produce, and in particular how we might describe the missing fourth term of this particular closed system. Very schematically, we may suppose that to a culture that organizes its rules according to ethical or "truth" categories, there might logically be opposed a culture that organized its "truth" categories and its ethics according to rules and methods, that is a culture that systematically rewrote what used to be ontological categories (being, meaning, goodness, and the like) in terms of the sheerly operational ones of rules of transformation, transcoding, infinite semiosis, and the like. The kinship Lotman has underscored with Foucault's enterprise, in *The Order of Things*,[23] confirms the suspicion that his fourth and still hypothetical type of culture can be none other than the "structuralist" moment celebrated in prophetic annunciation at the end of Foucault's work and sociologically unmasked by Jean Baudrillard as the very logic of consumer society itself—an autoproliferation of signifiers that have freed themselves from the myth and the ballast of all "natural" signifieds, the moment of metatheory, in which theories generate more theories, and of some new and postmodern, properly "textual" or schizophrenic aesthetic, in which sentences generate other sentences and texts still further texts.

The purpose of this hypothetical exercise is not to impute to Lotman a view of history that he might well not wish to endorse, but rather to demonstrate that underlying every such structural typology, whether it is grounded in the mechanism of linguistic tropes or in some other way, there can be found something from which the system was intended to free us, namely a narrative (and perhaps even teleological) "vision" or "philosophy" of history. As far as the tropes themselves are concerned, they are clearly unavailable for the construction of a typology or structural *combinatoire* unless their initial empirical multiplicity has been systematically reduced to some basic generative mechanism; this is indeed what we may observe in such contemporary rhetorical systems as those of the μ Group and in Hayden White's "tropics."[24] It will therefore come as no surprise to find that, whatever the official terms of this second underlying "system," it must necessarily be of another order of abstraction than the multiplicity of forms that it is called upon to organize and to order. We must then suspect that, even if this underlying system is described in terms of "master" tropes which organize surface tropes or figures, the status of such master tropes must ultimately be sought in a wholly different system altogether. My own experience suggests that this second, or "deep," system can always be grasped and rewritten in terms of something like a narrative or teleological vision of history.

Thus the structural attempt to reduce the multiplicity of empirical moments of the past or of other cultures to some fundamental typology or system would seem to be a failure, insofar as the surface categories of such narrative history find themselves smuggled back into the typology to lend it a generally disguised content. Nonetheless, even this apparent failure takes us a step forward, for if such categories are unavoidable, one may at least make a virtue out of necessity and propose a structural system that articulates them explicitly for the first time. As we will see shortly, such a system is that which is projected by the Marxist concept of the "mode of production."

Meanwhile, we must conclude this discussion of the option of a properly structural typology of history or culture by observing the inevitable: that the emphasis of this position on the logic of the historical object determines an imbalance in that feature which was strongest in the counterposition of existential historicism, namely the position of the historian-subject. The very conception of science—whether it be the "science" of some semiotics-yet-to-be-constructed or another kind—depends for its constitution on the mirage of that placeless scientific subject of knowledge which Lacan has conveniently termed the *sujet supposé savior*. Nonetheless, a certain reflexivity is posited in Lotman's scheme, insofar as the place of the semiotician is presumably to be reckoned into the metonymic moment of a rationalizing and scientific culture. Yet far from being the structuralist equivalent of some properly dialectical self-consciousness, this kind of reflexivity would seem to confront us with the logical paradox of a class that is a member of itself. The Utopian fourth culture of Foucault—a properly structuralist culture beyond the conventional scientific-rationalistic one—is surely at least partly motivated by the attempt to break out of this bind; yet neither the problem of the historian's place or self-consciousness, nor that of the Utopian moment, can be adequately dealt with within these systems.

VI

We must now mention, *pour mémoire,* the final option—after antiquarianism, existential historicism, and structural typology—which we have termed the Nietzschean position. Like the first of this series, of which it is in effect the inversion, this final option "solves" the dilemma of historicism by refusing the problem. In effect, for antiquarianism the problem of the relationship between past and present did not arise, since for it the present had no particularly privileged status. But was it not Hume who suggested that nothing but our own prejudices would be changed by the hypothesis that the world was created a mere instant ago, and that the whole archival and sedimented wealth of the "past's" traces—including Hume's complete works themselves, along with the documents that register this writer's historical "existence"—are nothing but an immense illusionary trompe l'oeil built into a synchronous present? Upon the foundation of Hume's paradox, then, there rises the ultimate "position" on the dilemmas of historicism, namely the view that the problem of the past is not a problem for the simple reason that the past does not exist:

> What is the object of history? It is quite simply, despite all the
> elaborations, equivocations, and qualifications of historians and
> philosophers, whatever is past...and yet, by definition, all that is
> past does not exist. To be accurate the object of history is whatever
> is *represented* as having hitherto existed. The essence of this represen-
> tation is preserved records and documents. History's object, the
> hitherto existing, does not exist except in the modality of its current
> existence, as representations....What the past *is* is determined by
> the content of the various ideological forms which operate within the
> parameters of historical knowledge. The content of the past—its
> nature, its periods and problems—is determined by the character of a
> particular ideological form. The particular modes of writing history
> invest this or that body of representations with the status of a record.
> Artifacts, washing lists, court rolls, kitchen middens, memoirs, are
> converted into *texts*—representations through which the real may be
> read. The text, constituted as a text by its reading, is at the mercy of
> this reading. Far from working on the *past*, the ostensible object of
> history, historical knowledge works on a body of *texts*. These texts
> are a product of historical knowledge. The writing of history is the
> production of texts which interpret these texts.[25]

This position, which draws the ultimate conclusion from structuralism's inaugural perception of the incommensurability between synchrony and diachrony, is to the conventional practice of the historian as a modernist—or, better still, a postmodernist, properly *textual*—aesthetic is to the aesthetic of traditional realistic representation. Indeed, the introduction of the very theme of representation into the discussion throws its terms and givens into a fresh light, subsuming it under an even broader theoretical and philosophical problem. For these writers, for example, Lenin's one great historical work. *The Development of Capitalism in Russia*, is only apparently a work of historiographic representation. Nor does their argument turn on the economic and statistical content of Lenin's text (Arthur Danto demonstrated some time ago that nonnarrative types of historical writing can always be transformed into essentially narrative or storytelling propositions).[26] Lenin's work does not aim in this sense to reconstitute a (more adequate) representation of the past; rather, such apparent representations are part of a theoretical (but also a political) practice in the present, and insert themselves into an ongoing polemic: "Lenin's book is a theoretical demolition of the arguments and evidence of Narodnism and evolutionism. 'Empirical' material—in fact, statistics and information, collected according to definite problems, by definite techniques, and within definite political and social purposes; Lenin had no illusions or fetishes about their purity—functions in this book as the object of criticism or as a source of illustration of a theoretical point."[27] To replace this interpretation of Lenin in a more familiar context, we may say that the older view according to which this particular textual signifier stands for and represents a particular signified or even a particular referent is here replaced by the view that the meaning of a signifier is generated by its work on previous signifiers alone. The classical view of this "textual" model of theory is, of course, Althusser's own: theoretical production is neither the representation of some real object nor direct work on the latter. Science "always works on 'generalized material' even when the latter takes on the form of a 'fact.'. . . It always works on preexistent concepts, on 'Vorstellungen.'. . . It does not 'work' on some pure and objective 'datum' which would be that of pure and absolute 'facts.' On the contrary, its business consists in *elaborating its own scientific facts* by means of the critique of *ideological 'facts'* elaborated by the more properly ideological theoretical practice that has preceded it."[28] Now, however, Hindess and Hirst draw the ultimate conclusion from this position—a conclusion Althusser has not been willing to take himself—and, thereby reproblematizing their own important book, provocatively close it with the following declaration: "The study of history is not only scientifically but also politically valueless. The object of history, the past, no matter how it is conceived, cannot affect present conditions. Historical events do not exist and can have no material effectivity in the present. . . . It is. . . the 'current situation' which it is the object of Marxist theory to elucidate and of Marxist political practice to act upon. All Marxist theory, however abstract it may be, however, general its field of application, exists to make possible the analysis of the current situation."[29] But if this is what historiography does anyhow—without realizing it, or under the delusion that it is "representing" past realities—then perhaps we can go on writing history as we did before; and it is conceivable that the Humean paradox would change nothing whatsoever in our life in what has become something of a Potemkin present.

Much of the same conclusion can be drawn from more explicitly Nietzschean contemporary versions of this position. Let Jean-François Lyotard, in his attack on current reinventions of Rousseau, serve as the spokesman for this view. Confronted with the polemic appeal to the radical social and cultural *difference* of primitive or tribal society (expressed, in this case, in the work of

Jean Baudrillard), Lyotard is willing to take the ultimate step: there never *were* any primitive societies to begin with ("Non, décidément, il faut le dire clairement: *il n'y a pas* du tout de sociétés primitives ou sauvages, nous sommes tous des sauvages, tous les sauvages sont des capitalistes-capitalisés[30]). There has never been anything but capitalism as far as the eye can see in time and space; there has never been anything but the present. Yet Lyotard's own call for a new "paganism," for a political revival of the old heterogeneity of the pagan gods (or "intensities")[31]—as well as his strategic reaffirmation of the oppositional underside of hegemonic classical philosophy, his defense of the sophists and the cynics against the dominant Platonic or Aristotelian tradition—suggests much the same "libidinal" practice of the past, and of its "names of history," whose program, whose "schizophrenic historicism," we have already seen outlined in Deleuze.

VII

The reader will already have suspected that the Marxist "solution" to the dilemma of historicism outlined here will consist in squaring the circle we have already traced, in positing a mode of Identity that is also one of radical Difference, and in producing a kind of *structural historicism*, in which the vital and, if one likes, properly libidinal investment of existential historicism in the past is somehow derived from or positioned within a conception of the logic of historical and cultural forms more satisfactory than that proposed by structural typology. We have already suggested that such a conception is to be found in the Marxian notion of the mode of production, whose various forms are conventionally enumerated as follows: hunting and gathering (primitive communism or the horde), neolithic agriculture (or the gens), the Asiatic mode of production (or so-called oriental despotism), the polis, slavery, feudalism, capitalism, and communism. These distinct forms are no longer to be considered "states" in some linear or evolutionary narrative which would be the "story" of human history, nor are they "necessary" moments in some teleological historical process. The local and empirical "transition" from one of these forms to another—as in the two great *loci classici* of Marxist historiography, the transition from primitive communism to power societies, and the transition from feudalism to capitalism—demands reconstruction, not as a narrative of emergence, but rather, as we have already suggested above, as a genealogy. Meanwhile, each of these synchronic forms designates, not merely a specific type of economic "production" or labor process and technology, but also a specific and original form of cultural and linguistic (or sign) production (along with the determinate place of the other traditional Marxian superstructures of the political, the juridical, the ideological, and so forth). It thus subsumes models like that of Lotman which seek to deal with cultural mechanisms in isolation (leaving aside here the fact that Lotman's is a model of cultural reproduction rather than of cultural production proper). Nor is there any reason that a contemporary Marxian model of social structure should not make a determinate place for the psychoanalytic "instance"—the construction of a particular "psychoanalytic" subject in this or that mode of production—and for the phenomenological—in particular the phenomenology of space and the organization of *Lebenswelt* or daily life in a given social formation. What needs to be stressed, however, is that all these various "instances" are dialectically modified according to the structural place assigned to them in the various modes of production; there cannot, therefore, be any question of the projection backward into radically different social formations of a concept of "production" drawn from capitalism,[32] any more than a dialectical perspective can accept the ahistorical assumption of certain psychoanalytic schools that the constituted subject, the unconscious, the Oedipus complex, desire, and the like—all theorized from modern or bourgeois psychic materials—remain constant throughout history.

As with my initial remarks on interpretation, I cannot do any more here than to assert answers to problems about the nature of a mode of production which I will argue in more detail elsewhere. Chief among such problems is the status of this concept itself, about which it has been observed—in a number of critiques of the formulations of this concept in Althusser and Balibar[33]—that it is something like Spinoza's "eternity," a timeless structure which must apparently effortlessly reproduce itself without change across the empirical vicissitudes of human history. Nor is the conventional Marxist appeal to the complementary concept of a "social formation"—the empirical historical society or culture in which a given mode of production realizes itself—any more satisfactory as theoretical solution, since it merely reintroduces that empiricism which it was the mission of a dialectical approach to discredit and to replace.

A solution to this problem can be sought in two directions. On the one hand, as we have already suggested, the Marxian concept of a mode of production is essentially a *differential* one, in which the formulation of a single mode of production (as, for instance, Marx's own model of capital) at once structurally projects the space of other possible modes of production by way of Difference, that is, by a systematic variation in the features or semes of any given initial mode. This is the sense in which each mode of production structurally *implies* all the others. What is important about this from our present standpoint is that the contemplation of any given mode of production (or the replacement of any cultural artifact within its specific mode of production) must always implicitly or explicitly involve a differential relationship to all the others.

But one can also argue this differential interrelationship in a nonstructuralizing way: from this second standpoint, the hypothesis of a structural *combinatoire* is unnecessary, since each "more advanced" mode of production includes the earlier ones, which it has had to suppress in its own emergence. These are therefore sedimented within a mode of production like capitalism, in which the earlier forms, along with their own specific forms of alienation and productivity, persist in a layered, "canceled" fashion. But not only is it vanquished modes of production from the past that thus survive in the "nonsynchronicity"[34] of the present mode; it is also clear that future modes of production are also at work in the present and can be detected most visibly in the various local forms of class struggle. If this is so, however, it becomes evident not only that no mode of production exists in any pure state, but also that we need a concept of the same level of abstraction to designate this contradictory overlay and structural coexistence of several modes of production in tension with one another. I suggest that this concept has been made available to us by the Chinese experience, and that this larger form, which subsumes the individual modes of production, be called "cultural revolution," it being understood that the recent Chinese practice of cultural revolution is merely one distinct historical type of cultural revolution, of which one must assume that there have existed quite different structural embodiments at all moments of human history (thus, for instance, to draw) only on familiar and traditional examples, Bachofen's hypothesis of the triumph of patriarchy over matriarchy is an attempt to thematize a properly *neolithic* cultural revolution; Max Weber's analysis of the Protestant ethic is a contribution to the study of a properly *bourgeois* cultural revolution; and so forth). Let me add in passing that this new unifying category of historical study seems to me the only one in terms of which the so-called human sciences can be reorganized in a properly materialistic way.

Yet it would seem that this system of modes of production and cultural revolutions at best regrounds only one of the options discussed above—that of structural typology or of the logic of the historical *object*—in some more satisfactory and totalizing way, and that we have not yet shown how it is able to provide a more adequate formulation for the problem of the place of the historian-subject, or of the present, as this imposed itself in our counterdiscussion of existential historicism. We have already touched on the way in which Marxism, as an absolute historicism, grounds the possibility of a comprehensive theory of past societies and cultures in the structure of the present, or of capitalism itself. Yet this would seem at best to reinvent some "place of truth," some ethnocentric privilege of our present as inheritors of world culture and as practitioners of rationalism and science, which is not visibly different from the imperializing hubris of conventional bourgeois science, and which would tend at the same time to confirm the current line of the *nouveaux philosophes* on the innate or intrinsic "Stalinism" of the Marxian worldview.

This ultimate dilemma, which turns on the status of the present and the place of the subject in it, needs to be restructured in three ways. First, we must try to rid ourselves of the habit of thinking about our (aesthetic) relationship to culturally or temporally distant artifacts as being a relationship between individual subjects (as in my *personal* reading of an *individual* text written by a biographical individual names Spenser or Juvenal, or even my personal attempt to invent an individual relationship to an oral story once told by an individual storyteller in a tribal society). It is not a question of dismissing the role of individual subjects in the reading process, but rather of grasping this obvious and concrete individual relationship as being itself a mediation for a nonindividual and more collective process: the confrontation of two distinct social forms or modes of production. We must try to accustom ourselves to a perspective in which every act of reading, every local interpretive practice, is grasped as the privileged vehicle through which two distinct modes of production confront and interrogate each other. Our individual reading thus becomes an allegorical figure for this essentially collective confrontation of two social forms.

If we can do this, I suggest that a second reformulation of the nature of this contact between present and past will gradually impose itself. We will no longer tend to see the past as some inert and dead object which we are called upon to resurrect, or to preserve, or to sustain, in our own living freedom; rather, the past will itself become an active agent in this process and will begin to come before us as a radically different life form which rises up to call our own form of life into question and to pass judgment on us, and through us on the social formation in which we exist. At that point, the very dynamics of the historical tribunal are unexpectedly and dialectically reversed: it is not we who sit in judgment on the past, but rather the past, the radical difference of other modes of production (and even of the immediate past of our own mode of production), which judges us, imposing the painful knowledge of what we are not, what we are no longer, what we are not yet. This is the sense in which the past speaks to us about our own virtual and unrealized "human potentialities," but it is not an edifying lesson or any leisure matter of personal or cultural "enrichment." Rather, it is a lesson of privation, which radically calls into question the commodified daily life, the reified spectacles, and the simulated experience of our own plastic-and-cellophane society; and this not merely on the level of content (as in Marx's familiar opposition of the object world of Greek epic to the contemporary world of the locomotive and the electric telegraph), but in the very experience of form and linguistic production itself, where the primacy of collective ritual, or the splendor of uncommodified value, or even the transparency of immediate personal relations of domination, at once stigmatizes the monadization, the privatized and instrumentalized speech, the commodity reification, of our own way of life. On this view, then, as for existential historicism, our concrete relationship with the past remains an existential experience, a galvanic and electrifying event, yet one that is far more disturbing and unsettling than in the comfortable aesthetic appreciation of the practitioners of late nineteenth-century historicism. Now, on the contrary, it is the past that sees us, and judges us remorselessly, without any sympathy for our complicity with the scraps of subjectivity we try to think of as our own fragmentary and authentic life experience.

Yet it is not only the past that thus judges us; and with this final rectification we touch at the originality of the Marxist position with respect to the other options that have been evoked above. For if the proper articulation of any concrete mode of production structurally implies the projection of all other conceivable modes, it follows that it implies the future as well and that the hermeneutic contact between present and past outlined here cannot fully be described without the articulation within it of what Ernst Bloch has called the Utopian impulse. Among the conditions of possibility of Marxism itself as a new type of dialectical thought was, as we have indicated above, the commodification of land and labor completed only by the emergence of capitalism; but if this were its only historical precondition, it could be argued that Marxism as such was merely a theoretical "reflection" of early or classical capitalism. It is, however, also the anticipatory expression of a future society, or, in the terms of our discussion above, the partisan comitment to that future or Utopian mode of production which seeks to emerge from the hegemonic mode of production of our own present. This is the final reason why Marxism is not, in the current sense, a "place of truth," why its subjects are not centered in some possession of dogma, but are rather very precisely historically decentered; only the Utopian future is a place of truth in this sense, and the privilege of contemporary life and of the present lies not in its possession, but at best in the rigorous judgment it may be felt to pass on us.

The fullest and most terrifying form of a Marxist hermeneutic act can therefore best be conveyed by those great moments in Sartre's *Condemned of Altona*, when the implacable gaze of the alien and incomprehensible inhabitants of the thirtieth century burns unanswerably upon a present steeped in torture, exploitation, and blood guilt: "Habitants masqués des plafonds . . . décapodes . . . siècles, voici mon siècle, solitaire et difforme, l'accusé. Mon client s'éventre de ses propres mains; ce que vous prenez pour une lymphe blanche, c'est du sang. . . . Répondez donc! Le trentième ne répond plus. Peut-être n'y aura-t-il plus de siècles après le nôtre. Pèut-être qu'une bombe aura soufflé les lumièrès. Tout sera mort: les yeux, les juges, le temps. Nuit. O tribunal de la nuit, toi qui fus, qui seras, qui es, j'ai été! j'ai été" Masked inhabitants of the ceilings. . .decapods. . .centuries, here is my own century, solitary, misbegotten, the accused. My client disembowels himself before your very eyes; what looks like lymph is really blood. . . . Answer me! The thirtieth century no longer answers. Maybe there are no centuries after this one. Maybe a bomb blew out all the lights. Everything will be dead: eyes, judges, time. Night. O great court of the night, you who were and always will be, who are—I have been! I have been).[35] Yet Franz's appeal to a silent and unimaginable posterity, with all its echoes of a more properly existentialist pathos, is not the only possible figure for this fullest relationship to history. Sartre's crabs are after all our own grandchildren or great grandchildren, Brecht's "Nachgeborenen"; and it is therefore fitting to conclude with the evocation of a rather different type of political art—Alain Tanner's film *Jonah Who Will Be 25 in the Year 2000*—with its play of postindividual collective relationships around the absent center of birth and of a new subject to come—to convey the sense of a hermeneutic relationship to the past which is able to grasp its own present as history only on condition it manages to keep the idea of the future, and of radical and Utopian transformation, alive.

Autumn 1979

Chapter 9
Periodizing the 60s

Nostalgic commemoration of the glories of the 60s and abject public confession of the decade's many failures and missed opportunities are two errors that cannot be avoided by some middle path that threads its way in between. The following sketch starts from the position that History is Necessity, that the 60s had to happen the way it did, and that its opportunities and failures were inextricably intertwined, marked by the objective constraints and openings of a determinate historical situation, of which I thus wish to offer a tentative and provisional model.

To speak of the "situation" of the 60s, however, is necessarily to think in terms of historical periods and to work with models of historical periodization, which are at the present moment theoretically unfashionable, to say the least. Leave aside the existential fact that the veterans of the decade, who have seen so many things change dramatically from year to year think more historically than their predecessors; the classification by generations has become as meaningful for us as it was for the Russians of the late nineteenth century, who sorted character types out with reference to specific decades. And intellectuals of a certain age now find it normal to justify their current positions by way of a historical narrative ("then the limits of Althusserianism began to be evident," etc.). Now, this is not the place for a theoretical justification of periodization in the writing of history, but to those who think that cultural periodization implies some massive kinship and homogeneity or identity within a given period, it may quickly be replied that it is surely only against a certain conception of what is historically dominant or hegemonic that the full value of the exceptional—what Raymond Williams calls the "residual" or "emergent"—can be assessed. Here, in any case, the "period" in question is understood not as some omnipresent and uniform shared style or way of thinking and acting, but rather as the sharing of an objective situation, to which a whole range of varied responses and creative innovations is then possible, but always within that situation's structural limits.

Yet a whole range of rather different theoretical objections will also bear on the selectiveness of such a historical narrative: if the critique of periodization questions the possibilities of diachrony, these involve the problems of synchrony and in particular of the relationship to be established between the various "levels" of historical change singled out for attention. Indeed, the present narrative will claim to say something meaningful about the 60s by way of brief sketches of but four of those levels: the history of philosophy, revolutionary political theory and practice, cultural production, and economic cycles (and this in a context limited essentially to the United States, France, and the Third World). Such selectiveness seems not merely to give equal historical weight to base and superstructure indifferently, but also to raise the specter of a practice of homologies—the kind of analogical parallelism in which the poetic production of Wallace Stevens is somehow "the same" as the political practice of Che Guevara—which have been thought abusive at least as far back as Spengler.

There is of course no reason why specialized and elite phenomena, such as the writing of poetry, cannot reveal historical trends and tendencies as vividly as "real life"—or perhaps even more visibly, in their isolation and semi-autonomy which approximates a laboratory situation. In any case, there is a fundamental difference between the present narrative and those of an older organic history that sought "expressive" unification through analogies and homologies between widely distinct levels of social life. Where the latter proposed identities between the forms on such various levels, what will be argued here is a series of significant homologies between the *breaks* in those forms and their development. What is at stake, then, is not some proposition about the organic unity of the 60s on all its levels, but rather a hypothesis about the rhythm and dynamics of the fundamental situation in which those very different levels develop according to their own internal laws.

At that point, what looked like a weakness in this historical or narrative procedure turns out to be an unexpected strength, particularly in allowing for some sort of "verification" of the separate strands of the narrative. One sometimes believes—especially in the area of culture and cultural histories and critiques—that an infinite number of narrative interpretations of history are possible, limited only by the ingenuity of the practitioners whose claim to originality depends on the novelty of the new theory of history they bring to market. It is more reassuring, then, to find the regularities hypothetically proposed for one field of activity (e.g., the cognitive, or the aesthetic, or the revolutionary) dramatically and surprisingly "confirmed" by the reappearance of just such regularities in a widely different and seemingly unrelated field, as will be the case with the economic in the present context.

At any rate, it will already have become clear that nothing like a history of the 60s in the traditional, narrative sense will be offered here. But historical representation is just as surely in crisis as its distant cousin, the linear novel, and for much the same reasons. The most intelligent "solution" to such a crisis does not consist in abandoning historiography altogether, as an impossible aim and an ideological category all at once, but rather—as in the modernist aesthetic itself—in reorganizing its traditional procedures on a different level. Althusser's proposal seems the wisest in this situation: as old-fashioned narrative or "realistic" historiography became problematical, the historian should reformulate her vocation—not any longer to produce some vivid representation of History "as it really happened," but rather to produce the *concept* of history. Such will at least be the gamble of the following pages.

1. Third World Beginnings

It does not seem particularly controversial to mark the beginnings of what will come to be called the 60s in the Third World with the great movement of decolonization in British and French Africa. It can be argued that the most characteristic expressions of a properly First World 60s are all later than this, whether they are understood in countercultural terms—drugs and rock—or in the political terms of a student New Left and a mass antiwar movement. Indeed, politically, a First World 60s owed much to Third-Worldism in terms of politicocultural models, as in a symbolic Maoism, and, moreover, found its mission in resistance to wars aimed precisely at stemming the new revolutionary forces in the Third World. Belden Fields has indeed suggested that the two First World nations in which the most powerful student mass movements emerged—the United States and France—became privileged political spaces precisely *because* these were two countries involved in colonial wars, although the French New Left appears after the resolution of the Algerian conflict. The one significant exception to all this is in many ways the most important First World political movement of all—the new black politics and the civil rights movement, which must be dated, not from the Supreme Court decision of 1954, but rather from the first sit-ins in Greensboro, North Carolina, in February of 1960. Yet it might be argued that this was also a movement of decolonization, and in any case the constant exchange and mutual influences between the American black movements and the various African and Caribbean ones are continuous and incalculable throughout this period.

The independence of Ghana (1957), the agony of the Congo (Lumumba was murdered in January 1961), the independence of France's sub-Saharan colonies following the Gaullist referendum of 1959, finally the Algerian

Revolution (which might plausibly mark our schema here with its internal high point, the Battle of Algiers, in January-March 1957, as with its diplomatic resolution in 1962)—all of these signal the convulsive birth of what will come in time to be known as the 60s:

> Not so very long ago, the earth numbered two thousand million inhabitants: five hundred million *men* and one thousand five hundred million *natives*. The former had the Word; the others merely had use of it.[1]

The 60s was, then, the period when all these "natives" became human be-ings, and this internally as well as externally: those inner colonized of the First World—"minorities," marginals, and women—fully as much as its external subjects and official "natives." The process can and has been described in a number of ways, each one of which implies a certain "vision of History" and a certain uniquely thematized reading of the 60s proper: it can be seen as a decisive and global chapter in Croce's conception of history as the history of human freedom; as a more classically Hegelian process of the coming to self-consciousness of subject peoples; as some post-Lukácsean or more Marcusean, New Left conception of the emergence of new "subjects of history" of a nonclass type (blacks, students, Third World peoples); or as some poststructuralist, Foucaultean notion (significantly anticipated by Sartre in the passage just quoted) of the conquest of the right to speak in a new collective voice, never before heard on the world stage—and of the concomitant dismissal of the intermediaries (liberals, First World intellectuals) who had hitherto claimed to talk in your name; not forgetting the more properly political rhetoric of self-determination or independence, or the more psychological and cultural rhetoric of new collective "identities."

It is, however, important to situate the emergence of these new collective "identities" or "subjects of history" in the historical situation which made that emergence possible, and in particular to relate the emergence of these new social and political categories (the colonized, race, marginality, gender, and the like) to something like a crisis in the more universal category that had hitherto seemed to subsume all the varieties of social resistance, namely the classical conception of social class. This is to be understood, however, not in some intellectual but rather in an institutional sense; it would be idealistic to suppose the deficiencies in the abstract idea of social class, and in particular in the Marxian conception of class struggle, can have been responsible for the emergence of what seem to be new nonclass forces. What can be noted, rather, is a crisis in the institutions through which a real class politics had however imperfectly been able to express itself. In this respect, the merge of the AFL and the CIO in 1955 can be seen as a fundamental "condition of possibility" for the unleashing of the new social and political dynamics of the 60s: that merger, a triumph of McCarthyism, secured the expulsion of the Communists from the

American labor movement, consolidated the new antipolitical "social contract" between American business and the American labor unions, and created a situation in which the privileges of a white male labor force take precedence over the demands of black and women workers and other minorities. These last have therefore no place in the classical institutions of an older working-class politics. They will thus be "liberated" from social class, in the charged and ambivalent sense that Marxism gives to that word (in the context of enclosure, for instance): they are separated from the older institutions and thus "released" to find new modes of social and political expression.

The virtual disappearance of the American Communist Party as a small but significant political force in American society in 1956 suggests another dimension to this general situation: the crisis of the American party is "overdetermined" by its repression under McCarthyism and by the "revolution" in the Soviet bloc unleashed by Khrushchev's de-Stalinization campaign, which will have analogous but distinct and specific equivalents for the European Communist parties. In France, in particular, after the brief moment of a Communist "humanism," developed essentially by philosophers in the eastern countries, and with the fall of Khrushchev himself and the definitive failure of his various experiments in 1964, an unparalleled situation emerges in which, virtually for the first time since the Congress of Tours in 1919, it becomes possible for radical intellectuals to conceive of revolutionary work outside and independent of the French Communist Party. (The older attitudes—"we know all about it, we don't like it much, but nothing is to be done politically without the CP"—are classically expressed in Sartre's own political journalism, in particular in *Les Communists et la paix.*) Now Trotskyism gets a new lease on life, and the new Maoist forms, followed by a whole explosion of extraparliamentary formations of all ideological complexions, the so-called groupuscules, offer the promise of a new kind of politics equally "liberated" from the traditional class categories.

Two further key events need to be noted here before we go on. For many of us, indeed, the crucial detonator—a new Year I, the palpable demonstration that revolution was not merely a historical concept and a museum piece but real and achievable—was furnished by a people whose imperialist subjugation had developed among North Americans a sympathy and a sense of fraternity we could never have for other Third World peoples in their struggle, except in an abstract and intellectual way. Yet by January 1, 1959, the Cuban Revolution remained symbolically ambiguous. It could be read as a Third World revolution of a type different from either the classical Leninist one or the Maoist experience, for it had a revolutionary strategy entirely its own, the *foco* theory, which we will discuss later. This great event also announces the impending 60s as a period of unexpected political innovation rather than as the confirmation of older social and conceptual schemes.

Meanwhile, personal testimony seems to make it clear that for many white

American students—in particular for many of those later active in the New Left—the assassination of President Kennedy played a significant role in delegitimizing the state itself and in discrediting the parliamentary process, seeming to mark the decisive end of the well-known passing of the torch to a younger generation of leadership, as well as the dramatic defeat of some new spirit of public or civic idealism. As for the reality of the appearance, it does not much matter that, in hindsight, such a view of the Kennedy presidency may be wholly erroneous, considering his conservatism and anticommunism, the gruesome gamble of the "missle crisis," and his responsibility for the American engagement in Vietnam itself. More significant, the legacy of the Kennedy regime to the development of a 60s politics may well have been the rhetoric of youth and of the "generation gap" which he exploited, but which outlived him and dialectically offered itself as an expressive form through which the political discontent of American students and young people could articulate itself.

Such were some of the preconditions or "conditions of possibility"—both in traditional working-class political institutions and in the arena of the legitimation of state power—for the "new" social forces of the 60s to develop as they did. Returning to these new forces, there is a way in which their ultimate fate marks the close of the 60s as well: the end of "Third-Worldism" in the U.S. and Europe largely predates the Chinese Thermidor, and coincides with the awareness of increasing institutional corruption in many of the newly independent states of Africa and the almost complete militarization of the Latin American regimes after the Chilean coup of 1973 (the later revolutionary triumphs in the former Portuguese colonies are henceforth felt to be "Marxist" rather than "Third-Worldist," whereas Vietnam vanishes from American consciousness as completely after the ultimate American withdrawal as did Algeria from French consciousness after the Evian accords of 1963). In the First World of the late 60s, there is certainly a return to a more internal politics, as the antiwar movement in the United States and May 68 in France testify. Yet the American movement remains organically linked to its Third World "occasion" in the Vietnam War itself, as well as to the Maoist inspiration of the Progressive Labor-type groups which emerge from SDS, such that the movement as a whole will lose its momentum as the war winds down and the draft ceases. In France, the "common program" of the left (1972)—in which the current Socialist government finds its origins—marks a new turn toward Gramscian models and a new kind of "Eurocommunist" spirit which owes very little to Third World antecedents of any kind. Finally, the black movement in the U.S. enters into a crisis at much the same time, as its dominant ideology—cultural nationalism, an ideology profoundly linked to Third World models—is exhausted. The women's movement also owed something to this kind of Third World inspiration, but it too, in the period 1972-74, will know an increasing articulation into relatively distinct ideological positions ("Bourgeois" feminism, lesbian separatism, socialist feminism).

For reasons enumerated above, and others, it seems plausible to mark the end of the 60s around 1972-74; the problem of this general "break" will be returned to at the end of this sketch. For the moment we must complete our characterization of the overall dynamic of Third World history during this period, particularly if it is granted that this dynamic or "narrative line" entertains some privileged relationship of influence on the unfolding of a First World 60s (through direct intervention—wars of national liberation—or through the prestige of exotic political models—most obviously, the Maoist one—or finally, owing to some global dynamic which both worlds share and respond to in relatively distinct ways).

This is, of course, the moment to observe that the "liberation" of new forces in the Third World is as ambiguous as this term frequently tends to be (freedom as separation from older systems); to put it more sharply, it is the moment to recall the obvious, that decolonization historically went hand in hand with neocolonialism, and that the graceful, grudging, or violent end of an old-fashioned imperialism certainly meant the end of one kind of domination but evidently also the invention and construction of a new kind—symbolically, something like the replacement of the British Empire by the International Monetary Fund. This is, incidentally, why the currently fashionable rhetoric of power and domination (Foucault is the most influential of these rhetoricians, but the basic displacement from the economic to the political is already made by Max Weber) is ultimately unsatisfactory; it is of course politically important to "contest" the various forms of power and domination, but the latter cannot be understood unless their functional relationships to economic exploitation are articulated—that is, until the political is once again subsumed beneath the economic. (On the other hand—particularly in the historicizing perspective of the present essay—it will obviously be a significant historical and social *symptom* that, in the mid-60s, people felt it necessary to express their sense of the situation and their projected praxis in a reified political language of power, domination, authority and antiauthoritarianism, and so forth: here, Second and Third World developments—with their conceptions of a "primacy of the political" under socialism—offer an interesting and curious cross-lighting.) Meanwhile, something similar can be said of the conceptions of collective identity and in particular of the poststructuralist slogan of the conquest of speech, of the right to speak in your own voice, for yourself; but to articulate new demands, in your own voice, is not necessarily to satisfy them, and to speak is not necessarily to achieve a Hegelian recognition from the Other (or at least then only in the more somber and baleful sense that the Other now has to take you into consideration in a new way and to invent new methods for dealing with that new presence you have achieved). In hindsight, the "materialist kernel" of this characteristic rhetoric or ideological vision of the 60s may be found in a more fundamental reflection on the nature of cultural revolution itself (now independent of its local and now historical Chinese manifestation).

The paradoxical, or dialectical, combination of decolonization and neocolonialism can perhaps best be grasped in economic terms by a reflection on the nature of another process whose beginning coincides with the general beginnings we have suggested for this period as a whole. This is a process generally described in the neutral but obviously ideological language of a technological "revolution" in agriculture: the so-called Green Revolution, with its new applications of chemical procedures to fertilization, its intensified strategies of mechanization, and its predictable celebration of progress and wonder-working technology, supposedly destined to free the world from hunger (the Green Revolution, incidentally, finds its Second World equivalent in Khrushchev's disastrous "virgin lands" experiment). But these are far from neutral achievements; nor is their export—essentially pioneered by the Kennedys—a benevolent and altruistic activity. In the nineteenth and early twentieth centuries, capitalist penetration of the Third World did not necessarily mean a capitalist transformation of the latter's traditional modes of production. Rather, they were for the most part left intact, "merely" exploited by a more political and military structure. The very enclave nature of these older agricultural modes—in combination with the violence of the occupier and that other violence, the introduction of money—established a sort of tributary relation that was beneficial to the imperialist metropolis for a considerable period. The Green Revolution carries this penetration and expansion of the "logic of capital" into a new stage.

The older village structure and precapitalist forms of agriculture are now systematically destroyed, to be replaced by an industrial agriculture whose effects are fully as disastrous as, and analogous to, the moment of enclosure in the emergence of capital in what was to become the First World. The "organic" social relations of village societies are now shattered, an enormous landless preproletariat "produced," which migrates to the urban areas (as the tremendous growth of Mexico City can testify), while new, more proletarian, wage-working forms of agricultural labor replaced the older collective or traditional kinds. Such ambiguous "liberation" needs to be described with all the dialectical ambivalence with which Marx and Engels celebrate the dynamism of capital itself in the *Manifesto* or the historical progress achieved by the British occupation of India.

The conception of the Third World 60s as a moment when all over the world chains and shackles of a classical imperialist kind were thrown off in a stirring wave of "wars of national liberation" is an altogether mythical simplification. Such resistance is generated as much by the new penetration of the Green Revolution as it is by the ultimate impatience with the older imperialist structures, the latter itself overdetermined by the historical spectacle of the supremacy of another former Third World entity, namely Japan, in its sweeping initial victories over the old imperial powers in World War II. Eric Wolf's indispensable *Peasant Wars of the Twentieth Century* (1969) underscores the relationship between possibilities of resistance, the development of a revolutionary ethos, and a certain constitutive distance from the more absolutely demoralizing social and economic logic of capital.

The final ambiguity with which we leave this topic is the following: the 60s, often imagined as a period when capital and First World power are in retreat all over the globe, can just as easily be conceptualized as a period when capital is in full dynamic and innovative expansion, equipped with a whole armature of fresh production techniques and new "means of production." It now remains to be seen whether this ambiguity, and the far greater specificity of the agricultural developments in the Third World, have any equivalent in the dynamics with which the 60s unfold in the advanced countries themselves.

2. The Politics of Otherness

If the history of philosophy is understood not as some sequence of timeless yet somehow finite positions in the eternal, but rather as the history of attempts to conceptualize a historical and social substance itself in constant dialectical transformation, whose aporias and contradictions mark all of those successive philosophies as determinate failures, yet failures from which we can read off something of the nature of the object on which they themselves came to grief—then it does not seem quite so farfetched to scan the more limited trajectory of that now highly specialized discipline for symptoms of the deeper rhythms of the "real" or "concrete" 60s itself.

As far as the history of philosophy during that period is concerned, one of the more influential versions of its story is told as follows: the gradual supersession of a hegemonic Sartrean existentialism (with its essentially phenomenological perspectives) by what is often loosely called "structuralism," namely, by a variety of new theoretical attempts which share at least a single fundamental "experience"—the discovery of the primacy of Language or the Symbolic (an area in which phenomenology and Sartrean existentialism remain relatively conventional or traditional). The moment of high structuralism—whose most influential monuments are seemingly not philosophical at all, but can be characterized, alongside the new linguistics itself, as linguistic transformations of anthropology and psychoanalysis by Claude Lévi-Strauss and Jacques Lacan respectively—is, however, inherently unstable and has the vocation of becoming a new type of universal mathesis, under pain of vanishing as one more intellectual fad. The breakdown products of that moment of high structuralism can then be seen, on the one hand, as the reduction to a kind of scientism, to sheer method and analytical technique (in *semiotics*); and, on the other hand, as the transformation of structuralist approaches into active ideologies in which ethical, political, and historical consequences are drawn from the hitherto more epistemological "structuralist" positions; this last is of course the moment of what is now generally known as *poststructuralism*, associated with familiar names like those of Foucault, Deleuze, Derrida, and so forth. That the paradigm, although obviously French in its references, is not merely local can be judged from an analogous mutation of the classical Frankfurt School via problems of communication, in the work of Habermas; or by the current revival or pragmatism in the work of Richard Rorty, which has a home-grown American "poststructuralist" feeling to it (Pierce after all having largely preceded and outclassed Saussure).

The crisis of the philosophical institution and the gradual extinction of the philosopher's classic political vocation, of which Sartre was for our time the supreme embodiment, can in some ways be said to be about the so-called death of the subject: the individual ego or personality, but also the supreme philosophical Subject, the cogito but also the *auteur* of the great philosophical *system*. It is certainly possible to see Sartre as one of the last great system builders of traditional philosophy (but then at least one dimension of classical existentialism must also be seen as an ideology or a metaphysic: that of the heroic pathos of existential choice and freedom in the void, and that of the "absurd," more particularly in Camus). Some of us also came to *Marxism* through dialectical elements in the early Sartre (he himself then turning to follow up this avenue in his own later, more Marxian work, such as the *Critique of Dialectical Reason* [1960]). But on balance the component of his work that underwent the richest practical elaboration at other people's hands as well as his own was his theory of interpersonal relations, his stunning rewrite of Hegel's Master/Slave chapter, his conception of the Look as the most concrete mode in which I relate to other subjects and struggle with them, the dimension of my alienation in my "being-for-other-people," in which each of us vainly attempts, by looking at the other, to turn the tables and transform the baleful alienating gaze of the Other into an object for my equally alienating gaze. Sartre will go on, in the *Critique*, to try to erect a more positive and political theory of group dynamics on this seemingly sterile territory; the struggle between two people now becoming dialectically transformed into the struggle between groups themselves. The *Critique* was an anticipatory work, however, whose import and significance would not finally be recognized until May 68 and beyond, whose rich consequences indeed have not even fully been drawn to this day. Suffice it to say, in the present context, that the *Critique* fails to reach its appointed terminus, and to complete the projected highway that was to have led from the individual subject of existential experience all the way to fully constituted social classes. It breaks down at the point of the constitution of small groups and is ultimately usable principally for ideologies of small guerilla bands (in a latter moment of the 60s) and of microgroups (at the period's end). The significance of this trajectory will soon be clear.

However, at the dawn of the 60s, the Sartrean paradigm of the Look and the struggle for recognition between individual subjects will also be appropriated dramatically for a very different model of political struggle, in Frantz Fanon's enormously influential vision (*The Wretched of the Earth* [1961]) of the struggle between Colonizer and Colonized, where the objectifying reversal of the Look is apocalyptically rewritten as the act of redemptive violence of Slave against Master, the moment when, in fear and the anxiety of death, the hierarchical positions of Self and Other, Center and Margin, are forcibly reversed, and when the subservient consciousness of the Colonized achieves collective identity and self-affirmation in the face of coloniziers in abject fight.

What is at once significant is the way in which what had been a technical philosophical subject (the "problem" of solipsism, the nature of relationships between individual subjects or "cogitos") has fallen into the world and become an explosive and scandalous political ideology: a piece of the old-fashioned technical philosophical system of high existentialism breaking off and migrating outside philosophy departments altogether, into a more frightening landscape of praxis and terror. Fanon's great myth could be read at the time, by those it appalled equally well as by those it energized, as an irresponsible call to mindless violence. In retrospect, and in the light of Fanon's other, clinical work (he was a psychiatrist working with victims of colonization and of the torture and terror of the Algerian war), it can more appropriately be read as a significant contributon to a whole theory of cultural revolution as the collective reeducation (or even collective psychoanalysis) of oppressed peoples or unrevolutionary working classes. Cultural revolution as a strategy for breaking the immemorial habits of subalternity and obedience which have become internalized as a kind of second nature in all the laborious and exploited classes in human history—such is the vaster problematic to which, today, Gramsci and Wilhelm Reich, Fanon and Rudolf Bahro, can be seen as contributing as richly as the more official practices of Maoism.

3. Digression on Maoism

But with this new and fateful reference, an awkward but unavoidable parenthetical digression is in order: Maoism, richest of all the great new ideologies of the 60s, will be a shadowy but central presence throughout this essay, yet owing to its very polyvalence it cannot be neatly inserted at any point or exhaustively confronted on its own. One understands, of course, why Left militants here and abroad, fatigued by Maoist dogmatisms, must have heaved a collective sigh of relief when the Chinese turn consigned "Maoism" itself to the ashcan of history. Theories, however, are often liberated on their own terms when they are thus radically disjoined from the practical interests of state power. Meanwhile, as I have suggested above, the symbolic terrain of the present debate is fully as much chosen and dictated by the Right as by Left survivors; and the current propaganda campaign, everywhere in the world, to Stalinize and discredit Maoism and the experience of the Chinese cultural revolution—now rewritten as yet another Gulag to the East—all of this, make no mistake about it, is part and parcel of the larger attempt to trash the 60s generally. It would not be prudent to abandon rapidly and without thoughtful reconsideration any of this terrain to the "other side."

As for the more ludicrous features of Western Third-Worldism generally—a kind of modern exotic or orientalist version of Marx's revolutionaries of 1848, who "anxiously conjure up the spirits of (the Great Revolution of 1789) to their service and borrow from them names, battle cries and costumes"[2]—these are now widely understood in a more cynical light, as in Régis Debray's remark: "In France, the Columbuses of political modernity thought that following Godards's *La Chinoise* they were discovering China in Paris, when in fact they were landing in California."[3]

Most paradoxical and fascinating of all, however, is the unexpected and unpredictable sequel to the Sino-Soviet split itself: the new Chinese rhetoric, intent on castigating the Soviet bureaucracy as revisionistic and "bourgeois," will have the curious effect of evacuating the class content of these slogans. There is then an inevitable terminological slippage and displacement: the new binary opposite to the term "bourgeois" will no longer be "proletarian" but rather "revolutionary," and the new qualifications for political judgments of this kind are no longer made in terms of class or party affiliation but rather in terms of personal life—your relationship to special privileges, to middle-class luxuries and dachas and managerial incomes and other perks—Mao Zedong's own monthly "salary," we are told, was something in the neighborhood of a hundred American dollars. As with all forms of anticommunism, this rhetoric can of course be appropriated by the anti-Marxist thematics of "bureaucracy," of the end of ideology and social class, and so forth. But it is important to understand how for Western militants what began to emerge from this at first merely tactical and rhetorical shift was a whole new political space, a space which will come to be articulated by the slogan "the personal is the political," and into which—in one of the most stunning and unforeseeable of historical turns—the women's movement will triumphantly move at the end of the decade, building a Yenan of a new and unpredictable kind which is still impregnable at the present moment.

4. The Withering Away of Philosophy

The limit as well as the strength of the stark Fanonian model of struggle was set by the relative simplicity of the colonial situation; this can be shown in two ways, first of all in the sequel to the "war of national independence." For with the Slave's symbolic and literal victory over the (now former) Master, the "politics of otherness" touches its limit as well; the rhetoric of a conquest of collective identity has then nowhere else to go but into a kind of secessionary logic of which black cultural nationalism and (later on) lesbian separatism are the most dramatic examples (the dialectic of cultural and linguistic independence in Quebec province would be yet another instructive one). But this result is also contradictory, insofar as the newly constituted group (we here pick up Sartre's account in the *Critique*) *needs* outside enemies to survive as a group, to produce and perpetuate a sense of collective cohesion and identity. Ultimately, in the absence of the clear-cut Manichean situation of the older imperialist period, this hard-won collective self-definition of a first moment of resistance will break up into the smaller and more comfortable unities of face-to-face microgroups (of which the official political sects are only one example).

The gradual waning of the Fanonian model can also be described from the perspective of what will shortly become its "structuralist" critique. On this view, it is still a model based on a conception of individual subjects, albeit mythical and collective ones. It is thereby both anthropomorphic and transparent, in the sense in which nothing intervenes between the great collective adversaries, between the Master and the Slave, between the Colonizer and the Colonized. Yet even in Hegel, there was always a third term, namely matter itself, the raw materials on which the Slave is made to labor and to work out a long and anonymous salvation through the rest of history. The "third term" of the 60s is, however, rather different from this. It was as though the protracted experiences of the earlier part of the decade gradually burned into the minds of the participants of specific lesson. In the United States, it was the experience of the interminable Vietnam War itself; in France, it was the astonishing and apparently invincible technocratic dynamism, and the seemingly unshakable inertia and resistance to de-Stalinization of the French Communist party; and everywhere, it was the tremendous expansion of the media apparatus and the culture of consumerism. This lesson might well be described as the discovery, within a hitherto antagonistic and "transparent" political praxis, of the opacity of the Institution itself as the radically transindividual, with its own inner dynamic and laws, which are not those of individual human action or intention, something which Sartre theorized in the *Critique* as the "pactico-inert," and which will take the definitive form, in competing "structuralism," of "structure" or "synchronic system," a realm of impersonal logic in terms of which human consciousness is itself little more than an "effect of structure."

On this reading, then, the new philosophical turn will be interpreted less in the idealistic perspective of some discovery of a new scientific truth (the Symbolic) than as the symptom of an essentially protopolitical and social experience, the shock of some new, hard, unconceptualized, resistant object which the older conceptuality cannot process and which thus gradually generates a whole new problematic. The conceptualization of this new problematic in the coding of linquistics or information theory may then be attributed to the unexpected explosion of information and messages of all kinds in the media revolution, which will be discussed in more detail in the following section. Suffice it to remark at this point that there is some historical irony in the way in which this moment, essentially the Third Technological Revolution in the West (electronics, nuclear energy)—in other words, a whole new step in the conquest of nature by human praxis—is philosophically greeted and conceptually expressed in a kind of thought officially designated as "antihumanist" and concerned to think what transcends or escapes human consciousness and intention. Similarly, the Second Technological Revolution of the late nineteenth century—an unparalleled quantum leap in human power over nature—was the moment of expression of a whole range of nihilisms associated with "modernity" or with high modernism in culture.

In the present context, the Althusserian experiment of the mid- to late 60s is the most revealing and suggestive of the various "structuralisms," since it was the only one to be explicitly political and indeed to have very wide-ranging political effects in Europe and Latin America. The story of Althusserianism can be told only schematically here: its initial thrust is twofold, against the unliquidated Stalinist tradition (strategically designated by the code words "Hegel" and "expressive causality" in Althusser's own texts), and against the "transparence" of the Eastern attempts to reinvent a Marxist humanism on the basis of the theory of alienation in Marx's early manuscripts. That Althusserianism is essentially a meditation on the "institutional" and on the opacity of the "practico-inert" may be judged by the three successive formulations of this object by Althusser himself in the course of the 60s: that of a "structure in dominance" or *structure à dominante* (in *For Marx*), that of "structural causality" (in *Reading Capital*), and that of "ideological state apparatuses" (in the essay of that name). What is less often remembered, but what should be perfectly obvious from any rereading of *For Marx*, is the origin of this new problematic in Maoism itself, and particularly in Mao Zedong's essay "On Contradiction," in which the notion of the complex, already-given *overdetermined* conjuncture of various kinds of antagonistic and nonantagonistic contradictions is mapped out.

The modification that will emerge from Althusser's "process of theoretical production" as it works over its Maoist "raw materials" can be conveyed by the problem and slogan of the "semi-autonomy" of the levels of social life (a problem already invoked in our opening pages). This formula will involve a struggle on two fronts: on the one hand, against the monism or "expressive causality" of Stalinism, in which the "levels" are identified, conflated, and brutally collapsed into one another (changes in economic production will be "the same" as political and cultural changes), and, on the other, against bourgeois avant-garde philosophy, which finds just such a denunciation of organic concepts of totality most congenial, but draws from it the consequence of a post- or anti-Marxist celebration of Nietzschean heterogeneity. The notion of a semi-autonomy of the various levels or instances, most notably of the political instance and of the dynamics of state power, will have enormous resonance (outstandingly in the work of Nicos Poulantzas), since it seems to reflect, and to offer a way of theorizing, the enormous growth of the state bureaucracy since the war, the "relative autonomy" of the state apparatus from any classical and reductive functionality in the service of big business, as well as the very active new terrain of political struggle presented by government or public sector workers. The theory could also be appealed to to justify a semi-autonomy in the cultural sphere, as well, and especially a semi-autonomous cultural politics, of a variety that ranges from Godard's films and *situationnisme* to the "festival" of May 68 and the Yippie movement here (not excluding, perhaps, even those forms of so-called terrorism that aimed, not at any classical seizure of state power, but rather at essentially pedagogical or informational demonstrations, e.g., "forcing the state to reveal its fundamentally fascist nature").

Nonetheless, the attempt to open up a semi-autonomy of the levels in one hand, while holding them altogether in the ultimate unity of some "structural totality" (with its still classical Marxian ultimately determining instance of the economic), tends under its own momentum, in the centrifugal force of the critique of totality it had itself elaborated, to self-destruct (most dramatically so in the trajectory of Hindess and Hirst). What will emerge is not merely a heterogeneity of *levels*—henceforth, semi-autonomy will relax into autonomy *tout court*, and it will be conceivable that in the decentered and "schizophrenic" world of late capitalism the various instances may really have no organic relationship to one another at all—but, more important, the idea will emerge that the struggles appropriate to each of these levels (purely political struggles, purely economic struggles, purely cultural struggles, purely "theoretical" struggles) may have no necessary relationship to one another either. With this ultimate "meltdown" of the Althusserian apparatus, we are in the (still contemporary) world of microgroups and micropolitics—variously theorized as local or molecular politics, but clearly characterized, however different the various conceptions are, as a repudiation of old-fashioned class and party politics of a "totalizing" kind, and most obviously epitomized by the challenge of the women's movement, whose unique new stategies and concerns cut across (or in some cases undermine and discredit altogether) many classical inherited forms of "public" or "official" political action, including the electoral kind. The repudiation of "theory" itself is an essentially masculine enterprise of "power through knowledge" in French feminism (see in particular the work of Luce Irigaray) may be taken as the final moment in this particular "withering away of philosophy."

Yet there is another way to read the density of Althusserianism, a way that will form the transition to our subsequent discussion of the transformation of the cultural sphere in the 60s; and this involves the significance of the slogan of "theory" itself as it comes to replace the older term "philosophy" throughout this period. The "discovery" of the Symbolic, the development of its linguistic-related thematics (as, e.g., in the notion of understanding as an essentially synchronic process, which influences the construction of relatively ahistorical "structures," such as the Althusserian one described above), is now to be correlated with a modification of the practice of the symbolic, of language itself in the "structuralist" tests, henceforth characterized as "theory," rather than work in a particular traditional discipline. Two features of this evolution, or mutation, must be stressed. The first is a consequence of the crisis in, or the disappearance of, classical *canon* of philosophical writings which necessarily results from the contestation of philosophy as a discipline and an institution. Henceforth, the new "philosophical" text will no longer draw its significance from an insertion into the issues and debates of the philosophical tradition, which means that its basic "intertextual" references become random, an *ad hoc* constellation that forms and dissolves on the occasion of each new text. The new text must necessarily be a commentary on other texts (indeed, that dependence on a body of texts to be glossed, rewritten, interconnected in fresh ways will now intensify if anything), yet those texts, drawn from the most wildly distant disciplines (anthropology, psychiatry, literature, history of science), will be selected in a seemingly arbitrary fashion: Mumford side by side with Antonin Artaud, Kant with Sade, pre-Socratic philosophy, President Schreber, a novel of Maurice Blanchot, Owen Lattimore on Mongolia, and a host of obscure Latin medical treatises from the eighteenth century. The vocation of what was formerly "philosophy" is thereby restructured and displaced: since there is no longer a tradition of philosophical problems in terms of which new positions and new statements can meaningfully be proposed, such works now tend toward what can be called metaphilosophy—the very different work of coordinating a series of pregiven, already constituted codes or systems of signifiers, of producing a discourse fashioned out of the already fashioned discourse of the constellation of *ad hoc* reference works. "Philosophy" thereby becomes radically occasional; one would want to call it disposable theory, the producton of a *metabook*, to be replaced by a different one next season, rather than the ambition to express a proposition, a position, or a system with greater "truth" value. (The obvious analogy with the evolution of literary and cultural studies today, with the crisis and disappearance of the latter's own canon of great books—the last one having been augmented to include the once recalcitrant "masterpieces" of high modernism—will be taken for granted in our next section.)

All of this can perhaps be grasped in a different way by tracing the effects of another significant feature of contemporary theory, namely its privileged theme in the so-called critique of representation. Traditional philosophy will now be grasped in those terms, as a practice of representation in which the philosophical text or system (misguidedly) attempts to express something other than itself, namely truth or meaning (which now stands as the "signified" to the "signifier" of the system). If, however, the whole aesthetic of representation is metaphysical and ideological, philosophical discourse can no longer entertain this vocation, and it must stand as the mere addition of another text to what is now conceived as an infinite chain of texts (not necessarily all verbal—daily life is a text, clothing is a text, state power is a text, that whole external world, about which "meaning" or "truth" were once asserted and which is now contemptuously characterized as the illusion of reference or the "referent," is an indeterminate superposition of texts of all kinds). Whence the significance of the currently fashionable slogan of "materialism," when sounded in the area of philosophy and theory: materialism here means the dissolution of any belief in "meaning" or in the "signified" conceived as ideas or concepts that are distinct from their linguistic expressions. However paradoxical a "materialist" philosophy may be in this respect, a "materialist theory of language" will clearly transform the very function and operation of "theory," since it opens up a dynamic in which it is no longer ideas, but rather texts, material texts, which struggle with one another. Theory so defined (and it will have become clear that the term now greatly transcends what used to be called philosophy and its specialized content) conceives of its vocation, not as the discovery of truth and the repudiation of error, but rather as a struggle about purely linguistic formulations, as the attempt to formulate verbal propositions (material language) in such a way that they are unable to imply unwanted or ideological consequences. Since this aim is evidently impossible to achieve, what emerges from the practice of theory—and this was most dramatic and visible during the high point of Althusserianism itself in 1967-68—is a violent and obsessive return to ideological critique in the new form of a perpetual guerrilla war among the material signifiers of textual formulations. With the transformation of philosophy into a material practice, however, we touch on a development that cannot fully be appreciated until it is replaced in the context of a general mutation of culture throughout this period, a context in which "theory" will come to be grasped as a specific (or semi-autonomous) form of what must be called postmodernism generally.

5. The Adventures of the Sign

Postmodernism is one significant framework in which to describe what happened to culture in the 60s, but a full discussion of this hotly contested concept is not possible here. Such a discussion would want to cover, among other things, the following features: that well-known poststructuralist theme, the "death" of the subject (including the creative subject, the *auteur* or the "genius"); the nature and function of a *culture of the simulacrum* (an idea developed out of Plato by Deleuze and Baudrillard to convey some specificity of a reproducible object world, not of copies or reproductions marked as such, but of a proliferation of trompe-l'oeil copies *without originals*); the relation of this last to media culture of the "society of the spectacle" (Debord), under two heads: (1) the peculiar new status of the image, the "material" or what might better be called the "literal," signifier: a materiality or literality from which the older sensory richness of the medium has been abstracted (just as on the other side of the dialectical relationship, the old individuality of the subject and his/her "brushstrokes" have equally been effaced); and (2) the emergence, in the work's temporality, of an aesthetic of *textuality* or what is often described as schizophrenic time; the eclipse, finally, of all depth, especially *historicity* itself, with the subsequent appearance of pastiche and nostalgia art (what the French call *la mode rétro*), and including the supersession of the accompanying models of depth-interpretation in philosophy (the various forms of hermeneutics, as well as the Freudian conception of "repression," of manifest and latent levels).

What is generally objected to in characterizations of this kind is the empirical observation that all these features can be abundantly located in this or that variety of high modernism; indeed, one of the difficulties in specifying postmodernism lies in its symbiotic or parasitical relationship to the latter. In effect, with the canonization of a hitherto scandalous, ugly, disonant, amoral, antisocial, bohemian high modernism offensive to the middle classes, its promotion to the very figure of high culture generally, and perhaps most important, its enshrinement in the academic institution, postmodernism emerges as a way of making creative space for artists now oppressed by those henceforth hegemonic modernist categories of irony, complexity, ambiguity, dense temporality, and particularly, aesthetic and utopian monumentality. In some analogous way, it will be said, high modernism itself won its autonomy from the preceding hegemonic realism (the symbolic language or mode of representation of classical or market capitalism). But there is a difference in that realism itself underwent a significant mutation: it became *naturalism* and at once generated the representation forms of mass culture (the narrative apparatus of the contemporary best seller is an invention of naturalism and one of the most stunningly successful of French cultural exports). High modernism and mass culture then develop in dialectical opposition and interrelationship with one another. It is precisely the waning of their opposition, and some new conflation of the forms of high and mass culture, that characterizes postmodernism itself.

The historical specificity of postmodernism must therefore finally be argued in terms of the social functionality of culture itself. As stated above, high modernism, whatever its overt political content, was oppositional and marginal within a middle-class Victorian or philistine or gilded age culture. Although postmodernism is equally offensive in all the respects enumerated (think of punk rock or pornography), it is no longer at all "oppositional" in that sense; indeed, it constitutes the very dominant or hegemonic aesthetic of consumer society itself and significantly serves the latter's commodity production as a virtual laboratory of new forms and fashions. The argument for a conception of postmodernism as a periodizing category is thus based on the presupposition that, even if *all* the formal features enumerated above were already present in the older high modernism, the very significance of those features changes when they become a cultural *dominant*, with a precise socioeconomic functionality.

At this point it may be well to shift the terms (or the "code") of our description to the seemingly more traditional one of a cultural "sphere," a conception developed by Herbert Marcuse in what is to my mind his single most important text, the great essay "The Affirmative Character of Culture" (1937). (It should be added that the conception of a "public sphere" generally is a very contemporary one in Germany in the works of Habermas and Negt and Kluge, where such a system of categories stands in interesting contrast to the code of "levels" or "instances" in French poststructuralism.) Marcuse there rehearses the paradoxical dialectic of the classical (German) aesthetic, which projects as play and "purposefulness without purpose" a Utopian realm of beauty and culture beyond the fallen empirical world of money and business activity, thereby winning a powerful critical and negative value through its capacity to condemn, by its own very existence, the totality of *what* is, at the same time forfeiting all ability to social or political intervention in what is, by virtue of its constitutive disjunction or autonomy from society and history.

The account therefore begins to concide in a suggestive way with the problematic of autonomous or semi-autonomous levels developed in the preceding section. To historicize Marcuse's dialectic, however, would demand that we take into account the possibility that in our time this very autonomy of the cultural sphere (or level or instance) may be in the process of modification; and that we develop the means to furnish a description of the process whereby such modification might take place, as well as of the prior process whereby culture became "autonomous" or "semi-autonomous" in the first place.

This requires recourse to yet another (unrelated) analytic code, one more generally familiar to us today, since it involves the now classical structural concept of the *sign*, with its two components, the signifier (the material vehicle or image—sound or printed word) and the signified (the mental image, meaning, or "conceptual" content), and a third component—the external object of the sign, its reference or "referent"—henceforth expelled from the unity and yet haunting it as a ghostly residual aftereffect (illusion or ideology). The scientific value of this conception of the sign will be bracketed here since we are concerned, on the one hand, to historicize it, to interpret it as a conceptual symptom of developments in the period, and, on the other, to "set it in motion," to see whether changes in its inner structure can offer some adequate small-scale emblem or electrocardiogram of changes and permutation in the cultural sphere generally throughout this period.

Such changes are already suggested by the fate of the "referent" in the "conditions of possibility" of the new structural concept of the sign (a significant ambiguity must be noted, however: theorists of the sign notoriously glide from a conception of reference as designating a "real" object outside the unity of signifier and signified to a position in which the signified itself—or meaning, or the idea or the concept of a thing—becomes somehow identified with the referent and stigmatized along with it; we will return to this below). Saussure, at the dawn of the semiotic revolution, liked to describe the relationship of signifier to signified as that of the two sides, the recto and verso, of a sheet of paper. In what is then a logical sequel, and a text that naturally enough becomes equally canonical, Borges will push "representation" to the point of imagining a map so rigorous and referential that it becomes coterminous with its object. The stage is then set for the structuralist emblem par excellence, the Moebius Strip, which succeeds in peeling itself off its referent altogether and thus achieves a free-floating closure in the void, a kind of absolute self-referentiality and autocirculatory from which all remaining traces of reference, or of any externality, have triumphantly been effaced.

To be even more eclectic about it, I will suggest that this process, seemingly internal to the sign itself, requires a supplementary explanatory code, that of the more universal process of reification and fragmentation at one with the logic of capital itself. Nonetheless, taken on its own terms, the inner convulsions of the sign is a useful initial figure of the process of transformation of culture generally, which must in some first moment (that described by Marcuse) separate itself from the "referent" the existing social and historical world itself, only in a subsequent stage of the 60s, in what is here termed "postmodernism," to develop further into some new and heightened, free-floating, self-referential "autonomy."

The problem now turns around this very term, "autonomy," with its paradoxical Althusserian modification, the concept of "semi-autonomy." The paradox is that the sign, as an "autonomous" unity in its own right as a realm divorced from the referent, can preserve that initial autonomy, and the unity and coherence demanded by it, only at the price of keeping a phantom of reference alive, as the ghostly reminder of its own outside or exterior, since this allows it closure, self-definition, and an essential boundary line. Marcuse's own tormented dialectic expresses this dramatically in the curious oscillation whereby his autonomous realm of beauty and culture returns upon some "real world" to judge and negate it, at the same time separating itself so radically from that real world as to become a place of mere illusion and impotent "ideals," the "infinite," and so on.

The first moment in the adventures of the sign is perplexing enough as to demand more concrete, if schematic, illustration in the most characteristic cultural productions themselves. It might well be demonstrated in the classical French *nouveau roman* (in particular the novels of Robbe-Grillet himself), which established its new language in the early 1960s, using systematic variations of narrative segments to "undermine" representation, yet in some sense confirming this last by teasing and stimulating an appetite for it.

Because an American illustration seems more appropriate, however, something similar may be seen in connection with the final and canonical form of high modernism in American poetry, namely the work of Wallace Stevens, which becomes, in the years following the poet's death in 1956, institutionalized in the university as a purer and more quintessential fulfillment of poetic language than the still impure (read: ideological and political) works of an Eliot or a Pound, and can therefore be numbered among the literary "events" of the early 60s. As Frank Lentricchia has shown, in *After the New Criticism*,[4] the serviceability of Stevens' poetic production for this normative and hegemonic role depends in large measure on the increasing conflation, in that work, of poetic practice and poetic theory:

> This endlessly elaborating poem
> Displays the theory of poetry
> As the life of poetry...

"Stevens" is therefore a locus and fulfillment of aesthetics and aesthetic theory fully as much as the latter's exemplar and privileged exegetical object; the theory or aesthetic ideology in question is very much an affirmation of the "autonomy" of the cultural sphere in the sense developed above, a valorization of the supreme power of the poetic imagination over the "reality" it produces. Stevens' work, therefore, offers an extraordinary laboratory situation in which to observe the autonomization of culture as a process: a detailed examination of his development (something for which we have no space here) would show how some initial "set toward" or "attention to" a kind of poetic *pensée sauvage*, the operation of great preconscious *stereotypes*, opens up a vast inner world in which little by little the images of things and their "ideas" begin to be substituted for the things themselves. Yet what distinguishes this experience in Stevens is the sense of a vast systematicity in all this, the operation of a whole set of cosmic oppositions far too complex to be reduced to the schemata of "structuralist" binary oppositions, yet akin to those in spirit, and somehow pregiven in the Symbolic Order of the mind, discoverable to the passive exploration of the "poetic imagination," that is, of some heightened and impersonal power of free asssociation in the realm of "objective spirit" or "objective culture." The examination would further show the strategic limitation of this process to landscape, the reduction of the ideas and images of things to the names for things, and finally to those irreducibles that are place names, among which the exotic has a privileged function (Key West, Oklahoma, Yucatan, Java). Here the poetic "totality" begins to trace a ghostly mimesis or *analogon* of the totality of the imperialist world system itself, with Third World materials in a similarly strategic, marginal, yet essential place (much as Adorno showed how Schoenberg's twelve-tone system unconsciously produced a formal imitation of the "total system" of capital). This very unconscious replication of the "real" totality of the world system in the mind is then what allows culture to separate itself as a closed and self-sufficient "system" in its own right: reduplication, and at the same time, floating above the real. It is an impulse shared by most of the great high modernisms, as has been shown most dramatically in the recent critiques of architectural modernism, in particular of the international style, whose great monumental objects constitute themselves, by protecting a protopolitical and utopian spirit of transformation *against* a fallen city fabric all around them and, as Venturi has demonstrated, end up necessarily displaying and speaking of themselves alone. Now, this also accounts for what must puzzle any serious reader of Stevens' verse, namely the extraordinary combination of verbal richness and experimental hollowness or impoverishment in it (the latter being attributable as well to the impersonality of the poetic imagination in Stevens, and to the essentially contemplative and epistemological stance of the subject in it, over and against the static object world of his landscapes).

The essential point here, however, is that this characteristic movement of the high modernist impulse needs to justify itself by way of an ideology, an ideological supplement which can generally be described as that of "existentialism" (the supreme fiction, the meaninglessness of a contingent object world unredeemed by the imagination, etc.). This is the most uninteresting and banal dimension of Stevens work, yet it betrays along with other existentialisms (e.g., Sartre's tree root in *Nausea)* that fatal seam or link that must be retained in order for the contingent, the "outside world," the meaningless referent, to be just present enough dramatically to be overcome within the language. Nowhere is this ultimate point so clearly deduced, over and over again, as in Stevens, in the eye of the blackbird, the angels, or the Sun itself—that last residual vanishing point of reference as distant as a dwarf star upon the horizon, yet which cannot disappear altogether without the whole vocation of poetry and the poetic imagination being called back into question. Stevens thus exemplifies for us the fundamental paradox of the "autonomy" of the cultural sphere: the sign can become autonomous only by remaining semi-autonomous, and the realm of culture can absolutize itself over against the real world only at the price of retaining a final tenuous sense of that exterior or external world of which it is the replication and the imaginary double.

All of this can also be demonstrated by showing what happens when, in a second moment, the perfectly logical conclusion is drawn that the referent is itself a myth and does not exist, a second moment hitherto described as postmodernism. Its trajectory can be seen as a movement from the older *Nouveau roman* to that of Sollers or of properly "schizophrenic" writing, or from the primacy of Stevens to that of John Ashbery. This new moment is a radical break (which can be localized around 1967 for reasons to be given later), but it is important to grasp it as dialectical, that is, as a passage from quantity to quality in which the *same* force, reaching a certain threshold of excess, in its prolongation now produces qualitatively distinct effects and seems to generate a whole new system.

That force has been described as reification, but we can now also begin to make some connections with another figural language used earlier: in a first moment, reification "liberated" the sign from its referent, but this is not a force to be released with impunity. Now, in a second moment, it continues its work of dissolution, penetrating the interior of the sign itself and liberating the signifier from the signified, or from meaning proper. This play, no longer of a realm of signs, but of pure or literal signifiers freed from the ballast of their signifieds, their former meanings, now generates a new kind of textuality in all the arts (and in philosophy as well, as we have seen above) and begins to project the mirage of some ultimate language of pure signifiers which is also frequently associated with schizophrenic discourse. (Indeed, the Lacanian theory of schizophrenia—a language disorder in which syntactical time breaks down and leaves a succession of empty signifiers, absolute moments of a perpetual present, behind itself—has offered one of the more influential explanations and ideological justifications for postmodernist textual practice.)

Such an account would have to be demonstrated in some detail by way of a concrete analysis of the postmodernist experience in all the arts today; but the present argument can be concluded by drawing the consequences of this second moment—the aculture of the signifier or of the simulacrum—for the whole problematic of some "autonomy" of the cultural sphere which has concerned us here. For that autonomous realm is not itself spared by the intensified process by which the classical sign is dissolved; if its autonomy depended paradoxically on its possibility of remaining "semi-autonomous" (in an Althusserian sense) and of preserving the last tenuous link with some ultimate referent (or, in Althusserian language, of preserving the ultimate unity of a properly "structural totality"), then evidently in the new cultural moment culture will have ceased to be autonomous, and the realm of an autonomous play of signs becomes impossible, when that ultimate final referent to which the balloon of the mind was moored is now definitively cut. The break-up of the sign in mid-air determines a fall back into a now absolutely fragmented and anarchic social reality; the broken pieces of language (the pure signifiers) now fall again into the world, as so many more pieces of material junk among all the other rusting and superannuated apparatuses and buildings that litter the commodity landscape and that strew the "collage city," the "delirious New York" of a postmodernist late capitalism in full crisis.

But, returning to a Marcusean terminology, all of this can also be said in a different way: with the eclipse of culture as an autonomous space or sphere, culture itself falls into the world, and the result is not its disappearance but its prodigious expansion, to the point where culture becomes coterminous with social life in general; now all the levels become "acculturated," and in the society of the spectacle, the image, or the simulacrum, everything has at length become cultural, from the superstructures down into the mechanisms of the infrastructure itself. If this development then places acutely on the agenda the neo-Gramscian problem of a new cultural politics today—in a social system in which the very status of both culture and politics have been profoundly, functionally, and structurally modified—it also renders problematic any further discussion of what used to be called "culture" proper, whose artifacts have become the random experiences of daily life itself.

6. In the Sierra Maestra

The preceding section will, however, have been little more than a lengthy excursion into a very specialized (or "elite") area, unless it can be shown that the dynamic therein visible, with something of the artificial simplification of the laboratory situation, finds striking analogies or homologies in very different and distant areas of social practice. It is precisely this replication of a common diachronic rhythm or "genetic code" which we will not observe in the very different realities of revolutionary practice and theory in the course of the 60s in the Third World.

From the beginning, the Cuban experience affirmed itself as an original one, as a new revolutionary model, to be radically distinguished from more traditional forms of revolutionary practice. *Foco* theory, indeed, as it was associated with Che Guevara and theorized in Regis Debray's influential handbook, *Revolution in the Revolution?* (1967), asserted itself (as the title of the book suggests) both against a more traditional Leninist conception of party practice and against the experience of the Chinese revolution in its first essential stage of the conquest of power (what will later come to be designated as "Maoism," China's own very different "revolution in the revolution," or Great Proletarian Cultural Revolution, will not become visible to the outside world until the moment when the fate of the Cuban strategy has been sealed).

A reading of Debray's text shows that *foco* strategy, the strategy of the mobile guerrilla base or revolutionary *foyer*, is conceived as yet a third term, as something distinct from *either* the traditional model of class struggle (an essentially *urban* proletariat rising against a bourgeoisie or ruling class) *or* the Chinese experience of a mass peasant movement in the countryside (and also has little in common with a Fanonian struggle for recognition between Colonizer and Colonized). The *foco*, or guerrilla operation, is conceptualized as being neither "in" nor "of" either country or city; geographically, of course, it is positioned in the countryside, yet that location is not the permanently "liberated territory" of the Yenan region, well beyond the reach of the enemy forces of Chiang Kai-shek or of the Japanese occupier. It is not indeed located in the cultivated area of the peasant fields at all, but rather in that third or nonplace which is the wilderness of the Sierra Maestra, neither country nor city, but rather a whole new element in which the guerrilla band moves in perpetual displacement.

This peculiarity of the way in which the spatial coordinates of the Cuban strategy is conceived has, then, immediate consequences for the way in which the class elements of the revolutionary movement are theorized. Neither city nor country; by the same token, paradoxically, the guerrillas themselves are grasped as being neither workers nor peasants (still less, intellectuals), but rather something entirely new, for which the prerevolutionary class society has no categories: new revolutionary subjects, forged in the guerrilla struggle indifferently out of the social material of peasants, city workers, or intellectuals, yet now largely transcending those class categories (just as this moment of Cuban theory will claim largely to transcend the older revolutionary ideologies predicted on class catagories, whether those of Trotskyist workerism, Maoist populism and peasant consciousness, or of Leninist vanguard intellectualism).

What becomes clear in a text like Debray's is that the guerrilla *foco*—so mobile as to be beyond geography in the static sense—is in and of itself a *figure* for the transformed, revolutionary society to come. Its revolutionary militants are not simply "soldiers" to whose specialized role and function one would then have to "add" supplementary roles in the revolutionary division of labor, such as political commissars and the political vanguard party itself, both explicitly rejected here. Rather, in them is abolished all such prerevolutionary divisions and categories. This conception of a newly emergent revolutionary "space"—situated outside the "real" political, social, and geographical world of country and city, and of the historical social classes, yet at one and the same time a figure or small-scale image and prefiguration of the revolutionary transformation of that real world—may be designated as a properly Utopian space, a Hegelian "inverted world," an autonomous revolutionary sphere, in which the fallen real world over against it is itself set right and transformed into a new socialist society.

For all practical purposes, this powerful model is exhausted, even before Che's own tragic death in Bolivia in 1967, with the failure of the guerrilla movements in Peru and Venezuela in 1966; not uncoincidentally, that failure will be accompanied by something like a disinvestment of revolutionary libido and fascination on the part of a First World Left, the return (with some leavening of the newer Maoism) to its own current situation," in the American antiwar movement and May 68. In Latin America, however, the radical strategy that effectively replaces *foco* theory is that of the so-called urban guerrilla movement, pioneered in Uruguay by the Tupamaros; it will have become clear that this break-up of the utopian space of the older guerrilla *foco*, the fall of politics back into the world in the form of a very different style of political practice indeed—one that seeks to dramatize features of state power, rather than, as in traditional revolutionary movements, to build toward some ultimate encounter with it—will be interpreted here as something of a structural equivalent to the final stage of the sign as characterized above.

Several qualifications must be made, however. For one thing, it is clear that this new form of political activity will be endowed, by association, with something of the tragic prestige of the Palestinian liberation movement, which comes into being in its contemporary form as a result of the Israeli seizure of the West Bank and the Gaza Strip in 1967, and which will thereafter become one of the dominant worldwide symbols of revolutionary praxis in the late 60s. Equally clearly, however, the struggle of this desperate and victimized people cannot be made to bear responsibility for the excesses of this kind of strategy elsewhere in the world, whose universal results (whether in Latin America, or with Cointelpro in the United States, or, belatedly, in West Germany and Italy) have been to legitimize an intensification of the repressive apparatus of state power.

This objective coincidence between a misguided assessment of the social and political situation on the part of Left militants (for the most part students and intellectuals eager to force a revolutionary conjuncture by voluntaristic acts) and a willing exploitation by the state of precisely those provocations suggests that what is often loosely called "terrorism" must be the object of complex and properly dialectical analysis. However rightly a responsible Left chooses to dissociate itself from such strategy (and the Marxian opposition to terrorism is an old and established tradition that goes back to the nineteenth century), it is important to remember that "terrorism," as a "concept," is also an ideologeme of the Right and must therefore be refused in that form. Along with the disaster films of the late 60s and early 70s, mass culture itself makes clear that "terrorism"—the image of the "terrorist"—is one of the privileged forms in which an ahistorical society imagines radical social change; meanwhile, an inspection of the content of the modern thriller or adventure story also makes it clear that the "otherness" of so-called terrorism has begun to replace older images of criminal "insanity" as an unexamined and seemingly "natural" motivation in the construction of plots—yet another sign of the ideological nature of this particular pseudoconcept. Understood in this way, "terrorism" is a collective obsession, a symptomatic fantasy of the American political unconscious, which demands decoding and analysis in its own right.

As for the thing itself, for all practical purposes it comes to an end with the Chilean coup in 1973 and the fall of virtually all the Latin American countries to various forms of military dictatorship. The belated reemergence of this kind of political activity in West Germany and in Italy must surely at least in part be attributed to the fascist past of these two countries, to their failure to liquidate that past after the war, and to a violent moral revulsion against it on the part of a segment of the youth and intellectuals who grew up in the 60s.

7. Return of the "Ultimately Determining Instance"

The two "breaks" that have emerged in the preceding section—one in the general area around 1967, the other in the immediate neighborhood of 1973—will not serve as the framework for a more general hypothesis about the periodization of the 60s in general. Beginning with the second of these, a whole series of other, seemingly unrelated events in the general area of 1972-74 suggests that this moment is not merely a decisive one on the relatively specialized level of Third World or Latin American radical politics, but signals the definitive end of what is called the 60s in a far more global way. In the First World, for example, the end of the draft and the withdrawal of American forces from Vietnam (in 1973) spell the end of the mass politics of the antiwar movement (the crisis of the New Left itself—which can be largely dated from the break-up of SDS in 1969—would seem related to the other break mentioned, to which we will return below), while the signing of the Common Program between the Communist party and the new Socialist party in France (as well as the wider currency of slogans associated with "Eurocommunism" at this time) would seem to mark a strategic turn away from the kinds of political activities associated with May 68 and its sequels. This is also the movement when as a result of the Yom Kippur war, the oil weapon emerges and administers a different kind of shock to the economies, the political strategies, and the daily life habits of the advanced countries. Concomitantly, on the more general cultural and ideological level, the intellectuals associated with the establishment itself (particularly in the United States) begin to recover from the fright and defensive posture that was theirs during the decade now ending, and again find their voices in a series of attacks on 60s culture and 60s politics, which, as was noted at the beginning, are not even yet at an end. One of the more influential documents was Lionel Trilling's *Sincerity and Authenticity* (1972), an Arnoldian call to reverse the tide of 60s' countercultural "barbarism." (This will, of course, be followed by the equally influential diagnosis of some 60s concept of "authenticity" in terms of a "culture of narcissism.") Meanwhile, in July 1973, some rather different "intellectuals," representing various concrete forms of political and economic power, will begin to rethink the failure in Vietnam in terms of a new global strategy for American and First World interests; their establishment of the Trilateral Commission will at least symbolically be a significant marker in the recovery of momentum by what must be called "the ruling classes." The emergence of a widely accepted new popular concept and term at this same time, the notion of the "multinational corporation," is also another symptom, signifying, as the authors of *Global Reach* have suggested, the moment when private business finds itself obliged to emerge in public as a visible "subject of history" and a visible actor on the world stage—think of the role of ITT in Chile—when the American government, having been badly burned by the failure of the Vietnam intervention, is generally reluctant to undertake further ventures of this kind.

For all these reasons it seems appropriate to mark the definitive end of the "60s" in the general area of 1972-74. But we have omitted until now the decisive element in any argument for a periodization or "punctuation" of this kind, and this new kind of material will direct our attention to a "level" or "instance" which has hitherto significantly been absent from the present discussion, namely the economic itself. For 1973-74 is the moment of the onset of a worldwide economic crisis, whose dynamic is still with us today, and which put a decisive full stop to the economic expansion and prosperity characteristic of the postwar period generally and of the 60s in particular. When we add to this another key economic marker—the recession in West Germany in 1966 and that in the other advanced countries, in particular in the United States a year or so later—we may well thereby find ourselves in a better position more formally to conceptualize the sense of a secondary break around 1967-68 which has begun to surface on the philosophical, cultural, and political levels as they were analyzed or "narrated" above.

Such confirmation by the economic "level" itself of periodizing reading derived from other, sample levels or instances of social life during the 60s will now perhaps put us in a better position to answer the two theoretical issues raised at the beginning of this essay. The first had to do with the validity of Marxist analysis for a period whose active political categories no longer seemed to be those of social class, and in which in a more general way traditional forms of Marxist theory and practice seemed to have entered a "crisis." The second involved the problem of some "unified field theory" in terms of which such seemingly distant realities as Third World peasant movements and First World mass culture (or indeed, more abstractly, intellectual or superstructural levels like philosophy and culture generally, and those of mass resistance and political practice) might conceptually be related in some coherent way.

A pathbreaking synthesis of Ernest Mandel, in his book *Late Capitalism*,[5] will suggest a hypothetical answer to both these questions at once. The book presents, among other things, an elaborate system of business cycles under capitalism, whose most familiar unit, the seven-to-ten-year alternation of boom, overproduction, recession, and economic recovery, adequately enough accounts for the midpoint break in the 60s suggested above.

Mandel's account of the worldwide crisis of 1974, however, draws on a far more controversial conception of vaster cycles of some thirty- to fifty-year periods each—cycles which are then obviously much more difficult to perceive experientially or "phenomenologically" insofar as they transcend the rhythms and limits of the biological life of individuals. These "Kondratiev waves" (named after the Soviet economist who hypothesized them) have, according to Mandel, been renewed four times since the eighteenth century, and are characterized by quantum leaps in the technology of production, which enable decisive increases in the rate of profit generally, until at length the advantages of the new production processes have been explored and exhausted and the cycle therewith comes to an end. The latest of these Kondratiev cycles is that marked by computer technology, nuclear energy, and the mechanization of agriculture (particularly in foodstuffs and also primary materials), which Mandel dates from 1940 in North America and the postwar period in the other imperialist countries; what is decisive in the present context is his notion that, with the worldwide recession of 1973-74, the dynamics of this latest "long wave" are spent.

The hypothesis is attractive, however, not only because of its abstract usefulness in confirming our periodization schemes, but also because of the actual analysis of this latest wave of capitalist expansion, and of the properly Marxian version he gives of a whole range of developments that have generally been thought to demonstrate the end of the "classical" capitalism theorized by Marx and to require this or that post-Marxist theory of social mutation (as in theories of consumer society, postindustrial society, and the like).

We have already described the way in which neocolonialism is characterized by the radically new technology (the so-called Green Revolution in agriculture: new machinery, new farming methods, and new types of chemical fertilizer and genetic experiments with hybrid plants and the like), with which capitalism transforms its relationship to its colonies from an old-fashioned imperialist control to market penetration, destroying the older village communities and creating a whole new wage-labor pool and lumpenproletariat. The militancy of the new social forces is at one and the same time a result of the "liberation" of peasants from the older self-sustaining village communities, and a movement of self-defense, generally originating in the stabler yet more isolated areas of a given Third World country, against what is rightly perceived as a far more thoroughgoing form of penetration and colonization than the older colonial armies.

It is now in terms of this process of "mechanization" that Mandel will make the link between the neocolonialist transformation of the Third World during the 60s and the emergence of that seemingly very different thing in the First World, variously termed consumer society, postindustrial society, media society, and the like:

> Far from representing a postindustrial society, late capitalism... constitutes *generalized universal industrialization* for the first time in history. Mechanization, standardization, overspecialization and parcellization of labor, which in the past determined only the realm of commodity production in actual industry, now penetrate into all sectors of social life. It is characteristic of late capitalism that agriculture is step by step becoming just as industrialized as industry, the sphere of circulation [e.g., credit cards and the like] just as much as the sphere of production, and recreation just as much as the organization of work. (p. 387)

With this last, Mandel touches on what he elsewhere calls the mechanization of the superstructure, or, in other words, the penetration of culture itself by what the Frankfurt School called the culture industry, and of which the growth of the media is only a part. We may thus generalize his description as follows: late capitalism in general (and the 60s in particular) constitute a process in which the last surviving internal and external zones of precapitalism—the last vestiges of noncommodified or traditional space within and outside the advanced world—are now ultimately penetrated and colonized in their turn. Late capitalism can therefore be described as the moment when the last vestiges of Nature which survived on into classical capitalism are at length eliminated: namely the Third World and the unconscious. The 60s will then have been the momentous transformational period when this systemic restructuring takes place on a global scale.

With such an account, our "unified field theory" of the 60s is given: the discovery of a single process at work in First and Third Worlds, in global economy, and in consciousness and culture, a properly *dialectical* process, in which "liberation" and domination are inextricably combined. We may now therefore proceed to a final characterization of the period as a whole.

The simplest yet most universal formulation surely remains the widely shared feeling that in the 60s, for a time, everything was possible; that this period, in other words, was a moment of a universal liberation, a global unbinding of energies. Mao Zedong's figure for this process is in this respect most revealing: "Our nation," he cried, "is like an atom. . . .When this atom's nucleus is smashed, the thermal energy released will have really tremendous power!"[6] The image evokes the emergence of a genuine mass democracy from the breakup of the older feudal and village structures, and from the therapeutic dissolution of the habits of those structures in cultural revolutions. Yet the effects of fission, the release of molecular energies, the unbinding of "material signifiers," can be a properly terrifying spectacle; and we now know that Mao Zedong himself drew back from the ultimate consequences of the process he had set in motion, when, at the supreme moment of the Cultural Revolution, that of the founding of the Shanghai Commune, he called a halt to the dissolution of the party apparatus and effectively reversed the direction of this collective experiment as a whole (with consequences only too obvious at the present time). In the West, also, the great explosions of the 60s have led, in the worldwide economic crisis, to powerful restorations of the social order and a renewal of the repressive power of the various state apparatuses.

Yet the forces these must now confront, contain, and control are new ones, on which the older methods do not necessarily work. We have described the 60s as a moment when the enlargement of capitalism on a global scale simultaneously produced an immense freeing or unbinding of social energies, a prodigious release of untheorized new forces: the ethnic forces of black and "minority," or Third World, movements everywhere, regionalisms, the development of new and militant bearers of "surplus consciousness" in the student and women's movements, as well as in a host of struggles of other kinds. Such newly released forces do not only not seem to compute in the dichotomous class model of traditional Marxism; they also seem to offer a realm of freedom and voluntarist possibility beyond the classical constraints of the economic infrastructure. Yet this sense of freedom and possibility—which is for the course of the 60s a momentarily objective reality, as well as (from the hindsight of the 80s) a historical illusion—can perhaps best be explained in terms of the superstructural movement and play enabled by the transition from one infrastructural or systemic stage of capitalism to another. The 60s were in that sense an immense and inflationary issuing of superstructural credit; a universal abandonment of the referential gold standard; an extraordinary printing up of ever more devalued signifiers. With the end of the 60s, with the world economic crisis, all the old infrastructural bills then slowly come due once more; and the 80s will be characterized by an effort, on a world scale, to proletarianize all those unbound social forces that gave the 60s their energy, by an extension of class struggle, in other words, into the farthest reaches of the globe as well as the most minute configurations of local institutions (such as the university system). The unifying force here is the new vocation of a henceforth global capitalism, which may also be expected to unify the unequal, fragmented, or local resistances to the process. And this is finally also the solution to the so-called crisis of Marxism and to the widely noted inapplicability of its forms of class analysis to the new social realities with which the 60s confronted us: "traditional" Marxism, if "untrue" during this period of a proliferation of new subjects of history, must necessarily become true again when the dreary realities of exploitation, extraction of surplus value, proletarianization, and the resistance to it in the form of class struggle, all slowly reassert themselves on a new and expanded world scale, as they seem currently in the process of doing.

1984

Notes

Notes

Unless otherwise indicated, all translations of foreign-language quotations are the author's.

Chapter 1.   The Vanishing Mediator; or, Max Weber as Storyteller

1. I have found the following studies useful: Herbert Marcuse, "Industrialization and Capitalism in the Work of Max Weber," *Negations* (Boston, 1968), pp. 201–26; Wolfgang J. Mommsen, "Universalgeschichtliches und politisches Denken bei Max Weber," *Historische Zeitschrift*, 201, no. 3 (December 1965), pp. 558–612; Eugène Fleischmann, "De Weber à Nietzsche," *Archives européennes de sociologie*, 5 (1964), pp. 190–238; Hans Gerth and C. Wright Mills, "Introduction," *From Max Weber* (New York, 1958), pp. 3–74; and particularly, Arthur Mitzman, *The Iron Cage: An Historical Interpretation of Max Weber* (New York, 1970).

2. Compare Weber: "For those to whom no causual explanation is adequate without an economic (or materialistic as it is unfortunately still called) interpretation, it may be remarked that I consider the influence of economic development on the fate of religious ideas to be very important and shall later attempt to show in our case the process of mutual adaptation of the two took place" (*The Protestant Ethic and the Spirit of Capitalism*, trans. Talcott Parsons, New York, 1958, p. 277, n. 84); and Engels: "According to the materialistic conception of history, the *ultimately* determining element in history is the production and reproduction of real life. More than this neither Marx nor I has ever asserted. Hence if somebody twists this into saying that the economic element is the *only* determining one he transforms that proposition into a meaningless, abstract, senseless phrase" (letter to Joseph Bloch, Sept. 21–22, 1890, in Marx and Engels, *Basic Writings on Politics and Philosophy*, ed. L. Feuer, New York, 1959, pp. 397–98).

3. H. Stuart Hughes, *Consciousness and Society* (New York, 1961), p. 298.

4. Sigmund Freud, "Mourning and Melancholia" (1917), in *General Psychological Theory* (New York, 1963), p. 165.

5. Ibid., pp. 165–66.

6. Thomas Aquinas, *Summa Theologica*, pt. 1, question 63, article 2.

7. Ibid., pt. 2, question 35, article 1.

8. Aristotle, *Metaphysics.*

9. Fleischman, "De Weber à Nietzsche," p. 237.

10. See Nietzsche, *Zarathustra,* pt. 2, "Von der Selbst-Ueberwindung," and *Jenseits von Gut und Böse,* "Wir Gelehrten," section 211.

11. Mommsen, "Universalgeschichtliches und politisches Denken," pp. 562-63.

12. "Science as a Vocation," in *From Max Weber,* p. 148.

13. "Introduction," in Max Weber, *Sociology of Religion* (Boston, 1963), p. xxxix, n. 11.

14. Marcuse, "Industrialization," p. 203.

15. A. J. Greimas, "Les Jeux des contraintes sémiotiques" (with Francois Rastier), in *Du Sens* Paris, 1970), pp. 135-55; translated as "The Interaction of Semiotic Constraints," in *Yale French Studies,* 41 (Spring 1968), pp. 86-105. For further discussion of this model, see my *Prison-House of Language* (Princeton, N.J., 1973) pp. 163-68.

16. Max Weber, *Gesammelte Aufsätze zur Wissenschaftslehre* (Tübingen, 1968), p. 565.

17. *Sociology of Religion,* p. 28.

18. Max Weber, *General Economic History* (New York, 1961), p. 265.

19. *Du Sens,* p. 104.

20. *Structural Anthropology,* trans. C. Jacobson and B. G. Schoepf (New York, 1967), p. 225, translation modified.

21. "Not only is a developed sense of responsibility absolutely indispensable, but in general also an attitude which, at least during working hours, is freed from continual calculations of how the customary wage may be earned with a maximum of comfort and a minimum of exertion. Labor must, on the contrary, be performed as if it were an absolute end in itself, a calling [*Beruf*]. But such an attitude is by no means a product of nature. It cannot be evoked by low wages or high ones alone, but can only be the product of a long and arduous process of education" *(The Protestant Ethic,* pp. 61-62).

22. Ibid., pp. 181-82.

23. Weber's study (1904-1905) doubtless has as its implicit target Karl Kautsky's *Vorläufer des Neueren Sozialismus* (1895), rather than Engels's older work on the *Peasant Wars in Germany* (1850).

24. Ibid., p. 183.

25. Ibid., p. 126.

26. Ibid., pp. 124-25.

27. Ibid., p. 121.

28. Not that Lévi-Strauss is unaware of the function of mediatory figures (which he explicitly discusses later in the same essay); his formula simply does not seem to accommodate them. But see for an alternate interpretation Elli Kaija Köngäs and Pierre Miranda, "Structural Models in Folklore," *Midwest Folklore,* 3, no. 3 (Fall 1962), pp. 137-39.

29. *General Economic History,* p. 267.

30. *Sociology of Religion,* pp. 47-48.

31. J. P. Sartre, *Search for a Method* (New York, 1968), p. 62; and for further discussion of Sartre's treatment of psychoanalysis, see my *Marxism and Form* (Princeton, N.J., 1972), pp. 214-29.

32. Charles Morazé, *The Triumph of the Middle Classes* (Cleveland, 1966), p. 82.

33. Mitzman, *Iron Cage,* pp. 8-9 .

34. Marianne Weber, *Max Weber: Ein Lebensbild* (Heidelberg, 1950), pp. 71-72.

35. "What seems incontestable is that either on or shortly after his parents' wedding anniversary he ordered his father out of his [i.e., Max, Jr.'s] house to permit his mother and himself the undisturbed enjoyment of one another's company. It was the first time that Weber had ever revealed to his father the full depths of his bitterness. And he never saw the old man alive again" (Mitzman, *Iron Cage,* p. 152). Weber's own nervous breakdown, an obvious self-punishment for

this half-symbolic, half-real "murder of the father," began six weeks to the day after the anniversary.

36. Marianne Weber, *Max Weber*, pp. 102ff.

37. See ibid., p. 275.

38. See *Structural Anthropology*.

39. Claude Lévi-Strauss, *The Raw and the Cooked*, trans. Don and Doreen Weightman (New York, 1969), p. 341, translation modified.

Chapter 2. Architecture and the Critique of Ideology

1. Manfredo Tafuri, *Theories and History of Architecture*, trans. Giorgio Verrecchia (New York, 1980), p. iii. Hereafter referred to as *T & H*.

2. Manfredo Tafuri, *Architecture and Utopia*, second ed., trans. Barbara Luigia La Penta (Cambridge, Mass., 1980). Hereafter referred to as *A & U*.

3. Karl Marx and Friedrich Engels, *The German Ideology*, ed. R. Pascal (New York, 1947).

4. Manfredo Tafuri and Francesco Dal Co., *Modern Architecture* (New York, 1979), p. 342. Hereafter referred to as *MA*.

5. See Daniel Bell's two books, *Postindustrial Society* (New York, 1973) and *The Cultural Contradictions of Capitalism* (New York, 1976).

6. The most systematic and powerful exposition of this theory is to be found in Ernest Mandel, *Late Capitalism* (London, 1978), on which I draw heavily here.

7. Karl Marx, *Contribution to a Critique of Political Economy* (New York, 1970), p. 21.

8. Karl Marx, *Capital*, vol. 1, trans. Ben Fowkes (London, 1976), p. 172.

9. See Jürgen Habermas, "Modernity versus Postmodernity," *New German Critique*, 22, (Winter 1981), pp. 3-18.

10. The critique of central planning, as in Peter Blake, as powerful and persuasive as it is, seems to me extremely ambiguous for the following reason: a perfectly correct and well-documented thesis of this kind can *also* be the occasion for the production of, or investment by, a whole ideology or metaphysics, most notably in the binary opposition between intention or plan and tradition or organic growth. This ideology is already present in Christopher Alexander, "A City Is Not a Tree," but its full-blown transformation into a metaphysic can be observed most dramatically in Deleuze and Guattari's "Rhizome" [in *Mille Plateaux*]. In this form, of course, it recapitulates the oldest counterrevolutionary position of all, that of Edmund Burke in the *Reflections on the French Revolution*, where Jacobin hubris is counterposed against the slow and organic growth of social life. On the political level, the Left traditions include a number of counterpositions that work against the emergence of such a stark and ideological opposition, especially in concepts of federation and the "withering away of the state" (the Paris Commune), of *autogestion* or worker's self-management, and of council communism. But in the area of architecture or urbanism it is rather hard to see what form such counterpositions might take. Least persuasive, to my mind, is the idea that people will rebuild their own dwellings as they go along (see, for example, P. Boudon, *Lived-In Architecture*, Cambridge, Mass., 1972, where the idea that Le Corbusier would have approved of all this, let alone intended it to happen that way, seems most disingenuous indeed). I have been attracted by Rem Koolhaas' *Delirious New York* (New York, 1978) for a rather different (and highly idiosyncratic) way of cutting through this ideological double-bind; he *historicizes* the dilemma by transforming "planning" into the unique and historical decision, in 1811, to impose the "grid" on Manhattan. From this single "centralized" decision, then, both the anarchy and the urban classicism (streets and blocks) at once develop.

11. A somewhat different example of such homogenizing repression can be found in Venturi's account of Frank Lloyd Wright's exclusion of the *diagonal*, in *Complexity and Contradiction in Architecture* (New York, 1977), p. 52.

12. Karl Marx, *Early Writings*, ed. Bottomore (New York, 1964), p. 210.

Chapter 3: Pleasure: A Political Issue

1. Roland Barthes, *Le Plaisir du texte* (Paris, 1973), pp. 37-38.
2. Laura Mulvey, "Visual Pleasure and Narrative Cinema," *Screen*, 16, no. 3 (Autumn 1976).
3. Barthes, *Le Plaisir du texte*, p. 82.
4. Edmund Burke, *A Philosophical Enquiry into the Origin of Our Ideas of the Sublime and Beautiful* (Notre Dame, Ind., 1968), p. 123.

Chapter 4. Of Islands and Trenches: Neutralization and the Production of Utopian Discourse

1. "From 1886, the year of the Haymarket Riots, until 1896, the year of the restoration of conservative hegemony. . . over one hundred works of Utopian fiction appeared." Jean Pfaelzer, "American Utopian Fiction, 1888-1896: The Political Origins of Form," in *The Minnesota Review*, 6, special issue entitled "Marxism and Utopia" (Spring 1976), p. 114.
2. Herbert Marcuse, "The End of Utopia," in *Five Lectures* (Boston, 1970), pp. 68-69.
3. A. H. Holz, L. Köfler, and W. Abendroth, *Gespräche mit Georg Lukács* (Hamburg, 1967), p. 93.
4. Ursula LeGuin, *The Dispossessed* (New York, 1974).
5. Louis Marin, *Utopiques: Jeux d'espaces* (Paris, 1973). This work is now available in English as *Utopics: Spatial Play*, trans. Robert A. Vollrath (Atlantic Highlands, N.J., 1984). Quotations are my translations of the French original. Two sets of page numbers are given in the text: the first refers to the French edition, the second to the 1984 translation.
6. All page references herein are to the edition of Edward Surtz (New Haven, Conn., 1964) .
7. See the chapter "Structural Study of Myth" in Lévi-Strauss, *Structural Anthropology* (New York, 1961), pp. 206-31.
8. See A. J. Greimas and François Rastier, "The Interaction of Semiotic Constraints," *Yale French Studies*, 41, special issue on "Game, Play, and Literature" (1968), pp. 86-105; and also Frédéric Nef, ed., *Structures élémentaires de la signification* (Brussels, 1976).
9. The Austin-Searle concept of a "speech act" would appear to belong in the category of the *énoncé,* an already completed and successful transmission of meaning; the confusion this concept sometimes gives rise to is probably attributable to the ambiguity of the term "act," which has led people to try to assimilate it to the opposite category, of praxis and production, of the emergence of meaning. See Stanley Fish, "How to Do Things with Austin and Searle: Speech Act Theory and Literary Criticism," *Modern Language Notes*, 91, no. 5 (October 1976), pp. 98-125.
10. Julia Kristeva, "La Sémiologie: Science critique et/ou critique de la science," in *Théorie d'ensemble* (Paris, 1968), p. 88.
11. See Georg Lukács, "Reification and the Consciousness of the Proletariat," in *History and Class Consciousness* (Cambridge, Mass., 1971), pp. 83-222; and for a theory of reification in consumer society, see Guy Debord, *La Société du spectacle* (Geneva, 1967).
12. Jonathan Swift, *Gulliver's Travels*, ed. Robert A. Greenberg (New York, 1970), p. 36, n. 1.
13. It may be conjectured that, after some interrogation, they will allow Morris to pass by. For an important reconsideration of the relationship of Morris (and beyond him of the Romantic tradition) to radical and revolutionary thought, see Edward Thompson, "Romanticism, Utopianism, and Moralism: The Case of William Morris," *New Left Review*, 99 (September-October 1976), pp. 83-111 (reprinted as the "Postscript" to William Morris, *Romantic to Revolutionary*, New York, Pantheon, 1977).
14. Xenakis' description of the cosmic vertical city is published in *Urbanisme: utopies et réalitiés*, ed. Françoise Choay (Paris, 1965), pp. 335-42.

15. See Bénichou, "La Demolition du heros," in *Les Morales du grand* siècle (Paris, 1948), pp. 97-111.

16. Pierre Macherey, *Pour une théorie de la production littéraire* (Paris, 1966).

17. Louis Marin, *Etudes sémiologiques* (Paris, 1971).

18. For a demonstration of this process, see Michel de Certeau's chapter on the travel narrative of Jean de Léry in *L'Ecriture de l'histoire* (Paris, 1975).

19. For more on the relationship between Utopia and disjunction, see my "World Reduction in LeGuin: The Emergence of Utopian Narrative," *Science-Fiction Studies*, 7 (vol. 2, no. 3; November 1975), pp. 221-30.

Chapter 5. The Politics of Theory: Ideological Positions in the Postmodernism Debate

1. The following analysis does not seem to me applicable to the work of the *boundary 2* group, who early on appropriated the term "postmodernism" in the rather different sense of a critique of establishment "modernist" thought.

2. This essay was written in Spring 1982.

3. See his "Modernity—An Incomplete Project," in *The Anti-Aesthetic*, ed. Hal Foster (Port Townsend, Wash. 1983), pp. 3-15. The essay was first published in *New German Critique*, 22 (Winter 1981), pp. 3-14, under the different title "Modernity versus Postmodernity."

4. The specific politics associated with the "Greens" would seem to constitute a reaction to this situation, rather than an exception from it.

5. See "Answering the Questions: What Is Postmodernism?" in J.-F. Lyotard, *The Postmodern Condition* (Minneapolis, 1984), pp. 71-82; the book itself focuses primarily on science and epistemology rather than on culture.

6. See in particular Manfredo Tafuri, *Architecture and Utopia*, trans. Barbara Luigia La Penta (Cambridge, Mass., 1976) and *Modern Architecture* with Francesco Dal Co (New York, 1979); and also my "Architecture and the Critique of Ideology," chapter 2 of this volume.

7. I have tried to do this in "Postmodernism, or, The Cultural Logic of Late Capitalism," *New Left Review*, 146 (July-August, 1984), pp. 53-92; my contribution to *The Anti-Aesthetic* is a fragment of this definitive version.

8. See, for example, Charles Jencks, *Late-Modern Architecture* (New York, 1980); here, however, Jencks shifts his usage of the term from the designation for a cultural dominant or period style to the name for one aesthetic movement among others.

Chapter 6. Beyond the Cave: Demystifying the Ideology of Modernism

1. Iris Murdoch, *The Unicorn* (London, 1963), p. 118.

2. See, for example, Ernst Fischer, *The Necessity of Art* (London, 1959), or Georg Lukács' *Aesthetik* (Berlin, 1963).

3. Hans-Georg Gadamer, *Wahrheit und Methode* (Tubingen, 1965), pp. 255-61.

4. Fredric Jameson, *Marxism and Form* (Princeton, 1972), pp. 309-26.

5. The modernist position is resumed in Renato Poggioli, *Theory of the Avant-Garde* (Cambridge, Mass., 1968) and eloquently defended in Nathalie Sarraute, *The Age of Suspicion* (New York, 1963). I should add that my really consequent treatment of it would also have necessarily to come to terms with what might be called the left-wing modernism of Brecht or of the *Tel Quel* group.

6. Gilles Deleuze and Félix Guattari, *Anti-Oepide* (Paris, 1972); translated as *Anti-Oedipus* by R. Hurley, M. Seem, and H. R. Lane (Minneapolis, 1983).

7. Gerald Prince, *A Grammar of Stories* (The Hague, 1973), p. 23.
8. See Umberto Eco, *Opera Aperta* (Milan, 1962).
9. *The Republic*, Book VII, trans. H. D. P. Lee (Baltimore, 1955), pp. 278-79.

Chapter 7. Reflections on the Brecht-Lukács Debate

1. For a complementary analysis of the internal contradictions of the idea of modernism, see Paul de Man, "Literary History and Literary Modernity," in *Blindness and Insight*, second ed. (Minneapolis, 1983).

2. See Werner Mittenzwei, "Die Brecht-Lukács Debatte," *Das Argument*, 46 (March 1968); Eugene Lunn, "Marxism and Art in the Era of Stalin and Hitler: A Comparison of Brecht and Lukács," *New German Critique*, 3 (Fall 1974), pp. 12-44; and, for the somewhat earlier period of the review *Die Linskskurve* (1928-32), Helga Gallas, *Marxistische Literaturtheorie-Kontroversen im Bund proletarisch-revolutionärer Schriftsteller* (Neuweid, 1971).

3. See Lunn, "Marxism and Art," pp. 16-18.

4. See in particular "Narrate or Describe?" in Georg Lukács, *Writer and Critic* (London, 1970).

5. For a persuasive yet self-critical statement of such a Brechtian modernism, see Colin McCabe, "Realism and the Cinema: Notes on Some Brechtian Theses," in *Screen*, 15, no. 2 (Summer 1974), pp. 7-27.

6. "You say that you are communists, people intent on changing a world no longer fit for habitation.... Yet were you in reality the cultural servants of the ruling classes, it would be cunning strategy on your part to make material things unrecognizable, since the struggle concerns things and it is in the world of things that your masters have the most to answer for." "Uber gegenstandslose Malerei," in *Schriften zur Literatur und Kunst* (Frankfurt, 1967), vol. 2, pp. 68-69.

7. See *Illuminations* (London, 1970) and "The Author as Producer," in *Understanding Brecht* (London, 1973); and for further developments in a radical theory of the media, see Jürgen Habermas, *Strukturwandel der Öffentlichkeit* (Neuwied, 1962); Hans-Magnus Enzensberger, *The Consciousness Industry* (New York, 1974); and Oskar Negt and Alexander Kluge, *Öffenlichkeit und Erfahrung* (Frankfurt, 1973).

8. The more recent French variant on this position—as in the work of Jean Baudrillard—enlarges the model to include the "socialist bloc" within this new dystopian entente.

9. Thomas Adorno, "Commitment," in *Aesthetics and Politics* (New York, 1979), p. 194.

10. For a pathbreaking Marxian corrective to Adorno's reading of the *Caucasian Chalk Circle*, see Darko Suvin, "Brecht's *Caucasian Chalk Circle* and Marxist Figuration: Open Dramaturgy as Open History," in *The Weapons of Criticism*, ed. Norman Rudick (Palo Alto, Calif., 1976).

11. See, for example, the instructive comments of Stanley Aronowitz on the cinema. "Unlike the important efforts of Japanese and European film-makers to fix the camera directly on the action and permit the scene to work "itself" out, American films are characterized by rapid camera work and sharp editing whose effect is to segment the action into one- or two-minute time slots, paralleling the prevailing styles of television production. The American moviegoer, having become accustomed in TV watching to commercial breaks in the action of a dramatic presentation, is believed to have become incapable of sustaining longer and slower action. Therefore the prevailing modes of film production rely on conceptions of dramatic time inherited from the more crass forms of commercial culture. The film-maker who subordinates the action and the characters to this concept of dramatic time reveals a politics inside technique that is far more insidious than 'reactionary' content. When viewed from this perspective, the film-maker such as Howard Hawks, who refuses to subordinate art to the requirements of segmented time, becomes more resistant to authoritarianism than the liberal or left-wing film-makers who are concerned

with the humanitarian content of film but have capitulated to techniques that totally reduce the audience to spectators." *False Promises* (New York, 1973), pp. 116–17.

Chapter 8. Marxism and Historicism

1. See in particular chaps. 5 and 9 of "The Object of *Capital*," in Louis Althusser et al., *Reading Capital*, trans. Ben Brewster (London, 1970). The most systematic critique of "Althusserianism," including a powerful reaffirmation of the historicist character of Marxism, is that of E. P. Thompson, in *The Poverty of Theory* (London, 1978).

2. See *The Political Unconscious* (Ithaca, 1981).

3. On this last, see the instructive exchange between J. H. Hexter and Christopher Hill in *The Times Literary Supplements* of 24 October and 7 November 1976.

4. The standard works on historicism are Ernst Troeltsch, *Der Historismus und seine Probleme* (Tübingen, 1922), and Friedrich Meinecke, *Die Entstehung des Historismus* (Munich, 1959). Enthusiastic and programmatic endorsements of historicism may be found in Karl Mannheim, "Historicism," in *Essays on the Sociology of Knowledge* (New York, 1952), pp. 84–133; and Erich Auerbach, *Mimesis* (Princeton, N.J., 1953), pp. 443–48, 473–80, 546–51. The basic structuralist critiques of historicism, besides that of Althusser himself (see n. 1), are surely those of Claude Lévi-Strauss, "History and Dialectic," in *The Savage Mind* (Chicago, 1966), pp. 245–69; and A. J. Greimas, "Structure et histoire," in *Du Sens* (Paris, 1970), pp. 103–16.

5. J. J. Bachofen, *Das Mutterrecht* (Frankfurt, 1975), p. 103.

6. Ibid., p. 8.

7. Letter to Antoine Meillet, 4 January 1894, in *Cahiers Ferdinand de Saussure*, 21 (1964), p. 93. And for a fuller discussion of Saussure's "synchronic" revolution, see my *Prison-House of Language* (Princeton, 1972), pp. 3–39.

8. On Boas' antievolutionism (and its relationship to his anti-Marxism), see Marvin Harris, *The Rise of Anthropological Theory* (New York, 1968), chap. 10.

9. Jules Michelet, *Histoire de la révolution française* (Paris, 1952), vol. 1, p. 203.

10. The *kerygma*, or "message," is the central category of Paul Ricoeur's narrative theology; see, for instance, his "Preface to Bultmann," in *The Conflict of Interpretations* (Chicago, 1974), pp. 381–401.

11. Michelet, *Histoire*, vol. 1, p. 412.

12. Gilles Deleuze and Félix Guattari, *Anti-Oedipus*, trans. R. Hurley, M. Seem, and H. R. Lane (Minneapolis, 1983), pp. 20–22.

13. Leo Tolstoy, *Journal*, 28 February 1897, quoted in Viktor Shklovsky, "Art as Technique," in *The Theory of Prose* (translated in L. T. Lemon and M. J. Reis, *Russian Formalist Criticism*, Lincoln, 1965, p. 12).

14. Karl Marx, *Capital*, trans. Ben Fowkes (Harmondsworth, 1976), I, 274, n. 4. And compare the fundamental observation in which Aristotle's inability to conceptualize the labor theory of value is grounded in the limits of his own mode of production: "Aristotle himself was unable to extract this fact, that, in the form of commodity-values, all labor is expressed as equal human labor and therefore as labor of equal quality, by inspection from the form of value, because Greek society was founded on the labor of slaves, hence had as its natural basis the inequality of men and of their labor-powers" (*Capital*, vol. 1, pp. 151–52). A more general historicist theory of the relationship between conceptual abstraction and commodification has been developed in Alfred Sohn-Rethel's important book, *Intellectual and Manual Labor* (London, 1978).

15. Maurice Godelier, *Horizon: Trajets marxists en anthropologie* (Paris, 1973), p. 303.

16. Walter Benjamin, "Theses on the Philosophy of History" (thesis 14), in *Illuminations*, trans. H. Zohn (New York, 1969), p. 261.

17. Ibid., pp. 255, 264 (theses 6 and 18 B).

18. See Y. M. Lotman and B. A. Uspensky, "On the Semiotic Mechanism of Culture," *New Literary History*, 9, no. 2 (Winter 1978), pp. 211- 32; and Lotman and Uspensky, *Tripologia della cultura* (Milan, 1975). The fundamental critique of Lotman's theory of culture from a Marxist standpoint is that of Stefan Zólkiewski, "Des principles de classement des texts de culture," *Semiotica*, 7, no. 1 (1973), pp. 1-18.

19. Lotman and Uspensky, "On the Semiotic Mechanism of Culture," p. 213.

20. Ibid., p. 217.

21. Y. M. Lotman, "Problèmes de la typologie des cultures," *Social Science Information*, 6, nos. 2-3 (April-June 1967), p. 33.

22. Lotman and Uspensky, "On the Semiotic Mechanism of Culture," pp. 218-19.

23. See ibid., p. 230, n. 5.

24. J. Dubois et al., *Rhétorique générale* (Paris, 1970); and Hayden White, *Tropics of Discourse* (Baltimore, 1979); and see my chapter 6 in *The Ideologies of Theory: Essays 1971-1986*, vol. 1: *Situations of Theory*.

25. Barry Hindess and Paul Hirst, *Pre-Capitalist Modes of Production* (London, 1975), pp. 309, 311.

26. Arthur C. Danto, *The Analytical Philosophy of History* (Cambridge, 1968).

27. Hindess and Hirst, *Pre-Capitalist Modes*, p. 323.

28. Louis Althusser, *Pour Marx* (Paris, 1965), p. 187.

29. Hindess and Hirst, *Pre-Capitalist Modes*, p. 312.

30. Jean-François Lyotard, *Économie libidinale* (Paris, 1974), p. 155.

31. See, for instance, his latest collection, *Rudiments paiens* (Paris, 1978).

32. This familiar objection to Marxist anthropology has been most recently expressed by Jean Baudrillard in *The Mirror of Production*, trans. M. Poster (St. Louis, 1975), esp. pp. 69-92.

33. See, for example, Perry Anderson, *Considerations on Western Marxism* (London, 1976), pp. 64-66; and Hindess and Hirst, *Pre-Capitalist Modes*, pp. 313-20; responses may be found in L. Althusser, *Éléments d'Autocritique* (Paris, 1974), and Pierre Macherey, *Hegel ou Spinoza* (Paris, 1979).

34. Ernst Bloch, "Nonsynchronism and Dialectics," *New German Critique*, 11 (Spring 1977), pp. 22-38.

35. J. P. Sartre, *Les Séquestrés d'Altona* (Paris, 1960), pp. 222-23.

Chapter 9. Periodizing the 60s

1. J. P. Sartre, "Preface" to Frantz Fanon, *The Wretched of the Earth*, trans. Constance Farrington (New York, 1965).

2. Karl Marx, *The Eighteenth Brumaire of Louis Bonaparte* (New York, 1969), p. 15.

3. Régis Debray, "A Modest Contribution," *New Literary Review*, 115 (May-June 1979), p. 58.

4. Frank Lentricchia, *After the New Criticism* (Chicago, 1980), esp. pp. 31-35.

5. Ernest Mandel, *Late Capitalism* (London, 1978).

6. Mao Zedong, *Chairman Mao Talks to the People*, ed. S. Schram (New York, 1974), pp. 92-93.

Index

Index

(Compiled by Richard Dienst)

Fredric Jameson is the William A. Lane, Jr., Professor of Comparative Literature and director of the Graduate Program in Literature and Theory at Duke University. He previously taught at Harvard University, the University of California (San Diego and Santa Cruz) and Yale University. Jameson's books include *The Political Unconscious, Sartre: The Origins of a Style, Marxism and Form,* and *The Prison-House of Language.* He is also a co-editor of the journal *Social Text.* Three other forthcoming books will deal with film, dialectical aesthetics, and postmodernism.